BIOMES OF THE EARTH

OCEANS

Trevor Day

Illustrations by
Richard Garratt

CHELSEA HOUSE
PUBLISHERS
An imprint of Infobase Publishing

Oceans

Chelsea House
An imprint of Infobase Publishing
132 West 31st Street
New York NY 10001

Library of Congress Cataloging-in-Publication Data
Day, Trevor
  Oceans / Trevor Day ; illustrations by Richard Garratt.
    p. cm. — (Biomes of the Earth)
  Includes bibliographical references and index.
  ISBN 0-8160-5327-8
  1. Marine ecology—Juvenile literature. 2. Ocean—Juvenile literature. I. Garratt, Richard, ill.
II. Title. III. Series.
  QH541.5.S3D36 2006
  577.7—dc22   2005009086

Chelsea House books are available at special discounts when purchased in bulk quantities for businesses, associations, institutions, or sales promotions. Please call our Special Sales Department in New York at (212) 967-8800 or (800) 322-8755.

You can find Chelsea House on the World Wide Web at http://www.chelseahouse.com

Text design by David Strelecky
Cover design by Cathy Rincon
Illustrations by Richard Garratt
Photo research by Elizabeth H. Oakes

Printed in China

CP Hermitage 10 9 8 7 6 5 4 3 2 1

This book is printed on acid-free paper.

From Richard Garratt:
To Chantal, who has lightened my darkness

CONTENTS

CHAPTER 3

THE CHEMISTRY AND PHYSICS OF THE OCEANS   53

CHAPTER 4

ATMOSPHERE AND THE OCEANS   69

CHAPTER 7

HISTORY AND EXPLORATION OF THE OCEANS

CHAPTER 8

THE USES OF THE OCEANS

PREFACE

Earth is a remarkable planet. There is nowhere else in our solar system where life can survive in such a great diversity of forms. As far as we can currently tell, our planet is unique. Isolated in the barren emptiness of space, here on Earth we are surrounded by a remarkable range of living things, from the bacteria that inhabit the soil to the great whales that migrate through the oceans, from the giant redwood trees of the Pacific forests to the mosses that grow on urban sidewalks. In a desolate universe, Earth teems with life in a bewildering variety of forms.

One of the most exciting things about the Earth is the rich pattern of plant and animal communities that exists over its surface. The hot, wet conditions of the equatorial regions support dense rain forests with tall canopies occupied by a wealth of animals, some of which may never touch the ground. The cold, bleak conditions of the polar regions, on the other hand, sustain a much lower variety of species of plants and animals, but those that do survive under such harsh conditions have remarkable adaptations to their testing environment. Between these two extremes lie many other types of complex communities, each well suited to the particular conditions of climate prevailing in its region. Scientists call these communities *biomes*.

The different biomes of the world have much in common with one another. Each has a plant component, which is responsible for trapping the energy of the Sun and making it available to the other members of the community. Each has grazing animals, both large and small, that take advantage of the store of energy found within the bodies of plants. Then come the predators, ranging from tiny spiders that feed upon even smaller insects to tigers, eagles, and polar bears that survive by preying upon large animals. All of these living things form a complicated network of feeding interactions, and, at the base of the system, microbes in the soil are ready to consume the energy-rich plant litter or dead animal flesh that remains. The biome, then, is an integrated unit within which each species plays its particular role.

This set of books aims to outline the main features of each of the Earth's major biomes. The biomes covered include the tundra habitats of polar regions and high mountains, the taiga (boreal forest) and temperate forests of somewhat warmer lands, the grasslands of the prairies and the tropical savanna, the deserts of the world's most arid locations, and the tropical forests of the equatorial regions. The wetlands of the world, together with river and lake habitats, do not lie neatly in climatic zones over the surface of the Earth but are scattered over the land. And the oceans are an exception to every rule. Massive in their extent, they form an interconnecting body of water extending down into unexplored depths, gently moved by global currents.

Humans have had an immense impact on the environment of the Earth over the past 10,000 years since the last Ice Age. There is no biome that remains unaffected by the presence of the human species. Indeed, we have created our own biome in the form of agricultural and urban lands, where people dwell in greatest densities. The farms and cities of the Earth have their own distinctive climates and natural history, so they can be regarded as a kind of artificial biome that people have created, and they are considered as a separate biome in this set.

Each biome is the subject of a separate volume. Each richly illustrated book describes the global distribution, the climate, the rocks and soils, the plants and animals, the history, and the environmental problems found within each biome. Together, the set provides students with a sound basis for understanding the wealth of the Earth's biodiversity, the factors that influence it, and the future dangers that face the planet and our species.

Is there any practical value in studying the biomes of the Earth? Perhaps the most compelling reason to understand the way in which biomes function is to enable us to conserve their rich biological resources. The world's productivity is the basis of the human food supply. The world's biodiversity holds a wealth of unknown treasures, sources of drugs and medicines that will help to improve the quality of life. Above all, the world's biomes are a constant source of wonder, excitement, recreation, and inspiration that feed not only our bodies but also our minds and spirits. These books aim to provide the information about biomes that readers need in order to understand their function, draw upon their resources, and, most of all, enjoy their diversity.

ACKNOWLEDGMENTS

I would like to thank the team that helped create this book: illustrator Richard Garratt, photo researcher Elizabeth Oakes, project editor Dorothy Cummings, and executive editor Frank K. Darmstadt, who commissioned and managed the project. A special thank-you to Peter and Norma Goodwright, who lent me the use of their cottage during difficult times. A final thank-you to my partner, Christina, who is unswerving in encouraging me and my work.

INTRODUCTION

A biome is a major region on Earth's surface. It contains a distinctive community of plants and animals that are adapted to the climate and environmental conditions that exist there. Hot deserts, for example, contain plants and animals that are adapted to high temperatures and scarcity of water. Tropical rain forest organisms, on the other hand, thrive at similar temperatures but where rainfall is much higher. Most biologists recognize about 10 biomes, nine of which occur on land. The 10th biome is the oceans.

The world's ocean is the vast expanse of salt water that covers more than two-thirds of the planet. It is many times larger than any other biome on Earth. Unlike the biomes on land, the ocean straddles all climates, from the hottest tropical regions to the chilly poles. The ocean is also a much more three-dimensional environment. On land most living things thrive in a narrow layer that extends from a few hundred feet into the air to a few tens of feet beneath the soil. There are a few exceptions, such as bacteria living in rocks two to three miles (about 3 to 5 km) below ground or floating 13 miles (about 20 km) high in the atmosphere. In the ocean, on the other hand, most of the seafloor is at least three miles (5 km) beneath the sea surface. Marine life thrives at many levels between the surface and the sea bottom. Most of Earth's living space lies in the ocean.

Chapter 1 explores the geography of the oceans. It explains the living space of the ocean, from the shores that border landmasses, to the greatest depths more than six miles (10 km) down. It describes the five regional oceans that make up the world's oceans and the seas and islands that are scattered among them.

Chapter 2 describes Earth's geology (the structure of the Earth and the processes occurring within it). It reveals how forces beneath the ground create and alter the basins that contain the oceans. Chapter 3 highlights water's unique physical and chemical properties. The chapter goes on to explain the properties of seawater and some important chemical changes that occur within the oceans. Chemicals are transformed—physically and chemically—as they are cycled between land, sea, and air. Petroleum oil and natural gas that are the lifeblood of modern societies are squeezed into existence beneath the ocean floor.

Chapter 4 explores the connections between Earth's atmosphere and the oceans. The ocean's warmth and moisture fuels air circulation that shapes our weather and climate. The movement of air masses, in turn, creates winds that steer ocean currents.

As chapter 5 explains, life has flourished in the oceans many times longer than it has on land. The chapter begins by considering how organisms might have evolved in the oceans and then goes on to survey the breadth of life found in the present-day oceans. Chapter 6, on ecology, reveals how different types of marine organism depend upon one another. It highlights the sea's most important, and unusual, biological communities.

Chapter 7 considers the history and exploration of the oceans, from the earliest rafts and reed boats to the latest submersibles and satellites. It reviews the brief history of oceanography—the scientific study of the ocean and its inhabitants—which is barely 150 years old.

As chapter 8 makes clear, the oceans provide many services people take for granted. Oceans are highways for transporting goods and military forces. People obtain food from them. Much of world's oil and natural gas comes from the seabed, and increasingly, the oceans provide precious minerals, medicinal drugs, sources of clean energy, and leisure opportunities.

Exploiting the oceans, as chapter 9 shows, has its environmental costs. People treat the ocean as a waste dump, they remove its creatures at an alarming rate, and they alter its habitats. These negative impacts affect everyone, whether it is the influence on climate change, the loss of food supplies, or the destruction of much of the world's natural beauty.

As the last chapter explains, keeping the oceans healthy means managing their resources. In the last 30 years international laws have been created to protect and manage the oceans. But effective action still falls far short of good intentions.

As I hope this book makes clear, what happens in the air and on land affects the oceans. What happens in the oceans affects us all.

CHAPTER 1

GEOGRAPHY
OF THE OCEANS

Seen from space, the Earth is partly shrouded in a swirling dance of clouds. The clouds move to reveal patches of green, brown, or yellow—the landmasses—amid a sea of blue—the oceans. Planet Earth would be better called planet Ocean.

The oceans cover 71 percent of Earth's surface—more than twice the area of the land. The oceans are deep too, averaging about 12,500 feet (3,800 m) in depth. They contain a huge amount of water. If all the mountains and valleys on Earth's surface were leveled, so that the Earth's surface was smooth, the oceans' water would still cover the surface by more than 8,200 feet (2,500 m).

Earth's water

Most (about 97 percent) of the water on Earth's surface is in the form of salty seawater in the oceans. That leaves only about 3 percent of water as freshwater, mostly in the form of massive ice sheets on land, or as water in lakes and rivers, or in the soil and shallow rocks below ground (groundwater).

Earth's water does not stay in one place. It is on the move. As the Sun's heat warms the surface of the oceans, water molecules escape from the sea surface and enter the air as water vapor. Worldwide, this process of evaporation—from the oceans, but also from lakes, rivers, and damp surfaces on land—loads the air with moisture. As the moisture rises and cools in the atmosphere, the water vapor forms droplets that create clouds. Winds blow the clouds across the Earth's surface and eventually the clouds unload their water. The water falls to Earth's surface as precipitation (usually in the form of rain, hail, or snow). Most of this precipitation (nearly four-fifths) happens over the ocean and returns the atmosphere's water back into the sea. That still leaves the one-fifth that

Earth viewed from Apollo 17. The Southern Ocean at bottom is shrouded in swirling clouds. To the right of Africa lies the Indian Ocean and to the left, the Atlantic Ocean. *(Courtesy of National Aeronautics and Space Administration)*

falls on land. Most of this soaks into the ground and fills spongelike spaces in soil and rock. Some water flows directly off the land to feed streams, rivers, and lakes. Much of this freshwater eventually flows into the sea at the mouths of rivers.

This cycling of water between sea, air, land, and freshwater is called, not surprisingly, the water cycle, or more technically, the hydrologic cycle (*hydro* from the Greek word for "water"). This cycle shapes the planet's surface and governs the distribution of life on it. On land, for example, flowing water and moving ice carve the land surface, wear away rock, cut valleys, and carry rock particles and dissolved substances from one place to another. The balance of water movement between sea, air, and land governs climate. For example, clouds shroud the Earth in an insulating layer, helping to trap the heat on Earth's surface. On the other hand, clouds reduce the amount of sunlight reaching Earth's surface and have a cooling effect. The balance between the heating and cooling effect varies with the type of cloud. And most important, clouds release rain.

The balance between evaporation and precipitation, together with local temperatures, determines which plants and animals live where. For example, the hot desert of the Sahara in North Africa has an average rainfall of less than 4.8 inches (120 mm) a year. Only a few kinds of animals and plants survive here. They include the fennec fox, which is active only at night; the addax antelope, which never drinks; and grasses that fold their leaves to reduce water loss. In the rain forests of the Amazon, on the other hand, rainfall exceeds 80 inches (200 cm) a year. The tropical rain forest biome is the most complex on land and harbors several million species—more than one-half of all land species.

Most organisms, from microscopic bacteria to blue whales and redwood trees, are at least 65 percent water. Although this "living" water is only a tiny fraction (less than 0.0001 percent) of all the water on the planet's surface, it is vitally important. Once communities of microbes, plants, and animals develop in a particular place, they change their physical and chemical environment. For example, rain forests—as their very name implies—create rain. Apart from releasing plentiful supplies of water into the air by evaporation, they release particles and chemicals that seed the creation of clouds.

The oceans are not only the world's major source of surface water. They are the main source of circulating heat. The oceans act like huge heat reserves, carrying warmth from the tropical regions toward the poles. Without oceans, the equator would be unbearably hot and a wide area around the poles would be permanently locked under several miles of ice. By spreading the heat from hot climates to cool, the oceans reduce temperature differences on Earth. The oceans have a profound influence on almost all life forms on Earth, not just those that live in the sea.

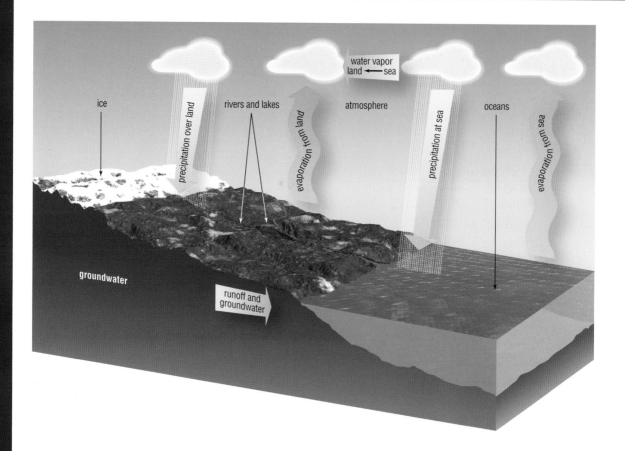

ice

water vapor
land ← sea

precipitation over land

rivers and lakes

evaporation from land

atmosphere

precipitation at sea

oceans

evaporation from sea

groundwater

runoff and
groundwater

The water (hydrologic) cycle. Water circulates between sea, air, and land.

The shape of the ocean floor

An ocean sits in one or more giant depressions on Earth's surface called basins. The bottom of an ocean—its seascape—is as dramatic as any landscape. If the seawater

The five oceans

Ocean (excluding some of its seas)	Area in square miles (km²)	Average depth in ft (m)	Volume in cubic miles (km³)
Pacific Ocean	58,957,258 (152,617,160)	13,874 (4,229)	154,960,672 (645,375,552)
Atlantic Ocean	31,563,463 (81,527,400)	12,391 (3,777)	73,902,416 (307,902,776)
Indian Ocean	26,064,036 (67,469,536)	12,720 (3,877)	62,780,380 (261,590,400)
Southern Ocean	8,102,165 (20,973,318)	11,188 (3,410)	17,165,720 (71,518,408)
Arctic Ocean	3,351,811 (8,676,520)	6,349 (1,935)	4,028,950 (16,790,582)

What is an ocean?

The continuous body of seawater covering 71 percent of Earth's surface is the ocean. Scientists who study the ocean, known as oceanographers, divide it into five major regions. The ocean regions are, from largest to smallest: the Pacific, Atlantic, Indian, Southern, and Arctic Oceans. Four of these are outlined by the shapes of the continents that separate them. The fifth, the Southern Ocean, is really a southern extension of the Pacific, Atlantic, and Indian Oceans. The International Hydrographic Organization (IHO)—the organization that decides the geographical boundaries in the ocean—only designated the Southern Ocean as a separate body of water in 2000.

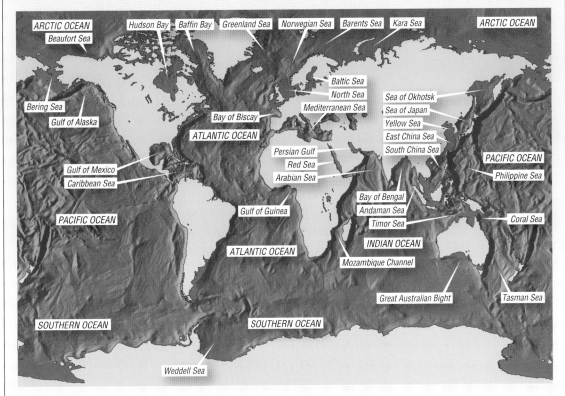

The world's oceans and some of their major seas, gulfs, and bays

could be drained from an ocean basin, its huge mountain ranges, deep canyons, and vast plains would be revealed. These features are even grander than those on land. The tallest mountain in the sea, the volcanic cone of Mauna Kea on the island of Hawaii, rises about 33,450 feet (10,200 m) above the ocean floor. Mount Everest, the tallest mountain on land, rises to "only" about 29,035 feet (8,850 m) above sea level. The river flowing through Hell's Canyon, Oregon—the deepest river gorge in North America and one of the world's deepest land canyons—lies 8,043 feet (2,452 m) beneath the canyon's east rim. By contrast, the Mariana Trench in the western Pacific Ocean descends to about 16,400 feet (5,000 m) below its flanking seafloor. At its deepest, this trench is 35,840 feet (10,924 m) beneath the sea surface and could swallow 29 Empire State Buildings stacked one on top of the other.

Most oceanographers describe the bottom of the ocean in three parts, or provinces: the continental margin, the deep-ocean floor, and the mid-ocean ridges.

The continental margin is the seawater-covered edge of a continent (one of the world's major landmasses). The continental margin has three parts: the shelf, the slope, and the rise. Extending from the seashore to a depth of about 500–650 feet (150–200 m) lies the gently sloping sea bottom of the continental shelf. Beyond this, at the shelf break, the slope gets steeper and falls away to depths greater than two miles (about 3 km). This is the continental slope, and it marks the submerged outer edge of the continent. At the bottom of the slope lies a gentler incline formed from sediments (small loose particles). These have washed off the land and the continental shelf and settled at the bottom of the steep slope over thousands of years to create the continental rise. Beyond this lies the flat expanse of the deep-ocean floor.

Deep canyons scar the continental shelf. Called submarine canyons, they can plunge to 9,840 feet (3,000 m) deep, as in the case of Monterey Canyon, the largest on the U.S. Pacific coast. This underwater canyon is of comparable size to Arizona's famous Grand Canyon.

How do submarine canyons form? The answer remained something of a mystery until the mid-1950s, when geologists discovered that underwater avalanches were snapping deep-sea telephone cables. These so-called turbidity currents are caused by sediment accumulating unevenly on the continental shelf. Eventually, a pile of sediment becomes too large and causes a major collapse, and rock, water, and suspended sediment rush down the continental slope, gouging out more sediment along the way. Once a canyon is created, occasional turbidity currents keep the canyon open, and even enlarge it.

The continental shelves only make up about 8 percent of the seafloor, but from the human perspective they are incredibly important. Being next to the land and covered in shallow water, they are the most accessible parts of the ocean realm. The combination of nutrients washed off the land and sunlight penetrating to the seabed favors the growth of marine plants. These plants, from microscopic plankton to seaweeds, thrive here. And where there are plants there is food for animals. As a result, the water covering the continental shelves contains many of the world's most important fisheries. Continental shelves also harbor many of the ocean's most productive yet endangered biological communities, such as coral reefs, seagrass meadows, and kelp beds. Many of these communities are at risk from land-based pollution and from disturbance by many kinds of human activity (see "Biodiversity," pages 199–200).

Beyond the continental margins, most of the deep-ocean floor is a flat expanse, called the abyssal plain, that lies at depths of 13,000–20,000 feet (about 4–6 km). The plain is covered in a layer of sediment that has settled over thousands or even millions of years. In the oldest parts of the ocean floor, which are more than 100 million years old, the sediment layer reaches more than 3,000 feet (about 1 km) thick. Here and there, features such as abyssal ridges and submerged volcanic cones called seamounts rise above the level of the sediment. At the edges of abyssal plains are trenches—the deepest parts of the ocean—that plunge to depths beyond 20,000 feet (about 6 km).

Imagine that people could walk across the drained bottom of the North Atlantic basin, leaving from eastern North America. After a 2,000-mile trek across a muddy abyssal plain they would come to a range of craggy "foothills." Climbing over these, they would see stretching to their right and left—

as far as they could see—a mountain range as tall as the Rockies. Reaching a summit, they would look into a rift—a flat-bottomed valley about 3,000 feet (nearly 1 km) across—hissing and sizzling with volcanic activity. The mountain range is a mid-ocean ridge. Its rift is the birthplace of new seafloor.

The mid-ocean ridge system is the longest chain of mountains on Earth. It meanders through all the Earth's oceans in a system more than 40,000 miles (65,000 km) long—much longer than the Andes, Rockies, and Himalayas combined. Lava (molten rock) erupting inside the ridge's rift gradually cools to form new oceanic crust—the rocky layer that makes up the ocean floor. Meanwhile, thousands of miles away, at the bottom of ocean trenches, ancient oceanic crust is sinking down beneath the Earth's surface and being destroyed. From the mid-ocean ridges to the deep trenches, seafloor is slowly moving, at the rate of one to six inches (about 2–15 cm) a year, from its birthplace to its place of destruction. This movement helps explain how the oceans change shape and the continents "drift" across Earth's surface over millions of years (see "Moving plates," pages 35–38).

In places seawater seeps through cracks on the flanks of a mid-ocean ridge into the ridge itself. There the water is

The floor of an ocean

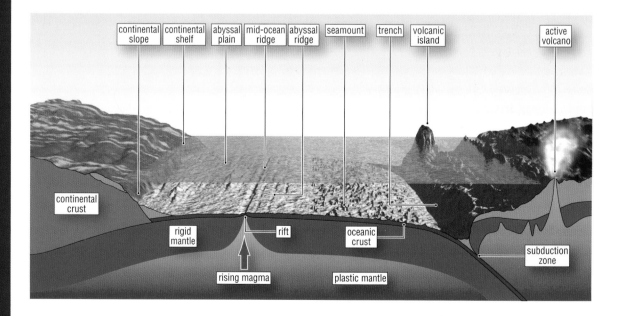

heated by volcanic rock until it seeps or bursts out through clefts on the rift valley floor, called hydrothermal or hotwater vents (from the Greek *therme* for "heat"). The exiting water is rich in minerals and can reach temperatures of 716°F (380°C). Since the late 1970s, when deep-sea hydrothermal vents were seen for the first time, scientists have been fascinated by the startling communities of microbes and animals that live alongside them (see "Hot vents and cold seeps," pages 157–158).

Seas and gulfs

People often use the words *sea* and *ocean* to mean the same thing. We can talk about going for a swim in the sea *or* ocean, or living in sea-front *or* an ocean-front property. Technically, however, a sea is a geographic region of an ocean. For example, the Sargasso Sea lies a few hundred miles off the Florida coast in the North Atlantic Ocean. The Sargasso is surrounded by a strong system of currents, which marks its boundary with the rest of the ocean. It also contains a unique community of plants and animals—floating seaweed and small, well-camouflaged fish and other small creatures that live among the weeds. The Sargasso Sea is a distinct part of the North Atlantic.

In fact, most seas, such as the Mediterranean Sea and Caribbean Sea of the North Atlantic, are partly or mostly surrounded by land. They are called marginal seas because they lie at the edges (margins) of the ocean. Gulfs and bays are alternative names for areas of seawater partly enclosed by land, as in the case of the Gulf of Mexico or the Bay of Bengal.

Parts of an ocean, such as the Sargasso Sea, have characteristic animal and plant communities because their distinctive environmental conditions allow some organisms to survive there and not others. The community of organisms living in an ocean region also depends upon when, and from where, animals and plants have colonized that area. If they entered the region millions of years ago and they have become more or less cut off from animals and plants in other regions, they may have evolved considerably in adapting to the local conditions. Over time, they may evolve to the point at which they have become new species. They are now reproductively isolated from (they cannot breed with) the forms from which they evolved and which may still exist elsewhere. This happens not only *within* an ocean but also *between* oceans. So, for example, the species of salmon found in the Atlantic Ocean are different from those found in the Pacific. Because an ocean's history and environmental conditions exert such an influence on the assemblage of organisms that inhabit it, it is appropriate to consider the different oceans in more detail before going any further.

The Pacific Ocean

The Pacific Ocean is the world's largest expanse of sea, covering nearly one-third of Earth's surface—more than 16 times the area of the 50 U.S. states. The Pacific Ocean stretches from the Arctic Ocean boundary near the North Pole to the Southern Ocean at the opposite pole. At its widest point, from the Americas in the east to Asia and Australia in the west, the Pacific is about 11,000 miles (17,700 km) across. Most geographers divide the Pacific's expanse into two: the North Pacific above the equator and the South Pacific below.

The Pacific Ocean is deep. It contains the Mariana Trench, the deepest place on Earth's surface. Altogether, the ocean holds nearly half of the world's seawater. If all the world's landmasses were scraped off at sea level and dumped into the Pacific Ocean basin, they would not fill it.

The Pacific gained its name from the Portuguese round-the-world explorer Ferdinand Magellan (ca. 1480–1521). In 1520 Magellan called the ocean *Mar Pacifico,* Portuguese for "The Calm Sea," because of his expedition's experience of its quiet waters. In fact, typhoons or tropical cyclones (the names for hurricanes in different parts of the Pacific) frequently batter communities around the Pacific. In addition, earthquakes, volcanoes, and landslides regularly shake the margins of the Pacific Ocean and trigger giant waves called tsunamis (Japanese for "harbor waves").

Few large rivers flow into the Pacific, so its coastal waters are largely undiluted by freshwater. The Pacific receives cold seawater from the Southern Ocean, but its connection with the Arctic Ocean is narrow, and little seawater flows between the two. The surface waters of the North Pacific are dominated by a circulating system of currents called a gyre. The North Pacific gyre flows clockwise, under the influence of the Earth's rotation (a phenomenon called the Coriolis effect; see "The effect of Earth's rotation," pages 71–73). A similar massive gyre in the South Pacific turns counterclockwise, influenced by the same effect.

The Pacific Ocean basin lies on several of Earth's massive plates (giant slabs of Earth's crust and underlying rock). Along the edges of the Pacific basin a series of trenches take ancient oceanic crust down beneath the surface of the Earth. The descending crust melts and feeds a system of volcanoes that erupt lava onto Earth's surface. Some volcanoes rise above the sea surface to form volcanic island chains. Others emerge on continental landmasses. Together, these volcanic systems almost encircle the Pacific. They form the aptly named "Ring of Fire."

While old seafloor is being destroyed, new seafloor is being created elsewhere. In the eastern Pacific a mid-ocean ridge system called the East Pacific Rise is laying down new seafloor at the rate of six inches (15 cm) width each year. Overall, however, Pacific seafloor is being destroyed at a faster rate than it is being replaced. As a result, the Pacific Ocean basin is gradually shrinking.

Thousands of volcanoes—most of them long extinct—rise up from the Pacific seafloor. Many remain submerged as seamounts. Others rise above the sea surface as volcanic islands. Where islands form in warm waters, coral reefs (rocky formations formed from the limestone skeletons of tiny animals) often grow on their flanks. In many cases these coral-rimmed islands gradually sink over millions of years.

Pacific Ocean data

Area	58,957,258 square miles (152,617,160 km^2)
Average depth	13,874 feet (4,229 m)
Maximum depth	35,840 feet (10,924 m) Mariana Trench
Volume	154,960,672 cubic miles (643,375,552 km^3)

When they disappear beneath the sea surface, the island's location is often marked by a ring of coral, a coral atoll (see the sidebar "Coral atolls," page 153). Thousands of these amazing structures lie scattered across the tropical and subtropical Pacific Ocean.

The Atlantic Ocean

The Atlantic Ocean gains its name from the mythical Greek Titan Atlas who held up the heavens. His name was given to the Atlas Mountains of North Africa, and the region of sea next to this mountain range became the Atlantic.

The Atlantic Ocean, at about nine times the size of the 50 U.S. states, is the second largest of the five oceans. It separates Europe and Africa from the Americas. For convenience, oceanographers divide it into two: the North Atlantic and the South Atlantic, separated by the equator.

The Mid-Atlantic Ridge runs snakelike, from north to south, down the center of the Atlantic. In places on or close to the ridge, volcanoes have risen up to create islands such as those of the Azores and, recently, Surtsey, near Iceland. Elsewhere, at the rift in the middle of the ridge, lava rises up and forms new seafloor. The plates on either side of the ridge are moving apart at the rate of at least one inch (2.5 cm) a year, carrying the continents with them. In consequence, the Atlantic Ocean is getting wider. It is at least 40 feet (12 m) wider than when Christopher Columbus sailed from Europe to the Bahamas in 1492. The continents on either side of the Atlantic have roughly interlocking shapes, like the pieces of a jigsaw puzzle, and this neat fit provided the German geologist Alfred Wegener (1880–1930) with evidence for his theory of continental drift in the early 20th century (see "Continental drift," pages 32–34).

In the North Atlantic the major system of ocean currents—the North Atlantic gyre—flows in a clockwise direction. In the west the gyre picks up warm water emerging from the Gulf of Mexico and carries it eastward across the Atlantic as the Gulf Stream. Much of this water then diverts northeast, toward the Arctic Ocean, as the North Atlantic Drift. The warming effect of the Gulf Stream and North Atlantic Drift

Atlantic Ocean data

Area	31,563,463 square miles (81,527,400 km^2)
Average depth	12,391 feet (3,777 m)
Maximum depth	28,232 feet (8,605 m) Puerto Rico Trench
Volume	73,902,416 cubic miles (307,902,776 km^3)

keeps northwest Europe unusually mild. Winter temperatures in London, England, are typically about 18°F (10°C) warmer than those on the mainland of Newfoundland, Canada, which lies at the same latitude but on the opposite side of the ocean and is cooled by a current flowing south from Baffin Bay.

In late summer and early fall the circulating warm water of the North Atlantic gyre feeds the surface waters of the tropical North Atlantic. Warm water heats the overlying air, and some of the water evaporates, releasing more heat energy into the air and creating warm updrafts of moist air. Some updrafts are sufficiently powerful to spawn hurricanes—violent tropical storms with wind speeds in excess of 74 mph (119 km/h), such as Hurricane Katrina, which struck the coasts of U.S. Gulf states in August 2005. That hurricane killed more than a thousand residents.

In the South Atlantic the counterclockwise gyre supplies tropical waters with seawater chilled by the Southern Ocean. As a result, the South Atlantic's tropical waters are too cool for hurricanes to form.

The Indian Ocean

The Indian Ocean, named after the subcontinent of India, is the third largest of the five oceans. Unlike the Pacific and Atlantic Oceans, the Indian Ocean lies mostly in the Southern Hemisphere (south of the equator), and its tropical waters are bounded to the north by landmasses. This arrangement sets up unusual seasonal changes that affect the northern Indian Ocean's currents and the climates of adjacent landmasses.

The present shape of the Indian Ocean basin can be traced to geological events of at least 130 million years ago. At that time, a southern supercontinent called Gondwana began to break up, creating most of the landmasses that now border the Indian Ocean. One of Gondwana's fragments split in two, with one piece drifting northward to become what we recognize today as Africa. The second piece remained in the far south. About 50 million years ago the southerly piece broke in two, creating Antarctica and Australia. Meanwhile, a large chunk of the African landmass tore free and drifted northward over millions of years, eventually colliding with Asia to form the Indian subcontinent. Remnants of this northward movement are visible as the Seychelles—islands in the northwest Indian Ocean that are fragments the moving India left scattered behind.

Today the Indian Ocean basin is dominated by a mid-ocean ridge system that extends from north to south in the shape of an upside-down *Y*. Elsewhere, hot spots (places where deep-lying molten rock has burned through Earth's crust) have created volcanic ridges, seamounts, and occasional volcanic islands. An Indian Ocean hot spot may be responsible for creating the longest straight-line feature on Earth, the Ninety East Ridge, which runs north to south close to longitude 90°E.

In the northeast Indian Ocean two massive river systems, the Ganges and Brahmaputra, empty sediment-laden freshwater into the Bay of Bengal. The rivers' load of particles discharged over many thousands of years has produced a sediment fan that extends across the seafloor more than 900 miles (1,450 km) from land.

As a rule, landmasses warm faster and cool more rapidly than the adjacent sea. During the Northern Hemisphere summer the Asian mainland warms more quickly than the adjacent northern Indian Ocean. Air expands and rises as it

Indian Ocean data

Area	26,064,036 square miles (67,469,536 km²)
Average depth	12,720 feet (3,877 m)
Maximum depth	23,376 feet (7,125 m) Java (Sunda) Trench
Volume	62,780,380 cubic miles (261,590,400 km³)

warms, and rising warm air over India in summer draws in moisture-laden monsoon winds from the Indian Ocean lying to the southwest. These summer monsoon winds, and their clouds, unload torrential rain onto India and some of its neighbors. The summer monsoons, blowing from the southwest, drive a northerly current along the African coast, feeding a clockwise gyre in the northern Indian Ocean in summer.

In winter the Indian subcontinent cools faster than the nearby ocean. Rising warm air now lies over the northwestern Indian Ocean, and the monsoon winds reverse direction, blowing from the northeast. This prompts a reversal in the direction of the northern Indian Ocean gyre, which now flows counterclockwise. This annual reversal of a major ocean gyre is unique to the northern Indian Ocean. The gyre in the southern Indian Ocean, like that in the South Pacific and South Atlantic, flows counterclockwise all year round.

Tropical cyclones (the Indian Ocean version of hurricanes) occasionally batter the Bay of Bengal. Their storm surges cause extensive flooding, sometimes with great loss of life. In 1970 the disruption produced by a cyclone killed at least 300,000 people in Bangladesh.

The Southern Ocean

The Southern Ocean, sometimes called the Antarctic Ocean, is the fourth-largest ocean. It surrounds the continent of Antarctica, which straddles the South Pole. Antarctica is the coldest place on Earth, yielding a record low temperature of –89.2°C (–128.6°F) in 1983. The Southern Ocean is partially frozen all year round.

In 2000 the International Hydrographic Organization (IHO), the organization that decides geographical names and boundaries in the ocean, designated the boundary of the Southern Ocean at latitude 60°S. This arrangement served practical and political purposes. The 60°S boundary coincides with the Antarctic Treaty boundary based on an international agreement that governs how Antarctica and its ocean waters should be used and protected. The natural boundary of the Southern Ocean is a feature called the Antarctic

Convergence. This lies mostly north of 60°S, but in some places reaches as far north as latitude 48°S. The Antarctic Convergence is where warm and cool currents mix. To the north of the Convergence surface waters are noticeably warmer than to the south.

Within the Southern Ocean two major systems of surface currents flow in opposite directions. The East Wind Drift hugs the Antarctic coast and flows from east to west. Farther north, and flowing west to east, lies the Antarctic Circumpolar Current. This ocean current is the world's largest in terms of volume. It carries about 100 times the water of all rivers combined. It is also the only ocean current to flow right around the world, uninterrupted by landmasses.

The Southern Ocean's floating ice forms in two ways: Some ice slides off Antarctica and breaks off (calves) as floating chunks (icebergs), and some of the seawater freezes to form sea ice.

Antarctica is almost entirely covered in a sheet of ice that averages about 5,750 feet (1,600 m) thick. This ice sheet—and the ice that extends from it over the surface of the Southern Ocean as ledges called ice shelves—contains an astonishing 90 percent of the permanent ice on Earth. This huge weight of ice has made Antarctica sink low in the ocean, so that its continental shelves reach more than 1,600 feet (490 m) deep—about three times the average depth of continental shelves in other oceans. To the north, beyond the Southern Ocean's basins, lie parts of the mid-ocean ridge system that continue through the Pacific, Atlantic, and Indian Oceans.

In the Antarctic winter, with coldest temperatures from June to September, seawater freezes at the surface of the Southern Ocean. This sea ice reaches more than 33 feet (10 m) thick and in places reaches more than 1,000 miles (1,600 km) from the Antarctic coast. In winter the Southern Ocean's floating ice covers an area five times its summer extent.

Each year several thousand floating chunks of ice calve from Antarctica's ice shelves as icebergs. Many of the icebergs are very wide and flat-topped. Some cover vast areas. One Antarctic iceberg was measured covering an area equivalent to the country of Belgium. The icebergs drift slowly north-

Southern Ocean data

Area	8,102,165 square miles (20,973,318 km^2)
Average depth	11,188 feet (3,410 m)
Maximum depth	23,737 feet (7,235 m) South Sandwich Trench
Volume	17,165,720 cubic miles (71,518,408 km^3)

ward for months on end, some reaching cool temperate waters before they melt away completely.

The Arctic Ocean

The Arctic Ocean is the smallest and shallowest of the five oceans. Lying north of latitude 66.5°N (the Arctic Circle), with the North Pole at its center, the Arctic Ocean is partially frozen all year round, rather like the Southern Ocean. But whereas the Southern Ocean is an ocean surrounding a continent, the Arctic Ocean is an ocean almost entirely surrounded by land. It is bordered to the south by North America, Greenland, and Europe and Asia (Eurasia). The ocean gains its name from the Greek *arktos* for "bear," referring to the northern constellation of stars called the Great Bear (*Ursa Major* in Latin), otherwise known as the Big Dipper.

The Arctic Ocean is also unusual in having the largest proportion of continental shelf of any ocean. Nearly half of the Arctic Ocean seabed is less than 660 feet (200 m) deep. In fact, the Arctic Ocean was only confirmed as a true ocean with a deep basin, rather than a shallow sea, in the 1890s. At that time the expedition of Norwegian explorer Fridtjof Nansen in the vessel *Fram* recorded soundings (depth readings) of more than 9,840 feet (3,000 m).

Floating sea ice (formed from frozen seawater) covers about half of the Arctic Ocean in summer and nearly all of it in winter. Seawater mixing between the Arctic and other oceans occurs mainly in the Atlantic, in the gap between Norway and Greenland. Here warm water from the North Atlantic Drift sweeps northward along the Norwegian coast. This Norwegian Current keeps much of Norway's coastline, and some of the Arctic Ocean, free of ice even in the depths of winter. A southward-flowing cool current leaves the Arctic

Arctic Ocean data

Area	3,351,811 square miles (8,676,520 km^2)
Average depth	6,349 feet (1,935 m)
Maximum depth	18,400 feet (5,680 m) Molloy Deep
Volume	4,028,950 cubic miles (16,790,582 km^3)

Ocean and flows past Greenland as the Greenland Current. It keeps Greenland's eastern coast locked in ice for most of the year. In the main expanse of the Arctic Ocean the overall movement of currents—and the ice floating on them—is in a clockwise direction.

Each year western Greenland's and northeast Canada's glaciers (slowly moving "rivers" of ice on land) shed more than 10,000 icebergs. The icebergs float south on the Labrador Current and some drift into the North Atlantic as far as the waters off Newfoundland before melting away. One of these icebergs collided with the RMS *Titanic* in 1912, sinking the ship with the loss of more than 1,500 lives. This tragic event prompted the establishment of the International Ice Patrol, which monitors the movement of North Atlantic icebergs and issues warnings to ships.

Marginal seas of the North Atlantic

To what extent do environmental factors, such as temperature and salinity, vary within an ocean? And how does this variation affect marine life? Conditions at the top of the ocean are very different from those at the bottom (see "Depth zones," pages 143–146). But even in the waters near the surface, environmental conditions vary from one location to another. These changes are particularly marked at the edges of the ocean, where the effect of land is greatest. About a dozen seas border the North Atlantic. Considering just three of these from different climatic zones illustrates how much their conditions can differ.

The Caribbean Sea lies between South and Central America, with Cuba to the north and the Caribbean Island groups of the Greater and Lesser Antilles to the east. Although the Caribbean Sea is now part of the Atlantic Ocean, more than 3 million years ago the Caribbean Sea was also joined to the Pacific. The narrow strip of land called the Isthmus of Panama now closes off this connection.

The bottom of the Caribbean Sea is probably part of the Pacific Ocean plate that has split away, and the Caribbean is more like a deep ocean basin than a shallow sea. Surface water flows into the Caribbean from the North Atlantic to the east, warms as it crosses the Caribbean, and then feeds the Gulf of Mexico to the north with warm water. Further warming in the Gulf produces Gulf Stream water that flows out into the North Atlantic.

Among the spectacular features of the Caribbean Sea are its widespread coral reefs. Scientists who study the fossil record, called paleontologists, have revealed that more than 60 percent of Caribbean coral species have arisen since the sea became separated from the Pacific. At the same time some coral species that were once widespread in the Caribbean became extinct. For example, several groups of reef-building corals are found on the Pacific side of the Isthmus of Panama but are now absent in the Caribbean.

The Mediterranean Sea lies between southern Europe, North Africa, and northwest Asia. It is a remnant of the Tethys Sea that 180 million years ago separated the world's two ancient supercontinents—Laurasia to the north and Gondwana to the south (see "The changing shape of the oceans," pages 39–42). Today the Mediterranean is connected to the North Atlantic through the narrow Strait of Gibraltar to the west and to the Black Sea through the Sea of Marmara to the east.

In 1869 excavators under the direction of the French diplomat Ferdinand de Lesseps (1805–94) completed the Suez Canal, which links the Mediterranean Sea to the Red Sea. Since that time several hundred Red Sea species have passed through the Suez Canal and established themselves in the Mediterranean Sea.

The surface flow of water in the Mediterranean is from the Atlantic Ocean through the Strait of Gibraltar and toward the Black Sea. At depths of 650–2,300 feet (200–700 m) there is a return flow of saltier than normal, nutrient-rich water. This loss of nutrients from the Mediterranean Sea to the Atlantic

Ocean helps account for the fairly low production of life in the Mediterranean compared with other marginal seas. Mediterranean waters do not contain coral reefs because they are too cool for reef-building coral polyps (see "The living reef," pages 151–154).

About 6 million years ago, during a long cold spell in Earth's history when sea levels fell, the Mediterranean Sea became cut off from the North Atlantic. The Mediterranean's water evaporated without being replaced so that the sea eventually dried up completely. Thick deposits of salt were left on what was once the floor of the Mediterranean Sea. All marine life in the Mediterranean Sea died out. Then, by about 5 million years ago, the global climate warmed and sea levels rose. North Atlantic water poured back into the Mediterranean basin near Gibraltar in what some geologists describe as "the world's biggest waterfall." All the Mediterranean Sea's animals and plants have evolved from ancestors that arrived within the last 5 million years.

Today the Mediterranean still loses water by evaporation at a great rate, and replacement is slow, so the salinity (saltiness) of Mediterranean water is generally slightly above that in the North Atlantic. The salinity of most ocean waters is about 35 parts per thousand (meaning 35 grams of salts per 1,000 grams of seawater). The Mediterranean averages 38 parts per thousand. Today the community of animals and plants in the Mediterranean is similar to that in the adjacent warm temperate waters of the North Atlantic, except for recent additions, such as the 140 or so species of zooplankton (animal plankton) that have arrived from the Red Sea.

The Baltic Sea is the shallow inland sea of northern Europe. Separated from the main body of the Atlantic Ocean by the North Sea, it is fed by several major rivers, notably the Vistula, Oder, and Neva. Because the Baltic's connection to the North Sea is narrow and evaporation is slow in the cool climate, the rivers' high input of freshwater strongly dilutes Baltic seawater. As a result, at the sea's northern end Baltic seawater is almost freshwater, with salinities less than five parts per thousand. At the Baltic's southern end, where it is connected to the North Sea, salinities reach 30 parts per thousand (less than the Atlantic's average of 35 parts per

ARCTIC OCEAN

Greenland Sea

Barents Sea

GREENLAND

Baffin Bay

Norwegian Sea

North Sea

Hudson Bay

Labrador Sea

Baltic Sea

ATLANTIC OCEAN

EUROPE

North Eastern
Atlantic Basin

NORTH
AMERICA

Mid-Atlantic Ridge

Azores

North American
Basin

Mediterranean Sea

Gulf of
Mexico

Canary Islands

Caribbean Sea

AFRICA

Cape Verde Islands

Cape Verde Basin

Guiana Basin

SOUTH
AMERICA

Gulf of Guinea

thousand). In addition, the Baltic Sea, unlike the North Sea, is separated from the warming effect of the North Atlantic Drift, so large areas of the Baltic Sea freeze in winter. These environmental conditions mean that only a restricted range of marine species survive in the Baltic Sea, such as those that can tolerate changing salinities. The Baltic—being so shallow and poorly flushed with seawater—does not disperse pollutants quickly, so contaminated water can take a long time to be flushed out of the Baltic. For such reasons, a restricted

The North Atlantic Ocean and its major seas, gulfs, and bays

range of organisms survives in the Baltic, but those that can—including clams, bristle worms, and amphipod crustaceans—have abundant food supplies and can flourish.

Different histories and different environmental conditions mean that these three marginal seas of the North Atlantic contain very different communities of organisms. Similar comparisons could be made for seas in other oceans, with similar striking contrasts.

Shores

Shores are the places where the land meets the sea: places where people can push their toes into coral sand, clamber over rocks to discover tide pools, or sink knee-deep in foul-smelling mud. They are magical places of recreation that bombard the senses: the rhythmic crashing of waves, the smell and taste of salty air, the sun and sea breeze against the skin.

Oceanographers define a shore quite precisely. A shore's lower boundary is the seabed that is exposed to the air by the very lowest tides. Its upper boundary is the edge of the land that is splashed by the biggest storm waves. Between these two lies the shore.

Inland of the shore is a coastal strip that is markedly affected by the nearby presence of the sea. Salty spray, for example, is blown inland onto the coastal strip and affects the kinds of plant life that can grow there. The winding boundary line between the shore and the coastal strip is called the coastline.

New shores are created by geological upheavals, when land sinks (subsides) or rises (uplifts) relative to the sea or land. Fresh land or seabed is brought to the edge of the sea. Once this happens, the shore becomes shaped gradually by the action of winds, waves, tides, and currents. Whether a shore is steep and rocky or gentle and sandy depends on the particular combination of physical, chemical, geological, and biological conditions. A starting point is the height and slope of the land relative to the sea. One factor that influences this is the distance of the shore from a plate boundary. Most of the U.S. Pacific coast lies close to a plate boundary, and in many places the coast is being uplifted; the result is coastal cliffs that tower above rocky shores, interspersed by occasional beaches. In stark contrast, the U.S. Atlantic coast is a long way from a plate boundary. The land here is slowly subsiding, bringing inland rock and soil into contact with the sea. Here, in many places, the beaches are wide, gently sloping, and sandy or muddy.

The seashore is a harsh environment. It is alternately exposed to the air when the tide falls, and then flooded with seawater when the tide rises. Animals and plants that stay on the shore contend with extremes. When the tide is low, seashore organisms may have to deal with baking sunlight on the one hand, which dries them out, or torrential rain on the other, which covers them in freshwater, not the salty seawater they are used to. Once the tide rises, they may be battered by waves or at the mercy of a host of marine grazers and predators. Those that can survive the demanding conditions reap rich rewards. Seaweeds can flourish in the shallow, sunbathed, nutrient-rich water. And for animals, the rising tide brings in abundant fresh supplies of food.

Estuaries and deltas

Estuaries are the coastal locations where rivers discharge into the sea—where freshwater mixes with seawater. Some estuaries, especially those with stark mudflats etched by creeks, seem to be the most forbidding places on a coast. But they are much more important—to people and to wildlife—than appearances suggest.

Geologists (scientists who study Earth's structure and the processes that affect it) generally recognize four kinds of estuaries, based on how they form, which, in turn, shapes their appearance. Chesapeake Bay, lying between Maryland and Virginia, is an example of a coastal plain estuary, so called because it is flat land around the mouth of a river that has been drowned by the sea. San Francisco Bay, on the other hand, with its fairly steep-sided borders, is a tectonic bay, formed when land subsided as a result of ground movement along faults (major fractures in the rock) such as the nearby San Andreas Fault.

Pamlico Sound, North Carolina, is a bar-built estuary. Such estuaries are shallow and separated from the open ocean by deposited sandbars or barrier islands (see "Sheltered shores," pages 48–51). Finally, fjords are deep U-shaped valleys that were originally gouged out by glaciers and have become flooded with seawater. They are common in coastal mountainous regions at high latitudes. Prime examples are visible on the west coasts of Alaska, Canada, and Norway.

A delta (named after the triangular Greek letter Δ) is a triangular or fan-shaped plain of sediment that sometimes forms at the mouth of a river. The largest, such as the Mississippi Delta and Egypt's Nile Delta, are more than 60 miles (about 100 km) across. They form where coastal currents fail to spread river-dumped mud and sand along the coast. Instead the sediment stays at the river mouth, eventually clogging it. The river then becomes restricted to several branched channels, called distributaries, that cross the low-lying delta.

Most estuaries contain plenty of mud—particles of clay and other fine material—brought down by the river. The mud settles on the estuary floor and sides, where it forms mudflats that become exposed at low tide. The close-packed particles in mud do not allow much oxygen to penetrate, so the mud is usually black and foul-smelling beneath the surface. Few animals are adapted to live in these oxygen-poor conditions, and among those that are able to, most live in the top inch or so or have burrows that bring in fresh supplies of water and oxygen.

The drastic changes in salinity (saltiness) pose another problem for creatures living in estuaries. At low tide, and especially after heavy rainfall, the river's water strongly dilutes the seawater of the estuary. When the tide is high, and river flow is reduced, the river's influence is minimal, and the estuary water can be nearly full-strength seawater. Only a fairly small range of marine organisms can tolerate such dramatic changes in salinity. But for those that can, the benefits are great. The river brings with it plentiful nutrients for the microbes (microscopic organisms) and simple plants that form the base of food chains and on which burrowing animals can feed (see "Food chains and food webs," pages

135–138). A single square foot of mud (about 0.1 m^2) can contain 300 burrowing clams. These and other mud dwellers provide food for thousands of birds that visit estuaries. The birds, in turn, provide a valuable environmental service. When they release their droppings on land, they recycle useful nutrients that were earlier washed off the land into rivers.

Coastal wetlands

Where coastal land gently slopes, as in many places on the U.S. Atlantic and Gulf coasts, a small rise or fall in sea level—as with rising and falling tides—means that large areas of coastal land becomes alternately flooded and then exposed to the air. The land here may become waterlogged with seawater, and only a few types of land plants can survive such salty conditions. In temperate regions these coastal wetlands are called salt marshes. In tropical and subtropical climates they form mangrove swamps (see "Missing mangroves," pages 212–213).

Many people are familiar with the strange, barren landscape of a North American or European salt marsh, where clumps of tough marsh plants grow between muddy creeks. In summer the air is filled with the song of skylarks. In winter flocks of gray geese arrive from their Arctic breeding grounds. At the salt marsh's seaward edge salt-tolerant cord grasses are almost the only land plants that survive. Toward the landward edge grow a limited range of rushes and grasses, as well as salt-tolerant succulents (fleshy-leaved, moisture-conserving plants) such as glasswort.

Salt marshes, like the muddy estuaries they often border, are demanding places for organisms to live, but they harbor hidden treasures. The salinity in the salt marsh varies from saltier than seawater to freshwater. The tough plants that survive here are difficult to digest, so local animals' main food supplies take the form of decayed plant material that microscopic organisms, particularly bacteria and fungi, have partially decomposed. Animals such as lugworms and clams feed on the microbes and partly decayed plant material found in and on the mud. These creatures are, in turn, food for larger animals such as fish and crabs. Wading birds such as plovers, sandpipers, and oystercatchers, and migratory birds such as ducks and geese, arrive at salt marshes in large flocks. The birds consume mud-living animals and fish and shellfish that live in the creeks. In some cases the birds breed here, too. Salt marshes provide safe havens because large predators from both land and sea find the maze of mud and creeks difficult to walk upon or swim through.

Salt marshes and mangrove swamps play a beneficial role, both for people and for the environment. First, the wetland's tangle of plant roots binds the mud and helps protect the coastal land from erosion by waves and currents. Second, the wetland mud behaves like a chemical processing factory. The mud particles attract and hold poisonous heavy metals such as lead and mercury. The roots of marsh plants absorb nitrates, such as those originating from fertilizers spread on agricultural land. The wetlands thus "clean" the water that passes through them, preventing many harmful substances from washing off the land and into the sea. Finally, coastal wetlands are important nurseries (places where young grow) for valuable fish and shellfish. The salt marsh creeks of the southeast United States serve as nurseries for the young of half the locally caught fish species. Fishers also harvest clams, oysters, and scallops from these creeks. In warmer climates the waters around the tangle of mangrove roots harbor the larvae of fish and shrimp that will disperse over a wide area when they grow into adults. When people drain or dig up salt marshes and mangrove swamps to build coastal developments, the wetlands' valuable environmental services are lost.

Islands

An island is a landmass, smaller than a continent, surrounded by water. The world's largest island, Greenland, is several times smaller than the world's smallest continent, Australia. The Pacific Ocean alone has at least 25,000 islands, many of which are barely a few tens of yards across. Most geographers recognize three types of marine island based on their origins: inshore islands, offshore islands, and oceanic islands.

Inshore islands lie on continental shelves. They were once joined to the continental mainland. Since that time sea levels have risen or the continental landmass has sunk (subsided) so that the land connection between the two has become submerged. The British Isles are islands of this type. Only 18,000 years ago, at the peak of the last ice age, they were connected to the European mainland. Since then, the glaciers and ice sheets that covered much of northern Europe have melted away. Seawater levels have risen by about 300 feet (90 m), and the land connection is now engulfed, with most lying at least 165 feet (50 m) beneath the North Sea and English Channel.

Offshore islands lie fairly close to continental landmasses but not on continental shelves. Some offshore islands were once connected to the nearby mainland, but they have been separated for millions of years. Others have never been part of the mainland. However, their closeness to the mainland—or their previous connection—means that they contain many of the same species of animals and plants that are found on the nearby continent. Many have colonized the islands by drifting on ocean currents, or, in the case of some animals, they have swum or flown across. Some offshore islands become refuges for animals that have died out on the mainland.

Madagascar, an offshore island cut off from Africa for many millions of years, today contains 30 species of prosimian (primitive members of the animal group that includes apes and monkeys). Many of these prosimian species, or closely related ones, have died out on mainland Africa, where they have lost out in competition with more recently evolved monkeys. On isolated Madagascar, however, which monkeys have not yet reached, the prosimians have survived.

Oceanic islands lie several hundred miles or more from the nearest mainland. Volcanoes that punched their way to the sea surface have created most of them.

Most oceanic islands are only a few tens of miles across, or less. But they are much more important than their size suggests. Because these islands are so remote, animals and plants that arrive there and set up breeding populations may evolve in isolation from their relatives elsewhere. Over many generations as the members of these populations adapt to life in their island home, those characteristics that equip them for survival are selected, and those individuals with these characteristics tend to be the ones that survive to breed. Over many generations the island animals and plants evolve to become slightly different from the mainland relatives from which they originated. As a result, some of the larger oceanic islands contain an unusually high proportion of species found nowhere else. For instance, biologists studying the animals and plants of the Galápagos Islands, lying in the Pacific Ocean about 600 miles (960 km) off Ecuador, have so far described about 5,000 species. Of these, about one-third are found nowhere else.

In the water, too, oceanic islands have great influence. Their sides deflect deep water toward the surface. This deep water is rich in nutrients that have come from the breakdown of waste matter and dead organisms. In the sunlit surface waters this injection of nutrients helps microscopic plantlike organisms called phytoplankton to grow. Animal plankton (zooplankton) feed on the phytoplankton, and they are consumed by fish, which in turn are eaten by larger fish and marine mammals. In warm clear waters, coral reefs grow on the flanks of islands, producing the most complex animal and plant communities in the ocean (see "The living reef," pages 151–154).

Seamounts

There are between 30,000 and 50,000 seamounts across the world. These extinct underwater volcanoes pepper the abyssal plains of the deep ocean, rising at least 3,280 feet (1,000 m) above the seafloor. They are magnets for marine life.

In the vast ocean expanses seamounts are like oases. As ocean currents sweep past a seamount, the seawater is swirled into eddies and pushed toward the surface. Nutrient-rich water rises near the surface, encouraging the growth of phytoplankton on which marine animals, directly or indirectly, depend for food. Above the seamount a rich community of marine life develops. Large predators, such as dolphins and sharks, will journey from one seamount to the next to harvest the schools of smaller fish that gather there.

These underwater mountains survive for millions of years. The larvae of bottom-dwelling animals—sponges, soft corals, sea anemones, crabs, sea squirts, and the like—settle there. Separated from other clusters of seamounts by hundreds of miles of flat, deep seabed, the creatures can evolve in isolation. As a result, many seamounts come to harbor an unusually high proportion of local species—species that are absent in other parts of the ocean. If the seamount rises to within a few dozen feet of the sea surface in tropical waters, hard corals—the kind that establish vibrant coral reef communities—will also grow there.

The importance of seamounts has only become apparent in the last 30 years. Technology now exists for divers to use underwater vehicles and sophisticated sonar devices to locate and explore these structures with greater ease.

CHAPTER 2

GEOLOGY OF THE OCEANS

Earth's structure

Various strands of evidence, such as the age of Moon rocks and meteorites, lead scientists to believe that the solar system (the Sun and its orbiting planets) formed about 4.6 billion years ago. The parts of the solar system came together from bits of space debris. These originated from the birth of matter in a universe-creating explosion some 13 billion years ago, which scientists call "the big bang."

When the solar system's larger planets, including Earth, began to assemble around the Sun, they were red-hot. Part of the reason for this is that when space debris collides at high speed, it releases its energy of movement as heat. When Earth began to assemble from this debris, it also contained many radioactive chemicals (those that break down of their own accord to release large amounts of energy). This generated more heat. The young planet Earth therefore formed as a fiery ball of melted substances. Within Earth the substances arranged themselves according to their density (heaviness). Under Earth's gravitational pull, less dense (lighter) material floated to the planet's surface, while denser (heavier) substances sank to the center of the planet. By about 4 billion years ago, Earth began to cool, and as it did so it formed an outer solid layer—a crust.

Today, Earth consists of several layers: crust and rigid upper mantle, two layers of mantle below these, and then an outer and inner core at the center. Scientists know this from indirect evidence. It is not yet possible to drill very far beneath Earth's surface. The deepest bore hole is about 7.5 miles (12 km) deep—reaching not even halfway through Earth's outer layer of rock on land, called the continental crust. However, scientists can gather useful information even at this depth. The temperature rise over this distance enables scientists to calculate Earth's likely temperature 1,865 miles (3,000 km) beneath the surface at the outer edge of the core. They work out this temperature to be an astonishing 7,050°F (3,900°C).

Scientists gain information about the chemical makeup of the deep crust and mantle from lava (molten rock) that erupts from volcanoes. Earthquakes also yield clues about the different layers. Earthquakes are shock waves in the ground produced when masses of rock underground suddenly slip past one another. The resulting shock waves travel in all directions through the rock. Scientists can detect the shock waves at the surface, using vibration-sensing instruments such as seismometers. Earthquakes produce three main types of shock waves, and how these waves are bent or bounced by the rock at different levels tells scientists about the size and consistency of Earth's layers.

The ground beneath our feet—the crust—seems solid enough, but deep below the surface, in the outer core, the rock is molten. Closer to the crust, in the mantle layer, lies a region called the *asthenosphere* (from *asthenos,* Greek for "weak") that is almost solid but acts like a liquid moving in slow motion. The rock we stand on "floats" on this layer and very slowly moves across the surface of Earth, up to a few inches a year.

Much of the rock on Earth's surface originally came from hot, molten rock, or magma, from within the mantle or deep crust. When this magma cooled, it became solid. Rock formed in this way is called igneous rock, and there are two common kinds: basalt and granite. Basalt is a fine-grained, dark rock that is rich in silica (Si) and magnesium (Mg). Basalt is denser (heavier) than granite, so it sinks lower on Earth's surface, where it makes giant hollows. In the past these depressions, or basins, filled with water, and they contain Earth's oceans. This basalt-rich surface layer of rock is called oceanic crust.

Granite, on the other hand, is coarse-grained, paler rock rich in silica and aluminum (Al). Granite is less dense (lighter) than basalt. It settles higher on Earth's surface, where it forms the continental crust of large landmasses. So the highs and lows on Earth's surface are present because of the nature of their underlying rock: The highs of granite have

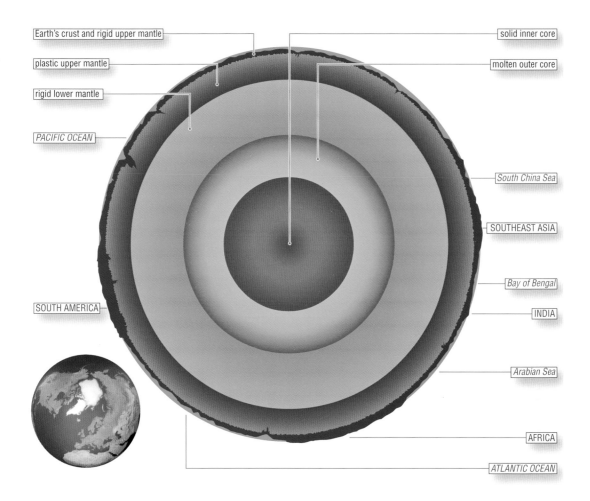

Earth's crust and rigid upper mantle

plastic upper mantle

rigid lower mantle

PACIFIC OCEAN

SOUTH AMERICA

solid inner core

molten outer core

South China Sea

SOUTHEAST ASIA

Bay of Bengal

INDIA

Arabian Sea

AFRICA

ATLANTIC OCEAN

A slice through the Earth

formed continents; the basalt-lined lows have filled with water to create oceans.

The oldest oceanic crust dates to about 200 million years ago, while the most ancient continental crust is 3.8 billion years old. Compared with continental crust, oceanic crust does not survive long. The reason for this, as will become apparent later, is the process of seafloor spreading (see "Seafloor spreading," pages 34–35).

Continental drift

As recently as the early 1960s many geologists believed that the continents were more or less fixed in position on the planet's surface. Evidence gathered since then, however, has forced geologists to rewrite their textbooks.

In about 1600 C.E. the Dutch mapmaker Abraham Ortelius noticed that the eastern coastlines of the Americas seemed to form a fairly snug fit with the western coastlines of Europe and Africa. This led him to speculate that the landmasses on opposite sides of the Atlantic might once have been joined. By the late 19th century various lines of evidence seemed to support this idea. For example, Africa and America shared similar kinds of coal deposits and other geological features. Fossils of the long-extinct aquatic reptile *Mesosaurus* were found on the west coast of southern Africa and the east coast of South America, but not in between. This distribution suggests that the two regions were once joined.

The first oceans

When did the first oceans form? And where did their water come from? About 4 billion years ago, as the solar system's planets continued to mop up debris from near space, the number of collisions diminished. With fewer collisions to superheat the planet, Earth began to cool. Earth's rock is "wet" (it contains water). As Earth's surface cooled, water escaping as steam from volcanoes gathered around Earth's surface rather than being driven off into space by the heat. Earth became shrouded in an atmosphere (the layer of gas that surrounds Earth) that was rich in water vapor. As the vapor cooled, it formed droplets that gathered together as clouds. Eventually, the clouds unloaded their water in a downpour that probably lasted thousands of years. This water filled any depressions on Earth's surface and formed the first oceans.

Earth has changed enormously since the first oceans formed. Not only have life forms evolved—beginning about 3.8 billion years ago—but the arrangement of the continents and the oceans must have undergone several cycles of change. Throughout that time wet rocks from space (meteorites) have struck the planet occasionally, adding more water. Comets—giant cosmic snowballs of ice and dirt—have struck Earth, too, adding water. A "rainfall" of miniature comets has probably sprinkled Earth's atmosphere with water over the last 4 billion years. Volcanoes continue to belch steam into the atmosphere, which will eventually fall as rain. All these sources account for the water found in the oceans today.

In 1912 Alfred Wegener (1880–1930), a German meteorologist, pieced together the available evidence about how continents might fit together and published his ideas in the German-language book *The Origin of Continents and Oceans*. Wegener suggested that all today's continents were once joined together in a supercontinent, which he called Pangaea. He believed that Pangaea broke into two supercontinents about 200 million years ago, yielding Laurasia to the north and Gondwana to the south. These supercontinents then broke apart and their fragments drifted across the surface of the Earth to become today's continents. Wegener's theory of continental drift, as it was called, was ridiculed at the time because scientists could not think of a reasonable mechanism that might cause continents to move. It would take nearly 50 years for scientists to find a convincing answer.

Seafloor spreading

After World War II, research institutions could buy surplus naval vessels fairly cheaply. Ships' equipment included sonar, or echo-sounding, devices that bounced sound waves off the seafloor to measure depth. Oceanographers could now begin systematically mapping the floor of the oceans in detail. By the mid-1950s a team that included Maurice Ewing, Bruce Heezen, and Marie Tharp, working at the Lamont-Doherty Geological Observatory in New York, had plotted the mid-ocean ridge system running down the middle of the Atlantic Ocean. They had also identified its central rift valley. Oceanographers worldwide were discovering that the ocean floors, far from being flat and boring, contained extensive mid-ocean ridge systems, deep trenches, and thousands of seamounts. By the late 1950s it was clear that many of the world's volcano and earthquake zones lie on or close to the system of ocean ridges and trenches. If plates existed, then at their edges (boundaries or margins) adjacent plates would be moving apart, colliding together, or sliding past one another. These movements could be the source of the earthquakes and volcanoes.

In 1960 two American geologists, Harry Hess (1906–69) and Robert Dietz (1914–95), came separately to the conclusion that oceanic crust is spreading from mid-ocean ridges. They suggested that moving rock in Earth's mantle, stirred by heat, was driving the process and causing plates on either side of the ridge to move apart. The continents, riding on some of these plates, were being carried along in the process.

By the late 1960s Hess and Dietz's "seafloor spreading" idea had been tested. Scientists were drilling into the sediment and crust on the deep-ocean floor. Using radiometric dating (dating techniques that involve assessing the decay of naturally radioactive atoms), they found that crust close to mid-ocean trenches was younger than that farther away. The layer of sediment close to a ridge was also thinner than that at a distance. This made sense because new crust would have less time to gather sediment. A most convincing piece of evidence came in the form of magnetic variation in oceanic crust.

The Earth behaves like a giant magnet. Earth's magnetic field causes iron particles on Earth's surface to align in a north-south direction. Every few hundred thousand years, however, Earth's magnetic field reverses. The South Pole, for example, comes to behave like the magnetic North Pole.

New rock that is laid down next to a mid-ocean ridge contains iron particles. In fresh, molten rock, the iron particles align with Earth's magnetic field. When the rock cools, the iron particles carry the "imprint" of Earth's magnetic field at the time. When Earth's magnetic field reverses, newly formed rock takes on the magnetic reversal. Scientists can detect this, and if seafloor is moving away from a ridge, the oceanic crust on either side should show a pattern of reversals—a series of magnetic "stripes" in the rock—that are a mirror image of each other. By the mid-1960s this is precisely what scientists had found. The evidence supported the idea of seafloor spreading, and this provided a great boost for the theory of plate tectonics—the modern theory that incorporates and extends Wegener's ideas about continental drift.

Moving plates

Today geologists agree that Earth's surface is made up of 13 or so giant plates that interlock like a giant jigsaw puzzle. The plates are slowly moving, and new material is being added to their edges at mid-ocean ridges and taken away in trenches. A plate contains crust and, attached to its underside, some rigid material from the outer mantle. The crust and rigid outer mantle are called *lithosphere* (from the Greek *lithos* for "rock"). The technical name for a plate is a *lithospheric,* or *tectonic, plate.* The modern theory that describes how plates are created, moved, and are destroyed, is called *plate tectonics* (from the Greek *tekton,* "to build").

Some of Earth's plates contain both continental and oceanic crust, so when they move, they carry the continents with them. Some of the plates contain only oceanic crust. What happens when two plates collide depends upon whether there is continental or oceanic crust at the boundary of collision.

When a plate that carries continental crust meets another carrying oceanic crust, the denser (heavier) oceanic crust slides beneath the lighter continental crust. This creates a deep dip in the ocean floor called a trench. As the oceanic plate descends beneath the continental one, friction between the two sets off occasional earthquakes. Oceanic crust melts in the mantle, and some of the lighter rock finds its way to the surface as lava in volcanoes. Near the western coast of South America the Nazca plate of the eastern Pacific is descending beneath the South American plate at a trench offshore. Earthquakes occur here, and volcanoes erupt through the Andes mountain range that runs parallel to the coast. The Andes themselves were created by the oceanic plate pushing against the continent, buckling the continental crust into mountains.

At a trench where two oceanic plates collide, both plates are of similar density but nevertheless one slides beneath the other. As in an oceanic plate–continental plate collision, earthquakes are triggered and volcanoes are produced, but the volcanoes often erupt under the sea rather than on a continent. If the volcanoes rise all the way to the sea surface, they produce an arc of islands, such as the Aleutian Islands off Alaska or the Mariana Islands of the western Pacific.

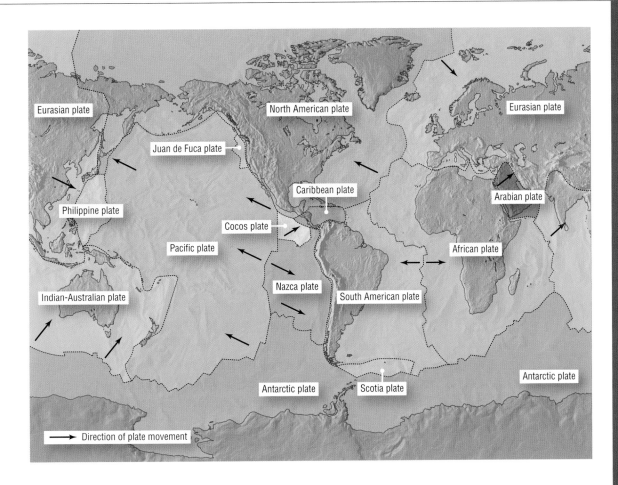

Eurasian plate

North American plate

Eurasian plate

Juan de Fuca plate

Caribbean plate

Arabian plate

Philippine plate

Cocos plate

African plate

Pacific plate

Nazca plate

Indian-Australian plate

South American plate

Antarctic plate

Antarctic plate

Scotia plate

→ Direction of plate movement

When two continental plates collide, both are light and neither slides into the mantle. Instead, as the landmasses push together, rocks distort under the pressure, and great mountain ranges squeeze into existence. The collision of Africa and Eurasia within the last 65 million years has created the eastern European Alps in this way.

Sometimes plates neither collide nor move apart but slide past each other. When this happens, friction (resistance to sliding) causes the surfaces to lock rather than slip, stresses build up, and then the plates unlock with a sudden release of energy that generates an earthquake. A good example of this kind of plate boundary—called a *transform fault*—is California's San Andreas Fault. Here the North American plate meets the Pacific plate. The sliding plates

Earth's plates. These are gigantic, slowly moving slabs of Earth's lithosphere.

make nearby San Francisco one of the most earthquake-prone cities in the world.

Birth and death of an ocean

How do ocean basins form in the first place? In the 1960s the Canadian scientist Tuzo Wilson (1908–93) suggested that an ocean basin has a life cycle (now called the Wilson cycle). Wilson's theory of how ocean basins are created also explains how continents might break apart, as happened in the case of the ancient supercontinent Pangaea and its offspring Laurasia and Gondwana.

The first stage of the Wilson cycle, the embryonic ocean, is a dry depression. This stage is illustrated by today's East African Rift Valley. Here a weakness in the continental crust, heated from below, has uplifted and split. An unsupported section of crust has sunk (subsided) to form a rift valley. The East African Rift Valley is not directly connected to the sea, but if it were, seawater would flood in to fill it. Such an event probably happened to the rift valley that formed between the African and Arabian plates some 20 million years ago. This rift valley has since widened to become the Red Sea.

The second stage of the Wilson cycle, the juvenile stage of an ocean, occurs when a rift valley floods, accompanied by seafloor spreading along its length, so that the land-masses on either side move apart. The Red Sea is at this stage today. Given another hundred million years or so, the Red Sea will probably have grown to become a mature ocean, the third stage.

The present-day Atlantic Ocean depicts the third stage of the Wilson cycle. The Atlantic began to form about 180 million years ago when a rift valley split Pangaea into Laurasia and Gondwana. The Atlantic is now a mature ocean and is still expanding. It will not, however, grow forever. Eventually, the rate of seafloor destruction in trenches will overtake the rate of seafloor creation at mid-ocean ridges, and the ocean will begin to shrink—as is the case for today's Pacific Ocean.

The Pacific Ocean basin illustrates the fourth stage of the Wilson cycle, the declining stage of an ocean. The Pacific Ocean continues to shrink as the surrounding plates override

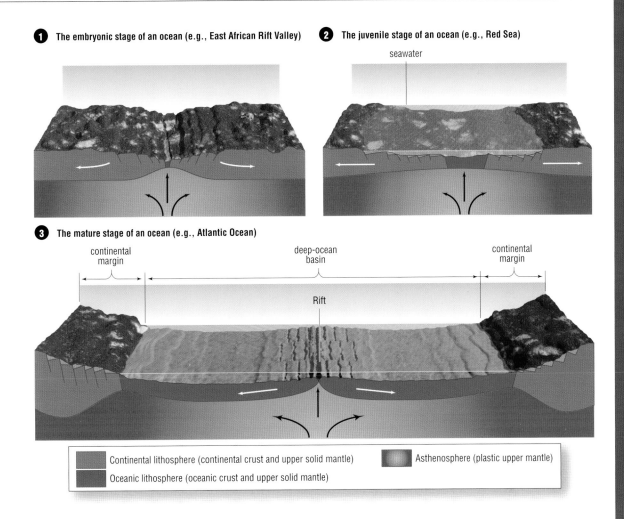

① The embryonic stage of an ocean (e.g., East African Rift Valley)

② The juvenile stage of an ocean (e.g., Red Sea)

seawater

③ The mature stage of an ocean (e.g., Atlantic Ocean)

continental margin   deep-ocean basin   continental margin

Rift

Continental lithosphere (continental crust and upper solid mantle)

Oceanic lithosphere (oceanic crust and upper solid mantle)

Asthenosphere (plastic upper mantle)

its edges. It will eventually reach the fifth, or terminal, stage. The present-day Mediterranean Sea illustrates this well. It is probably the largest remaining fragment of the ancient Tethys Sea. Eventually, the Mediterranean Sea may disappear entirely as North Africa and southern Europe collide, folding the continental crust and creating new mountains.

The changing shape of the oceans

Alfred Wegener's idea that today's continents were once joined together in a single supercontinent has been confirmed by analysis of the distribution of fossils, geological

The growth of an ocean, as explained by geologist Tuzo Wilson: An ocean basin grows from its embryonic stage as a flooded rift valley, then expands by seafloor spreading to become a mature ocean.

formations, and ancient climatic and magnetic records revealed in rocks. A textbook view of how the present-day continents and oceans came into being goes like this:

1. About 220 million years ago, soon after the start of the Age of Dinosaurs, the Earth's surface consisted of a single giant landmass, Pangaea, surrounded by a giant ocean, Panthalassa. Pangaea had two gigantic bays. One, the Sinus Borealis, lay in the far north. The other, the Tethys Sea, straddled the equator.

2. By 180 million years ago a rift had divided Pangaea into two supercontinents—Laurasia to the north and Gondwana to the south. The Tethys Sea flowed into the rift, marking the birth of the northern Atlantic Ocean.

3. By 130 million years ago a rift caused Gondwana to break up, releasing a fragment that was to move northward and form the Indian subcontinent. This event marked the birth of the Indian Ocean.

4. By 65 million years ago, the end of the Age of Dinosaurs, the southern Atlantic Ocean had been born from a rift between South America and Africa. The Sinus Borealis had moved to the North Pole to become the Arctic Ocean. The Atlantic Ocean had begun to spread and the Pacific Ocean to shrink, processes that continue to this day. North America and Europe were still joined together.

5. Within the last 60 million years, Antarctica and Australia separated, North America and Europe have parted as the Atlantic developed into a mature ocean, and the Indian subcontinent has collided with Eurasia creating the Himalayas. In the last 20 million years the Red Sea has formed around an extension of the northern Indian Ocean's mid-ocean ridge system. The Red Sea is probably an ocean in the making. Within the last 5 million years the Isthmus of Panama has bridged North and South America and separated the tropical Pacific from the tropical Atlantic.

(opposite page) *Continental drift and the changing shape of the oceans*

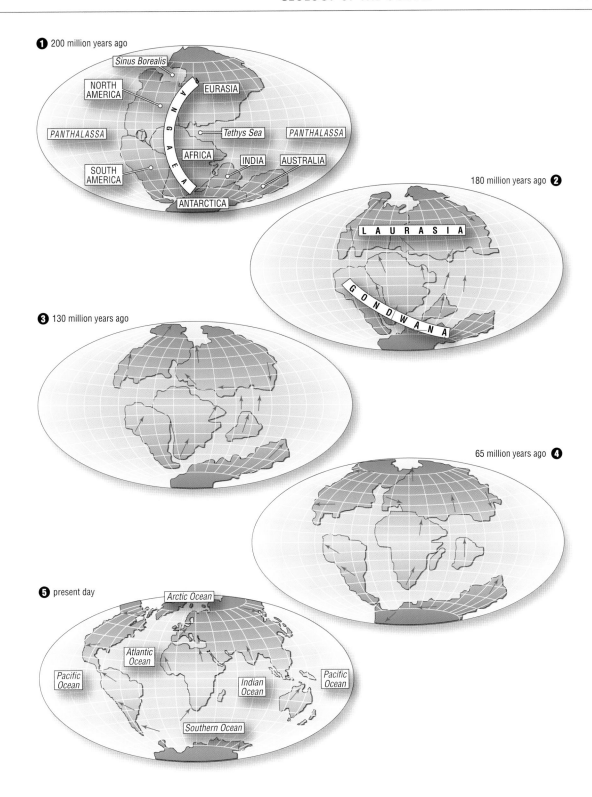

1 200 million years ago

Sinus Borealis
NORTH AMERICA
EURASIA
PANTHALASSA
Tethys Sea
PANTHALASSA
AFRICA
INDIA
AUSTRALIA
SOUTH AMERICA
ANTARCTICA
PANGAEA

2 180 million years ago

LAURASIA
GONDWANA

3 130 million years ago

4 65 million years ago

5 present day

Arctic Ocean
Atlantic Ocean
Pacific Ocean
Indian Ocean
Pacific Ocean
Southern Ocean

These five stages are snapshots in geological time. They are part of a continuing cycle of ocean creation and destruction, as continents break apart or merge. In 100 million years' time the arrangement of the oceans and continents will be quite different from the way it is today. The Red Sea may be an ocean, the widening Atlantic Ocean will have a much wider connection with the Arctic Ocean, and North and South America will probably separate, allowing tropical Atlantic and Pacific waters to mix freely once again.

Seafloor sediments

Environmentalist Rachel Carson (1907–64), in describing deep-ocean sediment in her 1941 book *Under the Sea Wind,* wrote of "the most stupendous 'snowfall' the Earth has ever seen." Carson's "snowfall" is the downward drift of sediment particles from above—day by day, year by year, millennium by millennium—that settle on the seabed. The drift will continue as long as there are oceans and continents.

Carson's snowfall contains small particles from many different sources. The particles fall through the water column (the vertical expanse of seawater from surface to seabed) under gravity. The snowfall carpets the seabed in a sediment layer that can reach 3,000 feet (900 m) thick on ancient oceanic crust.

The skeletons of once-living organisms, especially microscopic phytoplankton (plant plankton) and zooplankton (animal plankton), settle on the seabed to form skeleton-rich sediments called *oozes*. Some oozes are rich in silica from the skeletons of phytoplankton called *diatoms* or zooplankton called *radiolarians*. The 130-feet (40 m) high White Cliffs of Dover, on England's south coast, are made of chalky seabed sediments—squeezed together to form sedimentary rock and now uplifted to become land. These chalk deposits are remains of phytoplankton called *coccolithophores*. Examined under a microscope, a chalk sample reveals its structure of crushed skeletons.

Sediments that originate from land include fine grains of mud particles blown into the sea or carried there by rivers. The finest particles take a long time to settle, so they are often found in the deep ocean far from land. Larger particles settle closer to the coast, particularly near the mouths of rivers.

Some sediments arise from chemical reactions in seawater. Where hydrothermal (hot water) vents spew chemical-rich water into the deep ocean, chemicals react and settle out, covering the seabed in metal-rich deposits containing copper, cobalt, and nickel. Mining companies see these deposits as valuable sources of metal. Even stranger are the potato-sized lumps of rock scattered over much of the deep-ocean floor. It is a mystery as to exactly how these manganese or polymetallic (many-metal) nodules form. They seem to grow spontaneously on the seabed, attracting chemicals from the surrounding seawater. Most grow very slowly—at the rate of four inches (10 cm) or less every million years. Scientists have yet to understand why the nodules do not become smothered in fine sediment. The nodules are a potentially rich source of metal. Someday soon companies will probably gain permission to start dredging the oceans for them (see "The Law of the Sea Treaty," pages 217–218).

Dinosaur extinction

A dark band of sediment that dates to about 65 million years ago coincides with the extinction of the dinosaurs and the loss of many marine species. When scientists analyze the band, they find a layer rich in iridium, a metal common in meteorites. This finding led scientists to hunt for the 65-million-year-old impact site of a large meteorite. They found it in the Gulf of Mexico along the north coast of the Yucatán Peninsula. Seismic surveying revealed a 112-mile-wide (180 km) impact crater that could have been produced by a six-mile-wide (10 km) meteorite. Iridium-rich particles had been scattered in all directions around the crater. The explosive impact of the meteorite would have killed instantly nearly all life within a few hundred miles. The blast must have thrown enormous quantities of dust particles into the air, which changed Earth's climate temporarily. Sunlight was temporarily blocked, and Earth's temperature fell; next followed a period of global warming and acid rainfall. It is no wonder that many plants and animals—on land and in the sea—became extinct at this time.

Some deep-ocean sediment comes from space. Extraterrestrial particles—most of them less than 0.2 inches (.5 cm) across—sprinkle onto the sea surface and sink down to the seabed. However, at intervals of tens or hundreds of millions of years a giant meteorite impacts the Earth. When that happens, life on Earth is threatened, and many species become extinct (die out) in the aftermath of the impact.

Deep-ocean sediments provide a record of events happening in the land, sea, and air over millions of years. The types of particles that settle at a given time in Earth's history reflect the environmental conditions of the time. For example, in the last 200 years pollution by humans has left its trace on the topmost layers of deep-ocean sediments. Scientists can drill cores of sediment from the seabed and examine and interpret the layers of different ages to reveal life-changing events on Earth.

Changing sea levels

Locally, the level of the sea changes with the rising and falling tide (see "Tides," pages 81–84), and with changes in weather conditions (see "Hurricanes and sea fogs," pages 88–91). For example, along many coasts the sea level falls and rises twice a day with the ebb and flow of the tide. The difference in height between the highest and lowest tides reaches a remarkable 40 feet (12 m) in the Bay of Fundy, Canada—the highest tidal range anywhere in the world. The tidal effect can be increased or decreased by winds. Winds blowing toward a shore (onshore) will cause the water to pile up slightly next to the coast as a surge; winds blowing away from a shore (offshore) will have the opposite effect.

Changes in sea level in the open ocean are much less obvious but are detectable using remote sensing satellites. During an El Niño event (see "Upwelling and El Niño," pages 79–81), the slackening of trade winds causes the sea level in the western Pacific to drop by as much as six inches (15 cm).

Scientists take into account short-term changes in sea level to work out an average sea level for a given locality. By combining such data from many localities, they calculate a global sea level. The global sea level has probably risen by six inches (15 cm) in the last century, and the likely cause is global warming, a rise in average surface temperatures across the world. This has caused the world's seawater to expand slightly.

Very dramatic changes in sea level have happened within the last 100,000 years. During major cold spells in Earth's history, glaciers and ice sheets expanded outward from the poles. Rainwater stayed frozen on land rather than entering the sea, so sea levels fell. During the last ice age, which peaked about 18,000 years ago, the sea level dropped by about 560 feet (170 m). Since then, much of the ice on land has thawed, adding water to the oceans, and ocean water has expanded with the heat (water, like many substances, takes up more space when warmed). Sea levels have risen by 300 feet (90 m) or more, flooding many continental shelves that were previously exposed. Since that time, rising water has separated the British Isles from the European mainland. Today's North Sea, at 165–330 feet (50–100 m) deep, was a frozen landscape only 15,000 years ago. Where fish now swim, mammoths once roamed.

It is not just the sea that rises and falls. So does the land. This makes it quite tricky for scientists to calculate global sea level, because they need to take into account events on land as well as in the sea.

As Earth's plates move, stresses build up in places where the plates meet, triggering events such as earthquakes and volcanic eruptions. An earthquake can cause one section of land to rise by a yard or so, and another to fall, within the space of a few minutes. Volcanoes—by adding lava, or by causing snow and ice to melt—can make land levels rise or fall by many feet over a few hours or days. However, most changes in land level happen much more slowly, over periods of thousands or millions of years.

Since the end of the last ice age, melting ice sheets have lightened the load on many continents. Snow and ice weighs down the landscape, causing the landmass to sink slightly. With the thaw, added weight flows off the land, permitting the continental crust to rise. This does not happen overnight, however. There is a time lag of thousands of years. Scotland is still rising, and England sinking, as the tilted landmass of the British Isles rights itself after the thaw that began 15,000 years ago. Before this, northern Canada was covered in an ice sheet up to two miles (3 km) thick. Some geologists estimate that Hudson Bay—currently about 490 feet (150 m) below sea level—will form part of the land in tens of thousands of years, once the bay has finished "rebounding" after the thaw.

Evidence of dramatic changes in land and sea level is common. Chesapeake Bay, between Maryland and Virginia, is a river valley drowned by the sea since the last ice age. Raised beaches—ancient beaches left high and dry when the sea level fell or the land rose—are common as flat shelves of coastal land, such as those found near Point Reyes, California. Sedimentary rock, such as limestone or chalk formed by the squeezing of buried sediment under the seabed, is common on land. Mount Everest, the tallest land mountain, has a shale band near its summit, proving that this rock was once part of a continental shelf that has now been uplifted by more than three miles (about 5 km).

Shoreline processes

Once tectonic forces—those relating to the movement of Earth's plates—establish the shape and slope of a coastline, other processes come into play to alter it. These processes are grouped into two categories: erosion and deposition.

Erosion is the process of exposed material, such as rock or soil, being broken down and transported. Erosion involves natural breakdown by physical, chemical, and biological processes.

As for physical forces of erosion, on an exposed Atlantic rocky shore, 30-foot (9-m)-high storm waves slam into a cliff with a force similar to that of a space shuttle's main thrusters. The wave squeezes compressed air into crevices, then as the wave retreats, it creates a partial vacuum that makes the trapped air expand explosively. Under this onslaught the crevices enlarge, and pieces of rock become blasted off the cliff. At the base of the cliff storm waves can move boulders weighing hundreds of tons, scraping and scouring any surface across which they move. Sand and gravel, too, carried back and forth by the waves, scrape away at rocky surfaces, gradually wearing them down.

Among chemical processes of erosion, seawater gradually dissolves certain types of rock, such as limestone. On a stormy night, limestone cliffs can be cut back by three feet (1 m) by a combination of physical and chemical action. As for biological processes, mosses and lichens release carbon dioxide gas, which dissolves in water to form a weak acid. The acid is enough to speed up the breakdown of limestone rock on which these plants grow.

Deposition—the settling of particles—encompasses the other group of shoreline processes. Particles eroded from exposed parts of a coastline, such as cliffs, where the action of waves and currents is strong, are deposited in sheltered parts, such as bays and estuaries. On a rocky shore, erosion dominates. On sandy or muddy shores, deposition predominates.

Exposed shores

Exposed shores—those that are subjected to strong waves, winds, and currents—tend to be rocky, because any surface covering has been eroded to reveal the bedrock beneath. Cliffs are common on exposed shores, and their size and shape depends on the nature of the underlying rock and the impact of the forces of erosion. Soft, sedimentary rock such as limestone erodes more quickly than hard, igneous rock such as granite. Granite cliffs tend to have a jagged outline full of small nooks and crannies; limestone cliffs tend to have a smoother outline.

A newly established rocky coastline usually has headlands of harder rock that jut out into the sea. Sheltered bays of softer rock may lie in between. Sea waves breaking against the coast reach headlands first and bend around to attack them from all sides. As a result, the headlands erode, and particles worn away from the rock tend to gather in the bays in between. Over hundreds and thousands of years, as the headlands are cut back and the bays fill, the coastline tends to straighten.

As the exposed sea cliff gradually erodes under the onslaught of waves, a platform, or ledge, of rock develops at its base. Wave

View through a sea arch of the stacks known as the Twelve Apostles at Port Campbell, Victoria, Australia (Courtesy of Fred Bavendam/ Minden Pictures)

action may undercut the cliff face so that the upper part collapses, spreading rubble across the cliff base. If the wave-cut platform is exposed at low tide, it often reveals a boulder-strewn rocky ledge with scattered tide pools. Given enough time, the wave-cut platform may become wide enough that few waves ever reach the cliffs, and cliff erosion slows dramatically. Sand, gravel, or shingle (water-worn pebbles) may settle at the base of the cliff, creating a narrow beach.

As headlands erode, they develop distinctive features. Softer parts erode more quickly, creating sea caves. If a cave cuts right through a headland, it becomes a sea arch. If an arch collapses, it leaves behind towers of rock called *stacks*.

Sheltered shores

Sheltered shores develop where the action of waves, currents, and tides is less strong. In these places, such as bays and estuaries, the sea unloads its sediment in the form of mud, sand, or larger particles, and the sediment stays there rather than being swept away. Such shores are commonplace along the U.S. Atlantic and Gulf coasts and are found along parts of the California coast of the Pacific.

Larger, heavier particles settle more quickly than smaller, lighter particles, and once they have settled, they are more difficult to dislodge. So shingle and gravel (particle sizes greater than 0.08 inches, or 2 mm) gather on exposed, sloping shores. Sandy beaches are moderately sheltered and gather medium-size particles (0.0025 to 0.08 inches, or 0.063 to 2 mm). The most sheltered shores, such as those in and around estuaries, accumulate mud (particle sizes less than 0.0025 inches, or 0.063 mm).

The sediment that settles on a beach usually comes from a nearby location, but small particles may be carried hundreds of miles by rivers or by ocean currents. Beaches of sand, gravel, or shingle usually contain coarse mineral fragments eroded from nearby cliffs or coastal mountains. Desert sands can be blown onto shores to create beaches. Mud comes mostly from clay and other small particles emptied into the sea by rivers. In tropical or subtropical regions where there are no nearby rivers or mountains, beautiful pale, palm-fringed beaches may be biological in origin. On close inspection, the sand may consist of coral fragments from nearby reefs and pieces of shell from clams or marine snails.

Waves usually strike a beach at an angle, rather than "head on." This angled impact tends to move particles along the beach in the direction of prevailing winds and currents, a process called longshore drift. For example, on both U.S. Pacific and Atlantic coasts, the prevailing winds tend to move beach sediments in a southerly direction. Where bays are sheltered and the water is shallow, this movement produces characteristic depositional features. For example, on the downstream side of headlands a stretch of sand known as a spit may form roughly parallel to the shore. If this extends across the bay it becomes a bay barrier or bar. Where sand settles between an island and the mainland to create a connection, this is called a *tombolo.*

The barrier island is a characteristic depositional feature of many stretches of Atlantic and Gulf coast between Long

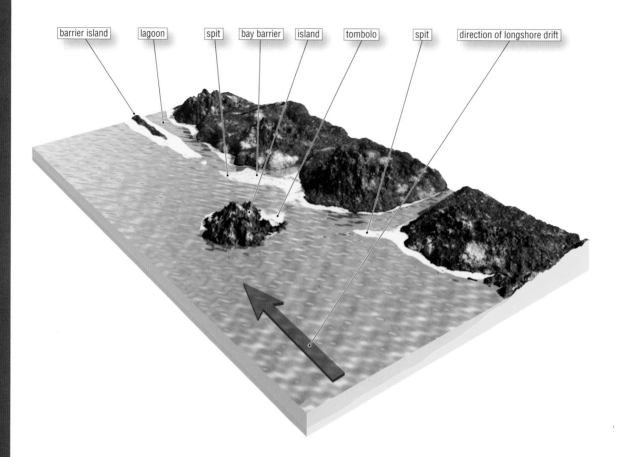

barrier island | lagoon | spit | bay barrier | island | tombolo | spit | direction of longshore drift

Common features of a sheltered shore

Island, New York, and southern Texas. These elongated, sandy islands run roughly parallel to the coast and get their name by forming a barrier to storm waves, so offering the coast some protection against erosion. How barrier islands are formed remains something of a mystery. Most experts agree that they formed since the last age, over which time sea levels have risen by some 300 feet (90 m). A popular explanation is that seawater flooded low-lying coastal land. After being transported down to river mouths by melting glaciers and ice sheets, sediment became deposited as bars and spits in shallow water. As sea levels rose further, the spits and bars lost their connection with the mainland and became islands.

However the barrier islands formed, today they offer prime real estate for those who want a beachfront property. As sites for development, however, barrier islands have their drawbacks. Unless protected by sea defenses, they are in danger of flooding, and they tend to shift under the action of waves and currents. The likelihood of this happening will increase in the face of rising sea levels as a result of global warming (see "Climate change," pages 91–93).

Effects at a distance

Regions of erosion are linked, over tens of miles, to regions of deposition. Some of the best examples of such systems are the four "beach compartments" that lie between Santa Barbara and La Jolla in Southern California. Each compartment has three sections: one or more rivers, a sandy beach, and, offshore, a submarine canyon. The rivers add sand to coastal water, which longshore currents distribute along the coast on the beach nearby. Eventually, the sand from the beach is washed to the head of a submarine canyon and is lost from the coastal system when it flows down the canyon and settles on the ocean floor beyond. Until recently, as fast as sand flowed down the submarine canyon, sand in the

---

Taming the coast

Coastal engineers design sea defenses to withstand the ocean's onslaught. They are guided by two principles. First, creating defenses alters the characteristics of the shore so the sea's behavior changes locally. Second, once sea defenses are in place, they need to be maintained and modified if they are to work. This is particularly the case now that sea levels are rising (see "Climate change," pages 91–93).

Many seaside communities see a sandy beach as a valuable recreational resource that they wish to conserve. To combat longshore drift, for example, local authorities will build groins—barriers running up the beach. As an observant visitor to a sandy beach will notice, sand gathers on the upcurrent side of a groin but is scoured away on the downcurrent side. Groins help stop beach erosion locally, but because sand is no longer swept away at the same rate, downcurrent of the beach of other shores can become starved of sand.

Managing beaches requires careful planning. In 1982 the local community at Ocean City, New Jersey, spent $5 million replacing the sand on their beach. The money and effort was wasted. The sea swept away the sand within 12 weeks.

beach compartment was being replaced by eroded material brought down the rivers. The sand on the beaches was constantly replenished.

This situation has changed. Local authorities in Southern California have been damming the rivers and lining the riverbanks with concrete. These developments provide local communities with hydroelectric power and offer them some protection against riverbanks flooding. But it has unintended effects. Much less sand now enters the beach compartments, and the beaches are being starved. If the process is unchecked, beaches will lose their sand and become rockier. Replenishing the sand artificially is likely to cost several million dollars a year for each beach compartment affected.

CHAPTER 3

THE CHEMISTRY AND PHYSICS OF THE OCEANS

The magic of water

To understand seawater chemistry, one first needs to understand something about the chemistry of water itself.

A water molecule is the smallest amount of water that exists. There are at least 1 billion billion water molecules in a drop of water on a pinhead. How water molecules behave with one another, and with other chemicals, gives water its unique physical and chemical properties.

A water molecule (H_2O) is an atom of oxygen (O) combined with two atoms of hydrogen (H). The structure of a water molecule is unusual. In most molecules with three atoms—carbon dioxide (CO_2), for example—the atoms arrange themselves in a straight line. A water molecule, however, is shaped more like a boomerang or a banana. It is bent in the middle.

Although a water molecule is electrically neutral overall, it has different electrical charges on its surface. The oxygen atom is slightly negative, and the two hydrogen atoms are slightly positive. Since opposite electrical charges attract, the slightly positive parts of one water molecule are attracted to the slightly negative part of another water molecule. This type of attraction is called hydrogen bonding. Combined with the fact that water molecules are bent, hydrogen bonding encourages water molecules to align with one another in geometric arrangements where they can. This helps create the beautiful star-shaped patterns of ice crystals found in snowflakes. The hydrogen bonding also produces many of water's other unusual properties.

Without hydrogen bonding, at normal temperatures water would be a gas like carbon dioxide. Hydrogen bonding makes water molecules less likely to fly apart and form a gas. It is for this reason that most of the water on Earth exists in a liquid

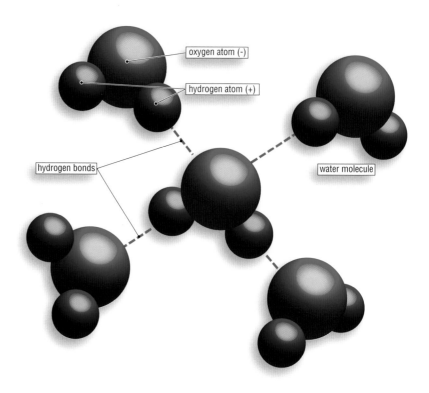

oxygen atom (-)

hydrogen atom (+)

hydrogen bonds

water molecule

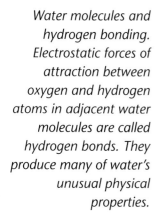

Water molecules and hydrogen bonding. Electrostatic forces of attraction between oxygen and hydrogen atoms in adjacent water molecules are called hydrogen bonds. They produce many of water's unusual physical properties.

form rather than as vapor. Water is also unusual among substances in that within the normal range of temperatures on Earth it exists in all three physical states: solid (ice), liquid, and gas (vapor).

Temperature and seawater

At sea level pure water freezes at 32°F (0°C) and boils at 212°F (100°C). If substances are dissolved in water, their presence changes the freezing and boiling points slightly. For example, seawater of average salinity at the sea surface freezes at 28.6°F (–1.9°C).

Water, like other liquids, gets denser (heavier) as it cools. So water at 39.2°F (4°C) is heavier than water at 42.8°F (6°C) and tends to sink below it, while warm water tends to rise above cool. When cool water sinks from the sea surface, other water moves across to replace it. Meanwhile, elsewhere, warm water rises to the surface to replace water that has sunk. This sinking and rising mixes ocean water and helps direct major ocean currents (see "Subsurface currents and climate control," pages 77–79).

Most liquids sink when they freeze. Water, again, is an exception. Below 39.2°F (4°C), as water approaches its freezing point, it becomes less dense as hydrogen bonding creates an open framework of ice crystals. In both freshwater and seawater, ice floats. If it did not, lakes, rivers, and polar seas would freeze solid. If that were the case, only the warmer regions of the planet would have liquid water, and large areas of the planet would be more or less uninhabitable. In reality, when polar seas freeze at the surface, water continues to circulate beneath the ice. The ice layer keeps warmer water away from the chilling air that might freeze it.

Temperature governs the rate of chemical reactions both inside and outside living organisms. Reactions are usually faster in warm conditions and slower in cool. Most marine species can thrive only in a fairly narrow range of temperatures, so environmental temperature is a key factor that influences where organisms live. Birds and mammals—which can control their body temperature internally—are among the exceptions. Arctic terns and humpback whales, for example, travel widely across the oceans, from polar to tropical waters (see "Marine migrations," pages 146–149).

In all but polar seas the oceans are three-layered for at least part of the year. A warm topmost layer is mixed by winds and currents and heated by the Sun. This layer reaches depths between 330 and 1,650 feet (100 and 500 m). Below this, extending over another 330 to 1,650 feet, is a layer across which the temperature drops rapidly, by between 9°F (5°C) and 15°C (27°F) from top to bottom. This is the thermocline (from the Greek word *klinein,* referring to "slope") and its steep temperature gradient acts as a barrier to the movement of many organisms. Some organisms, such as small shrimp-like animals called *copepods* (see "Zooplankton," pages 104–106), can pass through the thermocline on their daily travels, but many creatures cannot. The thermocline separates the warm surface waters from the cool waters of the deep ocean.

Below the thermocline the deep ocean's water is chilly, with temperatures between 32°F (0°C) and 41°F (5°C). In the

Ice

Ice in the sea takes two forms. Icebergs calve (break off) from the edge of glaciers and from ice sheets that spill into the sea. These floating chunks of ice, because they originate from precipitation over land, contain freshwater. Sea ice, on the other hand, is frozen seawater and contains salt.

In the Arctic and Southern Oceans, as the short polar summer comes to an end, floating ice crystals make the sea appear greasy. This "grease ice" thickens to form floating "pancakes" of ice that freeze together, creating ice floes. The floes crash into one another, buckling and overlapping, to build into mighty sheets of pack ice up to 16.5 feet (5 m) thick.

Pack ice contains varying amount of salts depending on how quickly it forms and how old it is. The water crystals in pack ice are pure water, but as the ice forms, salts separate out and gather in tiny spaces within the ice. Here they form pockets of very salty water, or brine. As the ice ages, some of the brine leaks out through miniature channels into the water beneath the ice. This cool salty water sinks to the sea bottom in polar seas. It helps drive a system of deepwater currents that distribute nutrients around the world's oceans (see "Subsurface currents and climate control," pages 77–79).

Antarctic sea ice in the foreground, with a tabular iceberg in the background (Courtesy of Tui de Roy/Minden Pictures)

deepest parts of the ocean, at the bottom of trenches, the water drops to 30.2°F (–1°C), which is below the normal freezing point of water. The water does not freeze because it is under such high pressure and because it contains salts that lower the freezing point. Only in places warmed by volcanic action, such as areas close to hydrothermal (hot-water) vents, does deep ocean water temperature rise above 41°F (5°C).

Since most of the deep ocean's water is remarkably constant in temperature, oceanographers attach great importance to even small temperature changes. By monitoring seawater temperature and salinity, they can track ocean currents that flow for thousands of miles. Each current has its own combination of temperature and salinity that differs slightly from that of other currents.

Light

The light people can see is just part of the electromagnetic spectrum—a range of waves that travel through matter and have both electrical and magnetic properties. The sunlight that strikes the Earth is "white" light. But as is apparent when raindrops bend sunlight to create a rainbow, sunlight is made up of a spectrum of visible colors, from red to violet. The various colors have different wavelengths; the lengths of their waves differ.

The colors we view are the light of different wavelengths bouncing off objects in our surroundings. Sand in bright sunlight looks yellow because yellow wavelengths of light are reflected from its surface. The sand absorbs other wavelengths of visible light, so we cannot see them.

When sunlight strikes the sea surface, the sea absorbs some wavelengths of light, while others pass readily through. Red wavelengths, for example, travel only 33 feet (10 m) deep or so, while blue light penetrates well beyond 330 feet (100 m) in clear water. This helps explain why clear seawater appears blue. Deeply penetrating blue wavelengths are reflected back to the sea surface, and you see them. Seawater's light-absorbing properties also explain why spectacular coral reefs can appear quite drab below 33 feet (10 m) or so. At this depth the penetrating sunlight no longer contains the

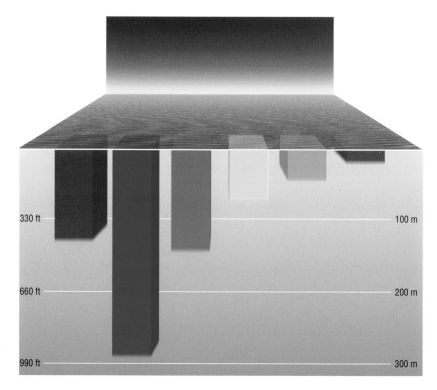

How far light penetrates in seawater. Blue wavelengths penetrate the most and red the least.

330 ft   100 m

660 ft   200 m

990 ft   300 m

full spectrum of visible colors. Seawater takes on a blue-green shade. A red sponge looks black rather than red because there are no red wavelengths to be reflected. At this depth it is only when the white light from an artificial source, such as a flashlight, shines onto the sponge that the animal's true color is revealed.

By about 330 feet (100 m) down in clear ocean water, 99 percent of the surface sunlight has been absorbed. For some animals living below this depth, where the background light is dim, being red is good camouflage. The animal appears black or gray against the faint light.

Particles floating in the water reflect or absorb light and therefore block light penetration. Many tropical and subtropical waters have relatively few particles floating in them, and the water appears clear blue. In temperate waters (those between tropical and polar latitudes) seawater often appears green because it is rich in nutrients that encourage the growth of tiny phytoplankton. These microscopic plants contain light-trapping pigments that give them a green color.

In coastal waters near rivers, seawater often looks coffee-colored because it contains suspended mud and sand.

Sunlight in seawater is a key factor that governs where marine life occurs. Even in the clearest waters there is not enough sunlight beyond a depth of 660 feet (200 m) to sustain photosynthesis, the process by which plants trap sunlight to make food. Marine plants, from microscopic phytoplankton to 330-foot (100-m)-long seaweeds, grow only in this top layer of the ocean, which is called, appropriately, the sunlit zone. The biggest mass of marine life lives in the top 3,300 feet (1,000 m) of the ocean. Sunlight does not reach beyond this depth, although in the inky depths below, some animals produce their own light (see "Depth zones," pages 143–146). Sunlight also warms the upper layers of the sea, and this warming effect stirs the oceans, drives ocean currents, and powers air circulation (see "Air movement," pages 70–71).

Sound

With the oceans averaging 12,500 feet (3,800 m) deep, and with sunlight penetrating only about 3,300 feet (1,000 m) at most, it is clear that using natural light is not an effective method for mapping the ocean floor. Even with lights mounted on underwater vehicles, only a tiny fraction of seafloor, a few tens of yards across, is revealed at any one time. Mapping with sound rather than light is the oceanographer's method of choice.

Underwater, sound waves travel far and fast, reaching distances of hundreds of miles at speeds of about 4,915 feet per second (about 1,500 m/s) in warm water, compared with ranges of tens of miles and speeds of about 1,080 feet per second (about 330 m/s) in air. By the 1920s oceanographers began using sonar (SOund Navigation And Ranging) to measure the depth of the ocean floor. This technique involves sending pulses of sound and measuring the time taken for the echo to return. Other things being equal, the longer it takes for the echo to return, the deeper the ocean floor. Today's sonar devices are very sophisticated. Those towed behind research vessels can scan a width of ocean floor many miles across and in a single day can produce data to map an area the size of Massachusetts. As the vessel moves forward, computers analyze the stream of sonar data to build up a three-dimensional map of the ocean floor.

The speed at which sound waves travel through water varies slightly with differences in temperature, pressure, and salinity (saltiness). Where these features change abruptly, they can act as a barrier to sound. At depths between about 1,000 and 3,300 feet (300 and 1,000 m), a natural barrier exists caused by the abrupt change in temperature, the thermocline. Sound waves tend to bounce back from this layer, or they become trapped within it. The overall effect is that the layer acts as a channel, allowing sounds to travel long distances sideways trapped within the layer.

Submarine commanders use this layer, called the sofar (SOund Fixing And Ranging) channel, for long-distance communication underwater. One species of whale, the humpback, even sings songs that travel hundreds of miles along the sofar channel (see the sidebar "Whale song," page 131).

In the 1990s oceanographer Walter Munk (1917–) and his team at the Scripps Institution of Oceanography used the sofar channel to measure seawater temperature. By sending low-pitched sound signals across the Pacific Ocean and measuring how long the signals took to reach their destinations, the team was able to pick up wide-area temperature differences of less than one hundredth of a degree centigrade (0.01°C). Comparing seawater temperatures from one year to the next offers a potentially cheap and effective means for monitoring global warming. The team's trials were halted in the late 1990s because environmentalists were concerned about the effect of the sound pulses on the sound communication and hearing of whales (see "Toothed whales," pages 127–129). Now that these concerns have been investigated, smaller-scale trials have continued since 2002.

Pressure

Each person on Earth's surface has a column of air up to 560 miles (900 km) high pressing down upon his or her head. The pressure of this column of air at sea level is called one atmosphere. As soon as a person dives beneath the sea surface, a column of seawater as well as a column of air pushes down upon her. And because water is so much denser (heavier) than air, one does not have to descend very far before the water pressure has a very noticeable effect. Simply diving 33 feet (10 m) beneath the surface doubles the pressure on the body. Such pressure changes alter the volume of air spaces within the body. For instance, a diver may experience pain or discomfort in the ears as the increased water pressure presses on the eardrums. One of the first things scuba instructors teach new divers is how to avert the problem by "clearing the ears." This involves pinching the nose and gently blowing to force air into the middle ear. This extra air pressure inside balances the raised pressure outside the eardrum. When the diver rises in the water column, the air in the middle ear expands. The pressure is relieved naturally by air being forced along the Eustachian tube connecting the middle ear to the throat.

When a swimmer makes a 33-foot (10-m) free dive from the surface (that is, without scuba gear) his or her air-filled lungs shrink to half the normal volume. When the swimmer returns to the surface, the pressure reverts to one atmosphere and the lungs return to normal size. The effect of pressure on fluids and solids in the body is much less noticeable because they do not change markedly in volume with changing pressure.

For many marine creatures, sudden pressure changes are enough to injure or kill. For example, when fishers haul in their catch from several hundred feet depth, the drop in pressure causes the fish's swim bladder (its air-filled buoyancy sac) to inflate like a balloon. This is often enough to kill the fish even if the fisher wants to return it to live for another day.

The high pressure underwater has other effects, too. It causes some gases in air to dissolve in the blood more readily than others, sometimes with harmful effects. For example, scuba divers who descend beyond 130 feet (40 m) and breathe pressurized air need to be aware of the dangers of "nitrogen narcosis." This drunken state is brought on by extra nitrogen dissolving in the blood, and it can influence a diver to take unwarranted risks. Mammals, such as seals and whales, which are adapted to diving, have special mechanisms to avoid such problems.

All in all, marine organisms are adapted to living at particular depths, and pressures, in the ocean. Most cannot withstand rapid changes in pressure, a situation that poses a particular problem for marine biologists who want to bring back live specimens from the deep ocean. These researchers need to use special pressurized containers. With water pressure increasing by one atmosphere for each 33 feet (10 m) of depth, the pressures across most of the ocean floor are at least 300 atmospheres. Underwater vehicles need to be highly engineered to withstand these immensely high pressures, which would crush the air spaces in normal craft (see "Underwater diving vehicles," pages 175–176).

Seawater chemistry

More substances dissolve in water than in any other liquid. One reason why water is such a good solvent (a liquid in which solids dissolve) is the presence of weak electrical charges on its atoms. Water molecules cluster around the ions (charged atoms) found in salts. Sodium chloride (common, or table, salt) is by far the most abundant salt in seawater.

Sodium chloride contains sodium ions (Na^+) and chloride ions (Cl^-) which, in their usual form, bond together to form salt crystals. Drop salt crystals in water, however, and water molecules gather around the salt's ions, pulling them out of the crystal so they dissolve. Water has the same effect on other salts.

Given that water is such a good solvent and is present in such large quantities at normal temperatures, it is not surprising that water is the liquid in which life processes take place. Most organisms are at least 65 percent water, and some marine organisms, such as jellyfish, are 95 percent water.

The main ingredients of seawater are the same the world over, and the balance of these different substances varies little from one ocean to the next. The average salinity of seawater is 35 parts of dissolved salts for each 1,000 parts of seawater. However, where freshwater flows into the sea at river estuaries, the concentration of dissolved salts can fall well below 30 parts per thousand. On the other hand, where water evaporates from seawater and is not replaced, the salt concentration rises. In the Red Sea salinities reach 41 parts per thousand.

These salinity differences are important for sea life. Most marine organisms can survive only in seawater of near normal salinity. However, some organisms live on shores and in estuaries where salinities change dramatically over the course of a few hours. They must either close themselves off from the changing conditions, as some clams and mussels do encased in their shells, or they must endure the change.

Some of the chemicals found in small quantities in seawater, such as nitrates, phosphates, and iron, vary in concentration from one part of the ocean to another. Marine plants depend upon these nutrients and cannot grow without them. The patchy distribution of life in the upper part of the sea is due, in large part, to the distribution of such nutrients in seawater.

Gases, too, dissolve in seawater, and their presence influences the distribution of life. Most organisms depend upon oxygen for the chemical reactions (called "respiration") that release energy from food. Oxygen dissolves in seawater and comes from two sources: oxygen absorbed from the air above the sea, and oxygen released by marine plants in the process of photosynthesis (by which plants trap sunlight and use it to make food).

Ocean currents carry oxygen-rich water from near the surface to the ocean depths, so few places—even in the deep ocean—are completely without oxygen. But there are some important exceptions. Near hydrothermal vents, for example, the chemicals in the hot vent water react with and use up the available oxygen. Vent animals (see "Hot vents and cold seeps," pages 157–158) have evolved that thrive without oxygen and even survive high levels of hydrogen sulfide— "rotten egg" gas—that is deadly to most organisms.

Chemical cycling

Where does the salt in seawater come from? According to an old Norse legend, a giant salt mill is grinding away on the seafloor to produce it. In fact, erosion is a major source of salt. Rocks on land are continually being worn away, and their chemicals wash into the sea. In addition, undersea volcanoes add substances to seawater, and volcanoes on land produce gases such as sulfur dioxide that dissolve in water droplets and fall as mildly acid raindrops into the sea. In the last 150 years or so, farms, towns, and industries have been adding a cocktail of chemicals to land, rivers, lakes, and the air, and one way or another, many of these find their way into the sea as pollutants (see "Pollution," page 200).

If salt is continually being added to the world's seawater, are the oceans getting saltier? It seems not. Scientists have examined the salt deposits left by ancient seas, and it appears that the salinity of seawater has remained almost constant for millions of years. For this to happen, it means that as fast as salt is added to the ocean it is being taken away. This also applies to many other chemicals in seawater.

Many of the sea's dissolved substances are removed when they attach to particles that settle on the seafloor. The particles become buried as more sediment piles on top. Eventually, the buried sediment becomes compacted to form sedimentary rock, such as limestone or shale. This way the chemicals are removed from the ocean system. Millions of years later, the seafloor may become uplifted onto the land when two tectonic plates collide. The chemicals eventually erode from the land and wash into the sea, so completing the cycle. However, many chemicals are recycled much more quickly than this, and living organisms form a vital link in the process.

Sulfur and carbon cycles

The element sulfur (S), in the form of the ion sulfate (SO_4^{2-}), is an important nutrient that helps plants to grow on land and in the sea. On land sulfur is lost when sulfate ions dissolve from rocks, leach from soils, and empty into rivers that eventually discharge into the sea. Some replacement occurs when volcanoes add sulfur dioxide (SO_2) gas to the air. When fossil fuels such as coal and gasoline are burned to power or heat towns, industrial complexes, and vehicles, this, too, releases sulfur dioxide. The gas usually dissolves in water to produce mildly acid rain, although the rain can become strongly acid when sulfur dioxide levels are high. Acid rainwater replaces some of the sulfur lost from land, but not all. Somehow, sulfur lost into the sea must be finding its way back onto land. But how?

The English scientist James Lovelock (1919–) suggested that the substance DMS (dimethyl sulfide) might be the missing piece of the puzzle. Various kinds of phytoplankton (microscopic plantlike organisms) produce DMS. In 1972 Lovelock and his colleagues found DMS in ocean waters stretching from the North Atlantic down to the Southern Ocean. Research in the 1980s showed that when phytoplankton release DMS, some enters the atmosphere. Here it reacts with oxygen to produce tiny droplets of sulfuric acid. Remarkably, these acid droplets cause rain clouds to form. When mildly acid rain falls to the ground, it helps renew the land's sulfur supplies, so completing the cycle.

The cycling of carbon between land, sea, and air is important because it is so closely linked with life on Earth. Living organisms are carbon-based. That is, the substances that build the cells and tissues of living organisms—substances

The carbon cycle. Carbon is cycled between land, sea, and air. Huge stores of carbon lie trapped in limestone beneath the ocean.

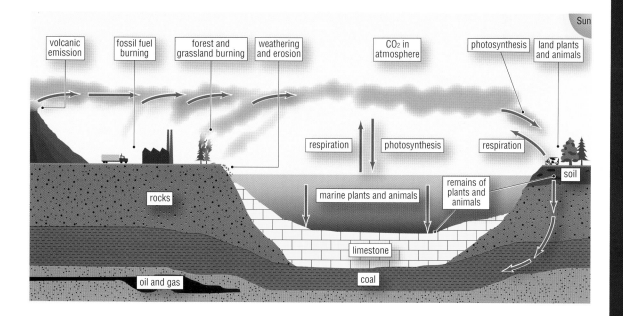

such as proteins, carbohydrates, fats, and DNA—are rich in carbon.

In the carbon cycle, plants absorb the gas carbon dioxide when they photosynthesize, and they use it to make the foods that they need (and that animals consume). When people burn fossil fuels, they add carbon dioxide to the atmosphere. The rise of carbon dioxide levels in the air, caused by towns, factories, and vehicles burning fossil fuels, is probably contributing to global warming (see "Climate change," pages 91–93).

Most people are familiar with the idea that forests on land are the "lungs" of the Earth. Trees take in carbon dioxide and give out oxygen, so "replenishing" the air. The microscopic plants of the ocean—the phytoplankton—do this as well. In this respect, they are as important as the plants on land.

Phytoplankton help recycle carbon between sea, air, and land. Carbon dioxide from the atmosphere dissolves in seawater, and marine phytoplankton absorb and chemically convert this carbon dioxide when they photosynthesize. They release carbon dioxide when they break down foods to release energy (the process of respiration). Some phytoplankton use carbon dioxide to build their bodies' calcium carbonate skeletons. When phytoplankton die, their skeletons often settle on the sea bottom, where they become buried and squeezed to form limestone deposits. This buried carbon from long-dead organisms is part of the "carbon sink"—carbon removed from circulation for millions of years.

In theory, if phytoplankton could be persuaded to photosynthesize more, they might help lower carbon dioxide levels in the air, and so counter global warming. Some marine scientists are experimenting with adding iron, a metal phytoplankton need that is sometimes in short supply, in order to encourage more photosynthesis. This trick is worth investigating, but "iron-seeding" could have unplanned effects on the environment, such as altering the grazing patterns of zooplankton and other animals in marine food webs (see "Food chains and food webs," pages 135–138). In any case, other human activities are continuing to add to marine pollution (see "Pollution," page 200). Some of this pollution kills phytoplankton, reducing photosynthesis overall. Like cutting down rainforests on land, polluting the seas may be damaging the lungs of the Earth.

Fossil fuels

Today, much of humankind's wealth originates from dead marine plankton that sank to the bottom of ancient seas. Over millions of years the plankton remains have become converted to the oil and natural gas that fuel our high-tech societies. Nations continue to fight wars to safeguard the supplies of these valuable fossil fuels.

Commonly, these fossil fuels form from marine plankton that are buried rapidly at the sea bottom on or near a continental shelf. If quickly covered by sediment, the organic (carbon-rich) remains do not decay as usual. Instead, over millions of years, as more sediment piles on top, the organic remains become squeezed and heated several thousand feet beneath the seafloor. Large carbon-based molecules—fats, proteins, complex carbohydrates, and so on—break down to simpler molecules that are the ingredients of crude petroleum oil. When the breakdown process continues further, petroleum oil eventually converts to natural gas, which is rich in methane.

To accumulate within the reach of drilling prospectors, oil and gas need to rise from deep deposits and gather in shallower places. Such locations include "traps" where a covering layer of impermeable (impassable) rock blocks the escape of oil or gas. Prospectors use seismic techniques—bouncing sound waves through overlying rock—to find the telltale signs of where a trap might lie.

Today many of the oil and gas deposits that prospectors exploit are found below the land, not under the sea. However, as prospectors exhaust the land reserves, the search for oil and gas reserves is moving under the seafloor beyond continental shelves. Today the deepest oil-producing rigs operate in 3,900 feet (1,190 m) of water, but test drillings are being carried out at about 7,700 feet (2,345 m).

On continental slopes and rises conditions may prevent plankton remains from converting to petroleum oil, but they nevertheless produce natural gas. When the gas bubbles onto the sea floor, the cold, high-pressure conditions cause the gas to combine with water to produce unusual crystals called gas hydrates.

Gas hydrate crystals are fragile. If they were raised from the seabed, they would break down spontaneously to release their gas. If a way could be found to harvest the crystals safely, their methane would be a valuable fuel source.

There is another reason to study gas hydrates. Methane is a greenhouse gas—a gas that traps infrared radiation and contributes to warming of the atmosphere. If global warming caused temperatures in the deep ocean to rise substantially, this might cause gas hydrate deposits to break down. If so, the ocean could release vast quantities of methane into the atmosphere, which would further add to global warming.

CHAPTER 4

ATMOSPHERE AND THE OCEANS

Atmosphere

Earth's atmosphere, the layer of air wrapped around the planet, is essential to life. It contains the oxygen that many organisms need; its clouds supply the land with water from the sea; and its circulation creates our weather and climate. The atmosphere acts as a protective blanket, helping ensure that Earth's surface gets neither too hot nor too cold for the survival of life. It also shields us from the most damaging effects of the Sun's rays.

Weather (studied by meteorologists) refers to the local atmospheric conditions—clear skies or rain, warm or cold, windy or still—that people experience from day to day. Climate (investigated by climatologists) is the average pattern of weather in a region over many years.

Compared with the dimensions of Earth, the atmosphere is very thin. If an inflated party balloon represented Earth, then the atmosphere would be about the same thickness as the balloon's stretched rubber wall.

The atmosphere reaches as high as 560 miles (900 km) above sea level at the equator; it is lower at the poles. Its bottom layer, the troposphere (from the Greek word for "sphere of change"), extends to some 10 miles (16 km) high and contains 80 percent of the atmosphere's mass of air and most of its water. Most of what people recognize as weather and climate takes place in the troposphere. All Earth's larger organisms (except for those people who enter higher levels of the atmosphere in aircraft or spacecraft) live in or below this layer.

The layer above the troposphere, rising to 164,000 feet (50 km) above ground, is the stratosphere (from the Greek word for "sphere of layers") because it contains various sublayers where different gases gather. Today people fly across the stratosphere in airplanes. Within the stratosphere lies the ozone layer, where sunlight converts oxygen (O_2) to ozone (O_3). This chemical reaction absorbs some of the ultraviolet radiation that would otherwise reach Earth's surface. Thus, formation of the ozone layer is a sign that dangerously high levels of ultraviolet (UV) radiation have been prevented from reaching Earth's life-forms. In high doses UV radiation causes mutations (changes in the genetic material of cells in living things) that can lead to cancers and other disorders.

Air movement

When air warms, it becomes less dense and rises because its constituent molecules move farther apart. When it cools, it becomes denser and sinks because the molecules it contains move closer together. The unequal heating of Earth's surface by the Sun, with air rising in some places and sinking in others, causes the atmosphere to circulate over the planet's surface.

The Tropics (that part of Earth's surface lying between the tropic of Cancer in the Northern Hemisphere and the tropic of Capricorn in the Southern Hemisphere) receives more sunlight than the poles. There are at least three explanations for this.

Near the equator the midday Sun rises high in the sky, and the Sun's rays are angled almost directly downward. By contrast, near the poles, the midday Sun rises low in the sky, and the Sun's rays hit Earth's surface at a shallow angle. At the poles sunlight is more likely to bounce off the atmosphere or off Earth's surface, rather than be absorbed. Also, the sunlight that is absorbed at the poles is spread over a wider area of Earth's curved surface. You can test this for yourself using a globe. Stand next to the globe and shine a flashlight beam onto the globe's surface from one side (as though you are the Sun directly above the equator). The flashlight beam produces a tight circle of light at the equator. Without changing your standing position, angle the flashlight so that it is now shining toward the North Pole. Notice how the flashlight beam produces a broad oval of light spread over Earth's curved surface. The brightness of light striking the poles is less than that reaching the Tropics. The same applies to sunlight.

Besides the intensity of the sunlight reaching Earth, how much sunlight is absorbed or reflected depends upon Earth's albedo (its whiteness or darkness). At the poles the ice and snow present there reflect sunlight well, so less heat is absorbed. In the Tropics, however, the landmasses are green, brown, or yellow and the sea is clear blue. These colors reflect less light, and consequently these regions absorb more of the Sun's heat energy.

If the Tropics heat up more than the poles, why don't equatorial regions simply get hotter and hotter? They do not because, as tropical regions warm, the moving oceans and atmosphere carry heat to other parts of the globe.

As tropical air warms, it rises. Low-level cool air moves in from higher latitudes (away from the Tropics) and replaces the air that has risen. Meanwhile, the warm air rises until it hits the tropopause (the cool boundary layer between troposphere and stratosphere). The air then travels across the upper troposphere toward the poles. As the air chills, it becomes denser and gradually sinks, providing cool air that will later return toward the Tropics. Put simply, there is an overall movement of warm air from the Tropics toward the poles at high altitude. There is a return flow of cooler air at low altitude, from the poles toward the equator.

This simple model of global air movement was first put forward by the English physicist Edmund Halley (1656–1742) in 1686. In the 1750s the model was modified by another Englishman, George Hadley (1686–1768), who recognized that the Earth's rotation would alter the direction of airflow.

The effect of Earth's rotation

Earth spins on its axis. If a person could hover high above the North Pole, Earth would be spinning counterclockwise beneath, rotating once every 24 hours. Earth's rotation causes most large-scale movements of water and wind on Earth's surface to turn rather than travel in straight lines. The Frenchman Gustave-Gaspard de Coriolis (1792–1843) investigated and described this effect in the 1830s, and it now bears his name.

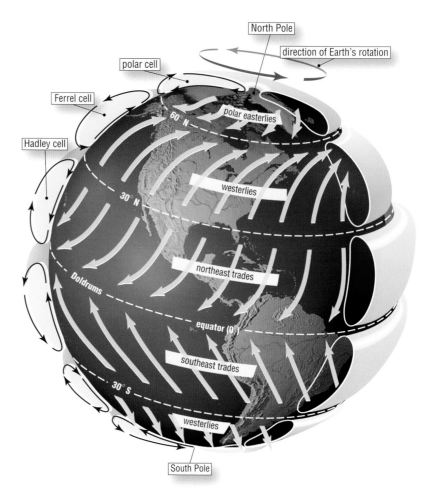

Global air circulation. Rising or falling air masses at different latitudes produce major wind systems at Earth's surface, which are turned by the Coriolis effect.

To understand the Coriolis effect, it helps to use a model globe or imagine a globe in the mind's eye. The Earth spins counterclockwise as seen from above the North Pole. For one rotation of the Earth, a point on the equator travels a lot farther through space (it follows a wide circle) than a point near the North Pole (which follows a tighter circle). The speed of rotation of a point at the equator is about 1,037 mph (1,670 km/h). A point in New York City, near latitude 40°N, rotates at about 794 mph (1,280 km/h). This means that as an object attempts to fly or sail northward from the equator, it experiences a slower speed of rotation. This has the effect of deflecting its movement to the right. An easy way to see or imagine this is with a finger slowly moving toward the pole as it gently rests on a model globe turning counterclockwise. The finger marks out a curved line moving toward the right.

Moving air experiences this turning effect, with the result that northward-moving winds are deflected to the right (or eastward) in the Northern Hemisphere. Winds moving northward form westerlies (winds blowing from the west). Southward-moving winds, because they are meeting higher speeds of rotation, are deflected to the left (or westward) in this hemisphere. They form easterlies or northeasterlies (winds blowing from the east or northeast respectively).

In the Southern Hemisphere similar wind patterns are established to those in the Northern Hemisphere. The overall effect of Earth's rotation on north-south air movements is to generate reliable westerly or easterly winds at different latitudes. For thousands of years seafarers in sailing ships have relied upon these winds for navigation and propulsion. Some wind systems are called "trade" winds, because sea traders depended upon them.

The Coriolis effect turns not just winds, but ocean currents, too. In the Northern Hemisphere the effect causes currents to turn to the right, producing clockwise circular systems of currents called gyres. In the Southern Hemisphere the turning effect is to the left, producing gyres that turn counterclockwise.

Global air circulation

In those parts of the world's oceans where the influences of landmasses are comparatively small, Hadley's model and the Coriolis effect offer a reasonable explanation for observed winds and climate patterns. Around the equator, between latitudes 5°S and 10°N, warm, humid air rises, creating a belt of low pressure called the intertropical convergence zone (ITCZ). Clouds and heavy rain are common here.

When rising air reaches the tropopause, it turns poleward. By about 30°N or 30°S the air has cooled sufficiently to sink back down to Earth's surface. These regions, called subtropical anticyclones, are high-pressure systems with characteristically warm, dry, still conditions. On land the world's great hot deserts, such as Africa's Sahara and Kalahari, are found here. At sea these latitudes are the so-called horse latitudes. In the days of sail, Spanish ships sailing to the West Indies became becalmed here; short of freshwater, horses on board died of thirst, and sailors threw them overboard.

Air moving at low altitude from the subtropical anticyclones toward the equator is deflected by the Coriolis effect. These moving air masses create the famous trade winds that are among the steadiest, most reliable winds in the open ocean.

Near the equator the trade winds die out in a region that British sailors called the doldrums (from an old English word meaning "dull"). Seafarers feared becoming becalmed here in windless conditions. The air circulations that rise at the ITCZ and descend at the subtropical anticyclones are called Hadley cells, named after George Hadley.

Some of the descending air at the ITCZ moves poleward, rather than toward the equator, and this movement forms part of a circulation of air masses between latitudes 30° and 60°. These so-called Ferrel cells, named after William Ferrel (1817–91), who identified them in 1856, include the low-altitude wind systems in middle latitudes called westerlies.

A third type of cell exists between latitudes 60° and 90°. These polar cells contain warm, poleward-moving air at high altitude. Cool air masses moving toward lower latitudes at low altitude, and deflected by the Coriolis effect, form the polar easterlies.

This broad overview of global air circulation does not take into account seasonal changes. Nor does it consider more localized wind systems, such as those generated by differences in rate of warming and cooling between land and sea, such as the monsoon winds of the northern Indian Ocean (see "The Indian Ocean," pages 13–15).

Surface currents

Oceanographers describe about 40 named currents at the surface of the oceans. Ocean currents are like rivers in the sea, carrying water from one place to another, but they are much larger than any river on land. The Gulf Stream alone carries several times more water than all rivers combined.

The ocean's surface currents are driven by winds. As a wind blows across the sea surface, friction between air and sea drags some of the water along. Because water is so dense, it is difficult to shift, so winds blowing for months on end produce ocean currents that are only a fraction of the wind speed. The fastest major surface currents in the world, the Gulf Stream of the North Atlantic and the Kuroshio Current of the North Pacific, flow at speeds of only 2.5–4.5 mph (4–7 km/h).

One might expect that surface currents flow in the same direction as the prevailing wind, but this is rarely the case. Within a particular hemisphere, winds and currents are turned in the same direction by the Coriolis effect. But because currents travel much more slowly than winds, slow movement of the current has a more marked turning effect.

The world's major surface currents. Warmer currents are shown in red, with cooler currents in blue.

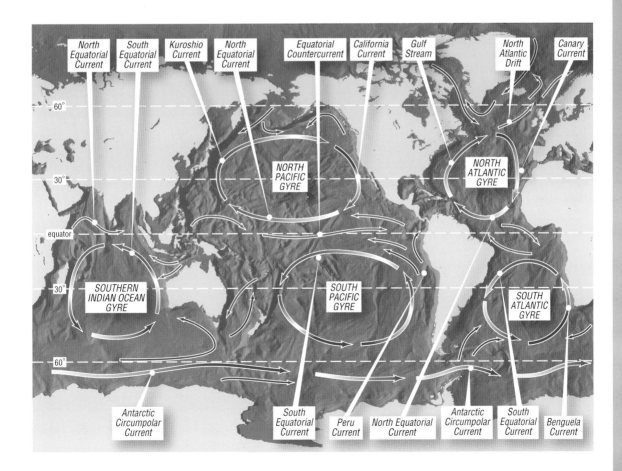

Current knowledge

Since ancient times knowledge of the direction and speed of ocean currents has made the difference between success and failure on long-distance sea voyages. Portuguese navigators of the late 15th century, trained in Prince Henry's School (see "The Portuguese explorers," pages 163–165), sailed a figure-of-eight course to West Africa and back, riding the currents of the North Atlantic and South Atlantic gyres. This route was longer but faster than sailing directly along the Atlantic coasts of Europe and Africa against winds and currents.

In the mid-18th century, statesman-to-be Benjamin Franklin (1706–90) was a colonial postmaster. He noticed that mail ships sailing from Europe to New England across the North Atlantic took two weeks' less time when they took a southerly route rather than a northerly one. Questioning sea captains, he discovered that on the northerly route they were sailing against the powerful Gulf Stream. Franklin's chart of the Gulf Stream, first published in 1770, enabled transatlantic traders to pick the best route—taking the Gulf Stream on the outward voyage and avoiding it on the return—for a swifter crossing.

Once a current is flowing, it is constrained by the shape of the ocean basin across which it moves. Landmasses and their continental shelves deflect currents, and coupled with the Coriolis effect, this produces circular systems of currents called gyres in the largest oceans. As a rule, gyres flow clockwise in the Northern Hemisphere and counterclockwise in the Southern. The gyre in the northern Indian Ocean is the partial exception to this rule. It reverses direction in the winter, when the monsoon winds change direction (see "The Indian Ocean," pages 13–15).

Currents on the western sides of gyres—such as the North Atlantic's Gulf Stream and the South Atlantic's Brazil Current—carry warm water away from the equator, and by transferring heat energy to the atmosphere, they warm neighboring landmasses. The Gulf Stream, for example, feeds the North Atlantic Drift, which keeps Iceland and northwest Europe much warmer than the chilly center of the Eurasian landmass.

On the eastern sides of gyres currents such as the North Pacific's California Current and the North Atlantic's Canary Current, carry cool water toward the equator. They have a cooling effect on neighboring landmasses. In summer onshore (sea to land) breezes from the California Current keep coastal air temperatures comparatively cool.

In the center of a gyre there is little movement of surface water, and this calm region of the sea can be a strange place where floating objects gather. In the center of the North Atlantic gyre lies the Sargasso Sea, with its covering of floating seaweed and unique community of plants and animals.

Subsurface currents and climate control

Most surface currents extend only a few hundred yards beneath the surface. The Florida Current and the Gulf Stream are among the exceptions; they extend to depths of 6,560 feet (2,000 m) and more. Because most surface currents are fairly shallow compared with the great depths of oceans, in total they contain only about 10 percent of the world's ocean water.

Whereas surface currents are driven by winds, subsurface currents are propelled mainly by differences in water density. Water, like air, usually sinks when cold and rises when warm. Strangely, subsurface currents are powered by the formation of sea ice in polar oceans.

When seawater freezes to form sea ice, it is the water content that freezes. Most of the salt separates out as a salty liquid, called brine, that eventually trickles through the ice. It makes the seawater beneath the ice more saline (salty). Cool, salty water is dense, and this water sinks to the ocean floor and then moves toward the equator. This ice-forming process—happening in the North Atlantic near Greenland and in the waters of the Southern Ocean around Antarctica— powers a deep circulation of seawater across the oceans. This descending water becomes bottom water and is replaced by subsurface currents of warm water at shallower levels originating from nearer the equator. Beneath the surface the flow of subsurface currents is, in fact, quite complex, with currents at different depths flowing in different directions.

With more than 80 percent of the world's seawater lying beneath the thermocline (the layer across which temperature changes markedly), the ocean's deep currents probably have a great influence on global climate, even if the effect is not obvious.

It is possible that if global warming continues (see "Climate change," pages 91–93) then Arctic sea ice might almost disappear in summer. If so, the Arctic's ice-making machine would temporarily stop. This would interrupt the production of cool, salty bottom water and might alter the flow of currents, both surface and subsurface, in the North Atlantic and beyond. For example, the Gulf Stream and the North Atlantic Drift might move southward, in which case they would no longer reach northwest Europe and moderate the climate there. The British Isles, for example, could be plunged into average winter tem-

The global conveyor belt: the circulation of seawater that connects warm, shallow currents with cool, deep currents

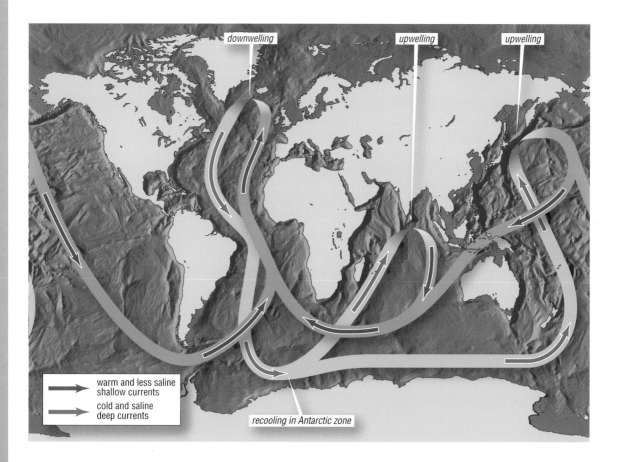

downwelling upwelling upwelling

warm and less saline shallow currents

cold and saline deep currents

recooling in Antarctic zone

peratures that are nine to 18°F (5 to 10°C) cooler than those today. The remains of cool-water foraminiferans (one-celled, animal-like marine organisms with shells made of calcium carbonate) in sediments at the bottom of the North Atlantic suggests that such an event has happened in the past, and more than once. The most recent occasion was about 11,000 years ago; a temporary climatic reversal called the Younger Dryas.

The disruption of deepwater circulation, if caused by prolonged global warming, could alter local climates across the globe, with some getting warmer and others cooler. Small changes in the path of ocean currents can also drastically alter where and when upwelling takes place.

Upwelling and El Niño

Upwelling is the rise of cool, subsurface water to the ocean's surface waters. It happens where surface currents move apart, as occurs at the equator and in subpolar waters, or where surface currents move water away from coastlines. The shift of surface water creates room for deeper water to rise up and fill the vacated space.

Upwelling is important because it brings nutrients to the sunlit surface waters where phytoplankton thrive. The combination of sunlight and nutrients fuels photosynthesis, and the multiplying phytoplankton provide food for other marine creatures. In the late 1990s more than one-third of the global catch of marine fish and squid came from upwelling regions.

Major regions of upwelling lie on the eastern sides of the Pacific and Atlantic Oceans. There, the combination of offshore winds and surface currents pulls surface water away from the coast for at least part of the year. Cool, nutrient-rich water rises up from below to fill the space. Plankton-feeding fish arrive to feed on the thriving phytoplankton and zooplankton, and the small fish, in turn, become food for larger creatures. Fishers harvest plankton-feeding fish such as anchovies, sardines, and herring off the Pacific coast of the Americas, and similar fisheries exist off the Atlantic coasts of Portugal, and northwest and southwest Africa. In these places the strength of coastal upwelling—and the size of the fish harvest—varies from year to year.

The phrase *El Niño* hits the headlines every few years, linked to extreme weather conditions such as torrential rain and floods in parts of the United States, Brazil, and Africa, and droughts in Australia, India, and Southeast Asia.

The term *El Niño* has taken on more than one meaning. To traditional sea fishermen of Peru and Ecuador, it refers to a slackening of trade winds that usually occurs around Christmastime and causes very warm water to appear at the surface in the eastern Pacific. El Niño is Spanish for "male child," and it refers to the birth of the Christ child. When the southeast Pacific trade winds slacken in December or January, warm water moves westward across the equatorial Pacific, and it blocks the upwelling off the South American coast. With the loss of nutrients the growth of phytoplankton slows, and the anchovies that feed on the plankton scatter. In a good year the Peruvian fishery is the largest anchovy fishery in the world. El Niño—the slackening of trade winds, warm surface water spreading eastward, and the reduction of upwelling—marks the end of the peak fishing season.

El Niño also refers to the headline-making major climatic event. Every two to seven years the slackening of southeast Pacific trade winds—the seasonal El Niño—happens much earlier than normal. The upwelling off the Peru-Chile coast is lost for months on end. The phytoplankton bonanza does not happen, and the plankton-eating fish do not gather. In that year the anchovy fishery is almost nonexistent, and fishers and wildlife suffer. This is an El Niño event, also called an El Niño year. Particularly strong El Niño events occurred in 1957–58, 1982–83, 1991–92, and 1997–98. In the 1957–58 event the population of seabirds off the Peru-Chile coast fell by about three-quarters. The anchovy catch during the 1982–83 event dropped to below 1 percent of a normal year. The strong 1997–98 El Niño was the first to be monitored closely by scientists using a system of temperature-sensing buoys in the equatorial Pacific along with the use of remote-sensing satellites. Scientists could predict the arrival of this El Niño six months before it happened.

Some climatologists liken an El Niño event to a pressure valve that helps stop the global climate from overheating. It is really part of a wider climatic feature called the El

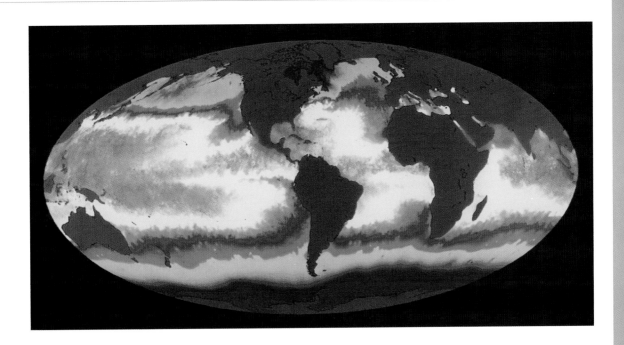

Niño–Southern Oscillation (ENSO) that links the southeast Pacific with the eastern Indian Ocean. When pressure is high in one region, like a seesaw, it is low in the other. During an El Niño event—with warm seawater in the southeast Pacific accompanied by rising warm, moist air and low sea-level pressures—alterations in the wind systems have ripple effects that influence weather patterns over thousands of miles. They cause unusual storms and torrential rain in parts of North and South America while parts of Africa, Southeast Asia, and Australia experience droughts.

If El Niño can be predicted, it can also be planned for. During an El Niño event, the Peru-Chile anchovy fishery may collapse, but if fishers can adapt to the changing conditions, they can catch high-value, warm-water fish, such as yellowfin tuna, skipjack tuna, and Spanish mackerel, that make an appearance off the Pacific coast of South America.

A computer-generated satellite image of global sea surface temperatures in the late fall/early winter of the Northern Hemisphere. The highest temperatures are coded red, with temperatures decreasing through oranges, yellows, greens, and blues. The tongue of cold water extending westward from South America is associated with upwelling. In El Niño years this tongue disappears much earlier in the season than usual. (Courtesy of National Aeronautics and Space Administration)

Tides

In most parts of the world local sea level rises and falls over the course of a day. This rhythmic rise and fall is called a tide, and in many places there are two rising (flood) tides and two falling (ebb) tides in about 24 hours. The difference in sea level between high and low tide is called the tidal range. In the Mediterranean Sea the tidal range is rarely more than 3 feet (0.9 m), but in the Bay of Fundy, on Canada's Atlantic coast, it can reach 52 feet (16 m).

Are tides important for marine life? For marine organisms living on shores and in the shallow waters of continental shelves, the answer is undoubtedly yes. An ebb tide can leave shore inhabitants high and dry until they are submerged again a few hours later. Tidal surges in shallow water produce strong currents that swimming creatures must battle against or be swept along by. Tidal surges and currents bring fresh supplies of seawater loaded with food and oxygen. Many shore or shallow-water organisms time their feeding to coincide with certain states of the tide. Tides also serve to distribute the eggs or larvae of marine organisms, and some shallow-water or shore-living creatures spawn when tides are highest or tidal currents strongest (see the sidebar "Coral snowstorm," page 154). As to what causes tides, the answer lies in the interaction of Earth, Moon, and Sun.

Earth spins on its axis once every 24 hours. At any given moment the gravitational attraction of the Moon pulls Earth's seawater toward it. This causes seawater to bulge toward the point on Earth that is nearest the Moon. At the same time a counterbalancing bulge forms on exactly the opposite side of the Earth (due to an effect called centripetal force). As Earth turns on its axis, the two bulges—one on either side of the Earth—travel around the planet. Where the bulges occur, it is high tide. In between the bulges, where some seawater has been withdrawn, it is low tide.

With two bulges (and two dips) tracking around Earth every 24 hours, one would expect exactly two high tides and two low tides a day at any location. However, the Moon advances slightly in its own orbit of the Earth, so the Earth has to turn slightly beyond its start point to catch up with the Moon, and this takes about 24 hours 50 minutes (a lunar day). In an idealized world each section of coastline would have two high tides and two low tides in a 24-hour, 50-minute period. But the real world is more complex.

Earth is not covered in seawater to a uniform depth, and ocean basins vary in shape and size. As tidal bulges move across Earth's surface, they are deflected and constrained by landmasses, continental shelves, and the shape of the ocean floor. The Coriolis effect also turns surges to the right or left (see "The effect of Earth's rotation," pages 71–73). These complicating factors cause tidal patterns to vary but in predictable ways. Many places, including most Atlantic coasts, have two tides of similar range each lunar day. Some places, such as parts of the Caribbean Sea, have two tides a day, but the tidal ranges are markedly different. The third pattern, as found in some parts of the Gulf of Mexico, is a single tide a day.

Tides follow a predictable pattern, but at a given place, the size of the tidal range varies from one week to the next. Apart from the Moon, another factor needs to be taken into account: the Sun. The Sun's gravitational attraction on Earth's seawater is less than that of the Moon (it is 400 times farther away from the Earth), but it nevertheless exerts a noticeable effect.

Earth completes an orbit of the Sun once every year. The Moon completes its orbit of the Earth once every 29.5 days, lunar month. Twice each lunar month the Sun and the Moon are in a straight line relative to the Earth. This happens at the full Moon (when the entire face of the Moon is visible from Earth) and the new Moon (when the Moon's face is completely in shadow and is seemingly invisible). At these times the gravitational attraction of the Sun adds to that of the Moon, and the tidal bulges are larger than normal. High tides are higher, low tides are lower, and tidal ranges are greater. These are the spring tides, so called because they "well up" or "spring," not because they are linked to a particular season of the year.

Halfway between one set of spring tides and the next, the Sun and Moon are at right angles relative to the Earth. Their gravitational attractions cancel each other out slightly, so tidal bulges are smaller. High tides are lower, low tides are higher, and tidal ranges are smaller. These are the neap tides. They happen around the Moon's first and third quarter (when half the face of the Moon is illuminated).

Oceanographers refer to tide tables to find the time and size of high and low tides in their locality. Although weather conditions, especially wind and air pressure changes, cause these tides to vary slightly from those predicted, the tide tables offer a reliable guide.

Waves

Most ocean waves are created by winds. When air blows across the sea surface, friction between wind and sea sculpts the surface into ripples. If the wind is strong enough and blows for long enough, the ripples build to become waves. The highest point of a wave is its crest, and the lowest point, its trough. The stronger the wind, and the longer it blows across the sea surface, the taller the wave it creates. In 1933 a ship's officer measured a storm wave at 112 feet (34 m) high—the largest on record. Even hurricanes with wind speeds reaching 106 mph (170 km/h) rarely raise storm waves higher than 43 feet (13 m).

Out at sea, winds whip up waves that have sharp peaks. As waves move away from the place where they were created, their outline smoothes, and a series of such waves becomes a swell.

How tides are generated. The gravitational attraction of the Moon, and to a lesser extent the Sun, generates tides. The tidal range is largest (spring tides) when the Moon and Sun are in alignment relative to Earth. The tidal range is smallest (neap tides) when the Moon and Sun are at right angles.

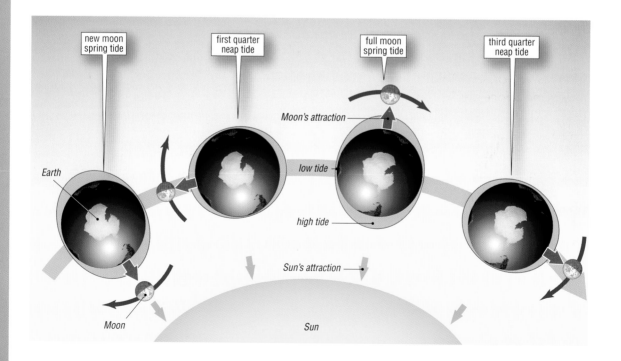

The waves we observe out at sea are usually a tumbled mix of waves of different sizes arriving from various directions. Where two wave crests meet, the wave grows. Where a wave and a trough come together, they partly cancel each other out.

When a wave passes by at sea, what a person sees is an up-and-down movement of the water traveling along the sea surface. Unlike winds and ocean currents, waves out at sea do not push objects along the sea surface. Instead, the wave crest pushes a floating object up and forward, and then the wave trough brings it back again. This is a circular motion, and the object returns to its starting point. Similar circular movements are happening in the water beneath the wave, so that the wave stirs the seawater, helping to distribute oxygen and nutrients a few yards beneath the surface, depending on the size of the wave.

When normal sea waves reach shallow water, their circular motion is blocked as they "touch bottom." The wave crest topples forward, and the wave breaks to crash as surf. Breaking waves do push objects along the sea surface, and even right up the beach, as any surfer can testify. Where shallow water and shore form a gentle slope, arriving waves unleash their energy gradually. These are the shores that surfers prefer. They can "ride the tube" over a long distance. Where shore and sea floor steeply shelve, crashing waves release their considerable energy over a much shorter distance.

Waves are one of the main agents of coastal erosion (see "Shoreline processes," pages 46–47). On rocky shores storm waves lift boulders and erode the base of cliffs. On sandy shores waves strike the shore at an angle, shifting the sand along the shore as longshore drift (see "Sheltered shores," pages 48–51).

Unusually large "rogue" waves develop when a series of storm waves meet an oncoming current that slows and builds them. This happens off the coast of southeast Africa, where storm waves moving north from the Southern Ocean meet the Agulhas Current flowing south. The waves build to 65 feet (20 m) and more—enough to swamp even large vessels. Since 1990 more than 20 ships have been sunk or damaged by rogue waves in these waters. Now vessels are encouraged to avoid the Agulhas Current by sailing around it.

Across the world the shipping industry loses one ship a week. At least some of these are due to rogue waves. The latest research reveals that some rare, steep-sided rogue waves seemingly grow out of nowhere in the deep ocean, and they do not follow the normal rules for waves. Unpredictable rogue waves can be deadly, but some other kinds of waves are much larger still.

Seismic sea waves (tsunamis)

In the early hours of December 26, 2004, villagers along the coastline of northern Sumatra, Indonesia, felt the ground shake, and minutes later heard a sound like the blast of a jet engine coming from the sea. The roar came from a tsunami—a giant wave. In the hours that followed, the giant wave rippled outward from an Indian Ocean trench to engulf seashore communities from Thailand in the east to Somalia, Africa, in the west, claiming about 300,000 human lives. The last major tsunami to hit this region was in 1883, when a volcano on the island of Krakatoa, off the coast of Java, exploded into life. It triggered tsunamis that reached 115 feet (35 m) high and swept across the Indian Ocean killing an estimated 36,000 people.

Tsunamis wreak their havoc in shallow water and along coastlines. These waves are not created by winds but are triggered by sudden, massive disturbances of water. The waves are like the ripples spreading out from a rock thrown into a pond, but on a gigantic scale. These giant waves are caused by earthquakes, landslides, volcanic eruptions, or, on very rare occasions, by meteorite impacts (see the sidebar "Dinosaur extinction," page 43). Called seismic sea waves or tsunamis (from the Japanese word for "harbor wave"), such waves are sometimes mistakenly called tidal waves because they look like a surge of water on a rising tide.

The displacement of water that generated the December 26 tsunami was produced by a several-yard-high uplift of the seabed associated with a massive earthquake in the Sunda trench region lying close to western Sumatra. The tsunami rippled outward from this location, taking a few minutes to reach the provincial capital of Aceh, northern Sumatra, and devastating the city. The wave progressed across the Indian Ocean, taking about two hours to reach Thailand and Sri Lanka, more than three hours to arrive in the Maldives, and nearly eight hours to travel to the East African coast.

At sea, tsunamis are only a yard or two high on the surface, with tens of miles between crest and trough. A tsunami usually consists of several waves and each is spread out over such a vast area that it passes by unnoticed. But traveling at the speed of an airliner—some 435 mph (700 km/h)—tsunamis slow down in shallow water and gradually build. By the time they reach a shore, they have slowed to a fraction of their original speed but can be tens of yards tall. The wall of water sweeps ashore, smashing boats and buildings and carrying them hundreds of yards inland. In many fishing communities smashed by the December 26 tsunami, fishers were out at sea in boats when the tsunami struck. They barely noticed it pass by, but when they returned to shore, they found their communities devastated. A tsunami's destructiveness is caused by three major processes: the direct effect of the wave impact, seawater flooding inland, and the erosion of coastal areas by the surge of water as it moves back and forth (see sidebar).

The 2004 tsunami—the most destructive on record—has caused geologists to reappraise the tsunami hazard. Previously, geologists thought the biggest danger from tsunamis lay in the Pacific Ocean, with its ring of geologically active plate boundaries. The December 26, 2004, disaster confirmed that major tsunamis can spring to life in unexpected places.

The Pacific Ocean, on average, experiences two life-threatening tsunamis each year. They are produced by volcanic or earthquake activity in the Ring of Fire (see "The Pacific Ocean," pages 10–12). The Pacific Tsunami Warning Center (PTWC), which monitors them, has its headquarters in Hawaii. It issues warnings of impending tsunamis, giving people time to move away from a threatened shore to higher ground. Usually the tsunamis travel long distances, giving people several hours' warning of their arrival. However, if a tsunami were to originate near a populated coastline, such as in the Cascadia subduction zone off the Pacific coast of North America, people might have only a few minutes to flee to safer ground.

Tsunamis are a hazard in the Atlantic Ocean, and the Caribbean, Mediterranean, and Black Seas, as well as in the Pacific Ocean and the eastern Indian Ocean. In all these regions geological activity at plate boundaries produces earthquakes, volcanoes, or landslides that can cause water displacements of sufficient size to generate tsunamis. At the beginning of 2005, regions outside the Pacific Ocean did not have tsunami monitoring and warning systems equivalent to those operated by the PTWC.

In January 2005, in the aftermath of the December 26 tsunami, UNESCO (the United Nations Educational, Scientific and Cultural Organization) announced its intention to help coordinate a global strategy for implementing tsunami early warning systems. Specialists estimated that a tsunami early warning system could be up and running in the eastern Indian Ocean by mid-2006. Such a system would need to incorporate several elements utilized by the PTWC. This includes seismic monitoring systems to detect earthquakes and other tsunami-generating events, plus sea-level registering buoys, water pressure detectors, and tide gauges that monitor passing waves. This seismic and sea-level data is then rapidly compiled, analyzed, and interpreted to estimate the risk of impending tsunamis. A warning can then be communicated to civil authorities in at-risk regions so they can take emergency action. Local communities can then evacuate endangered coastal areas according to preagreed plans.

Hurricanes and sea fogs

The sea warms and cools much more slowly than the air or the land, and in doing so, it stores and releases vast amounts of heat energy. The flow of heat energy and moisture from sea to air shapes much of Earth's weather. Here are considered two of the more extreme weather conditions than take place in the air above the oceans, hurricanes and sea fogs.

A hurricane, or tropical cyclone, is a violent tropical storm born at sea. It is a circular weather system with wind speeds greater than 74 mph (119 km/h) and very low sea-level pressures at its center (commonly 950 millibars or less, compared

Aftermath of the December 26, 2004, tsunami

Within weeks of the December 26 tsunami, scientists recognized the enormous impact of this giant wave on many ecosystems bordering the eastern Indian Ocean. The force of the tsunami physically damaged numerous coral reefs and sea-grass meadows. In thousands of isolated locations, animals and plants were swept ashore and left stranded. The effect on the different members of shallow-water communities was far from uniform. Many large fish were killed as they were borne along by the wave, while smaller animals that could anchor themselves on the seabed survived.

The sediment stirred up by the tsunami smothered some coral reefs and sea grass meadows. In the wake of the giant wave, many noxious substances and vast amounts of debris found their way into the sea. Raw sewage was swept offshore, and as animals, plants, and human bodies decomposed, so nutrient levels in the seawater rose while oxygen levels fell (see "Pollution," page 200). Nonbiodegradable debris such as plastic items were swept out to sea, while decomposing timber from smashed boats, buildings, and fallen trees would continue to degrade local seawater quality for many years to come. Exotic fish, mollusk, and crustacean species—introduced to the region for aquaculture and kept separate from natural marine communities—were swept into the sea where they could come into contact with native species (see "Alien invasions," pages 210–211).

The December 26 tsunami resculpted many shores and estuaries, although the damage was reduced where coral reefs and mangrove forests were well maintained and acted as barriers. The various effects of the tsunami in altering the physical, chemical, and biological structure of coastal ecosystems in the eastern Indian Ocean will probably not emerge until scientists have monitored these systems for many years.

In February 2005 more than 1 million coastal inhabitants across several countries—with their communities smashed, their boats wrecked, and the biological resources on which they rely disrupted—were depending on food relief and medical aid for their very survival.

with normal air pressure of 1,000 millibars). Tropical cyclones in the Atlantic and eastern North Pacific are called hurricanes. In the western North Pacific meteorologists call them typhoons, and in the Bay of Bengal and around Australia, they are simply called cyclones.

Hurricanes are born in the warmest, tropical regions of the ocean, where sea temperatures in the top 195 feet (60 m) of the water column are at least 80°F (27°C). North Atlantic hurricanes that strike the Caribbean, Central America, and the southeastern United States usually originate from storms off the coast of western Africa in late summer and early fall.

The energy that fuels a tropical cyclone is latent heat that is absorbed by water that evaporates from the sea surface. Latent heat is the heat energy absorbed or released when a substance changes from one physical state to another, in this case from a liquid to a gas. When clouds form, latent heat energy is released, as water vapor turns to liquid, and this energy release warms the surrounding air. This warming lowers air density and causes air to rise, generating updrafts and strong surface winds. When this happens over warm water—typically at latitudes of five to 15 degrees—the Coriolis effect causes the storm system to rotate. When wind speeds rise above 74 mph (119 km/h), the storm graduates from a tropical storm to a tropical cyclone.

A mature cyclone consists of bands of rain clouds spiraling around a calm center, called the eye. The weather system may reach 600 miles (about 1,000 km) across and contain hundreds of thunderstorms. The tropical cyclone gradually dies out when it moves over cooler water, or onto land, and its supply of heat energy is cut off.

The more powerful tropical cyclones rank among the most destructive weather systems on Earth. Hurricane winds reaching more than 110 mph (about 180 km/h) collapse buildings, uproot trees, and throw small boats through the air.

A storm surge is the mound of sea piled up ahead of an approaching hurricane or created by the low-pressure zone at its center. It can reach 23 feet (7 m) tall when coupled with a local high tide and can cause devastating coastal flooding. In November 1970 a tropical cyclone in the Bay of Bengal produced a storm surge that engulfed delta land in Bangladesh, killing about half a million people.

A tropical cyclone's torrential rain may cause flash flooding inland as well as along the coast. Rainfall of 12–24 inches (300–600 mm) has been recorded in a single day. In 1998 downpours from Hurricane Mitch set off mudslides in El Salvador, Honduras, and Nicaragua that killed at least 9,000 people. In 1999 Hurricane Floyd's greatest damage to south-eastern and eastern U.S. states came from torrential rain that caused inland flooding.

Sea fogs, in stark contrast to hurricanes, are quiet weather phenomena that form in cool air or above cool water. Temporary fogs form when rising moist air from a warm surface current meets cold air. When suddenly cooled, the water vapor condenses into tiny droplets to create fog. More persistent fog forms where warm, moist air crosses a cold ocean current. This happens off the coast of California, where warm sea air passes over the cold California Current. Sea fog forms in both ways where cool air above the Labrador Current mixes with warm air above the Gulf Stream. This happens in the vicinity of the Grand Banks off Newfoundland, Canada, where over the centuries, hundreds of vessels have collided in the thick fog.

Climate change

Global warming is a rise in average temperatures across the planet. The big question is, is it happening? And if so, what is the cause, and is there something people can do about it? An international team of scientists called the Intergovernmental Panel on Climate Change (IPCC) met in 1990, 1995, and 2000 to consider the answers to these questions.

There are major problems in assessing whether climate warming is taking place. Global climate is the sum total of local climates across the globe. Even if global warming is taking place, some places will be becoming cooler as others warm. Working out all the checks and balances is a complex process, and ideally measurements over decades are needed to see the trend. One of the best ways to monitor global warming may be to measure the temperature of subsurface ocean water (see "Sound," pages 59–60). Even a small temperature rise in the global conveyor belt system could give a forewarning of a dramatic change in global climate.

Global climate has varied naturally in the last 10,000 years, becoming 10.8°F (6°C) warmer in some periods than in others. If global warming is happening now, is it just part of a natural cycle, or is some human influence at work?

Among IPCC scientists the consensus is that human activities are releasing high levels of greenhouse gases into the atmosphere, and this is causing an "enhanced greenhouse effect" that is overheating the planet.

What is the greenhouse effect? Some of the gases that occur naturally in the atmosphere—carbon dioxide and methane, for example—absorb infrared radiation emitted from Earth's surface. They are called greenhouse gases because, like the glass in a greenhouse, they absorb outgoing infrared radiation and trap heat energy as they do so. On a sunny day in winter, for example, the air in a greenhouse becomes much warmer than the air outside, partly because of this effect. On a global scale greenhouse gases trap heat in the atmosphere and warm Earth's surface.

The greenhouse effect is a natural process that has been happening through much of the planet's life. Without it, the Earth today would probably be at least 54°F (30°C) cooler. The problem lies in human activities "enhancing" the greenhouse effect. When people burn large quantities of fossil fuels—oil products, natural gas, coal, and so on—the activity releases extra carbon dioxide into the atmosphere. This increases the greenhouse effect, trapping more heat energy in the atmosphere, and thus slightly warming the planet.

By analyzing the record of carbon dioxide trapped in polar ice over the last few hundred years, scientists have discovered that atmospheric carbon dioxide levels have risen by one-quarter in the last 150 years. Recent temperature measurements across the globe reveal that the 1990s were the hottest decade since records began. Global warming appears to be happening. Since the late 1990s, for example, the thickness and coverage of Arctic sea ice has declined—perhaps an early warning sign of global warming.

In 1998 many coral reefs across the Indian Ocean turned white. This "coral bleaching" comes about when coral polyps eject their partner algae (see "Coral grief," pages 213–215). The bleaching event can be enough to kill the coral polyps that build the reef.

The 1998 coral bleaching event coincided with the 1997–98 El Niño, when surface water temperatures in parts of the Indian and Pacific Oceans rose by 1.8 to 3.6°F (1 to 2°C) above the seasonal normal, enough to cause some polyps to eject their algae. Some scientists suspect that El Niño years may become more frequent and more intense as global warming worsens.

In their 2001 report the IPCC made their best estimate on climate change, predicting that Earth's surface would warm by 5.2°F (2.9°C) during the 21st century. If this occurs, then sea levels will probably rise by about 20 inches (50 cm) on average. Most of this rise will come about through seawater expanding slightly as it warms. Such a sea-level rise would be sufficient to threaten low-lying countries. Much of Bangladesh, for instance, is less than six feet (1.8 m) above high tide levels, and many of the Maldives' islands of the Indian Ocean rise to only three to six feet (0.9–1.8 m) above the current highest tides.

In any case, global warming by an enhanced greenhouse effect is likely to make weather patterns more extreme and unpredictable. Ocean currents, changing direction only slightly, would bring heat and moisture to new locations and deny it to others that currently receive it. Storms may become more intense and droughts more severe.

The best approach to counter human-induced global warming is to curb the release of greenhouse gases. But many countries are acting too little and too late. The United States, for example, has refused to sign up to the 1997 Kyoto Protocol to cut greenhouse gas emissions. By June 2005, representatives of more than 140 countries had signed this international treaty. On average, each person in the United States still produces, through the products and services they consume, about twice as much greenhouse gas as each person in Europe.

CHAPTER 5

BIOLOGY OF THE OCEANS

Life's beginnings

Scientists have found fossils of simple, single-celled organisms that date back at least 3.5 million years. This means that life has existed on planet Earth for at least three-quarters of its history.

Biologists argue about what precisely distinguishes living things from nonliving things. Most agree, however, that there are several characteristics that any aspiring organism should have. The first is a cellular structure. The simplest organisms are just a single speck of living matter—a cell—that has a boundary layer, a membrane, which separates the cell from the outer world. The most complex organisms—whether blue whales, human beings, or redwood trees—contain billions of cells.

Other characteristics of living organisms are that all are able to grow and reproduce. All living things also have bodies that are rich in the element carbon. This is a major constituent of the complex chemicals that make up the bodies of organisms, particularly carbohydrates (sugars and starches), fats, and proteins. Some living things make these substances from simpler ones, as in the case of most plants and some bacteria. Many gain them from other organisms (as animals do) by consuming them. Either way, the overall process is called nutrition. Organisms break down some complex chemicals in the process of respiration to power living processes. In the process, they create waste substances that must be removed (excreted). Organisms are also responsive to environmental change (they are sensitive), and they have moving body parts. Finally, in most organisms the chemical deoxyribonucleic acid (DNA) provides the blueprint of instructions for controlling the day-to-day functioning of cells. It also provides the set of instructions to make new cells and, in fact, to create new organisms (offspring).

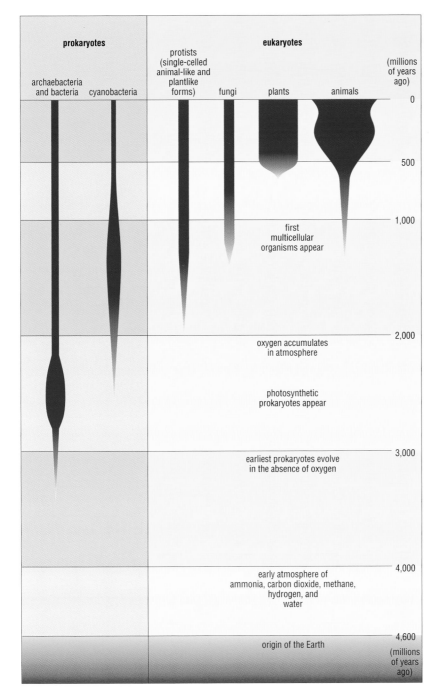

Evolution of life on Earth. As physical and chemical conditions on Earth's surface have changed over millions of years, new groups of organisms have evolved that can exploit the altered conditions.

It is not known whether Earth's first organisms came from meteorites or comets that "seeded" the Earth with microbes (microscopic organisms), or whether such organisms evolved from nonliving matter here on Earth. However, once organisms were established on Earth, they evolved.

Evolution is the natural process of change in the characteristics of populations over many generations. The changes are passed on through genes and accumulate, from one generation to the next, to the extent that they can give rise to new species. In this way, all species on Earth today are believed to have evolved from preexisting species.

A species is a population of organisms that interbreed to produce offspring that themselves can interbreed. For example, the pink salmon (*Oncorhynchus gorbuscha*) and the sockeye salmon (*Oncorhynchus nerka*) are closely related species of fish from the North Pacific. In nature they do not interbreed.

In 1858 naturalists Charles Darwin (1809–82) and Alfred Russell Wallace (1823–1913) put forward convincing arguments for the mechanism of evolution at a meeting of the Linnaean Society in London. In the following year Darwin published his groundbreaking arguments for evolution in his book *On the Origin of Species by Means of Natural Selection*. The fact of evolution and its likely mechanism, natural selection, is accepted by almost all biologists today.

The process of natural selection can be explained like this. Within a population of a species, some individuals are better than others at managing the demands of their environment. They may be better at gaining food, more successful at avoiding predators, or more attractive to potential mates. These individuals are more likely to survive, mate, and leave offspring than some individuals with less favorable characteristics. The characteristics of the better-surviving individuals—provided they can be passed on to offspring through the genetic material (DNA)—are likely to gather in the population over generations. In this way the population *adapts* to its environment and *evolves* by the natural selection of its members. This process, given enough time, can lead to the formation of populations of the same original species that are now reproductively isolated from one another. If the populations were brought together, they would no longer interbreed. They have evolved to the point that they are now separate species.

The evidence in favor of evolution and natural selection is, at present, overwhelming. Many lines of evidence, from the dating of rocks and the progression of fossils found in them to the genetic makeup of present-day organisms and similarities and differences among species, point to the conclusion that complex organisms have evolved from simpler ones.

Until recently, most ideas about where Earth's earliest organisms lived centered on tide pools at the edge of ancient seas. There are several good reasons why biologists suspect that Earth's earliest organisms originated in the sea, rather than on land or in freshwater.

First, the earliest known fossils are found in marine deposits. These fossilized microbes resemble cyanobacteria (blue-green algae) that today are found in pillarlike rocky structures called *stromatolites*. Today, stromatolites grow in shallow seawater in isolated parts of Western Australia and a few other places in the world.

Second, organisms are mostly water. Water is often scarce on land, but it is superabundant in lakes and rivers, and, of course, in the oceans. The concentration of chemicals in the body fluids of living organisms is much closer to that of seawater than freshwater, suggesting a seawater origin.

Third, for most of Earth's history, conditions on land were hostile to life. The atmosphere of the early Earth was without oxygen, which would later shield Earth against the Sun's damaging ultraviolet (UV) rays. High doses of UV radiation cause mutations (genetic changes in cells), some of which lead to cancers. However, several yards depth of water is enough to filter out most UV radiation, and organisms living below this depth are probably safe from its most damaging effects. It is only within the last 500 million to 600 million years that an oxygen-enriched atmosphere has blocked enough UV radiation to allow organisms to colonize the land.

All in all, the sea—or its edges—is a promising environment for earliest life. However, discoveries within the last 20 years suggest other possibilities. Simple forms of bacteria called *archaebacteria,* such as those found today close to deep-sea hydrothermal vents (see "Hot vents and cold seeps," pages 157–158) and in sulfur springs on land, may resemble the earliest bacteria. And "rock-eating" bacteria have been found more than a mile beneath the land surface. These extreme environments are contenders for the habitats of early life. Nevertheless, it is undoubtedly true that for most of Earth's history the great majority of life-forms evolved in the oceans.

The procession of life

The earliest of Earth's organisms were probably archaebacteria ("archae" from the Greek *archaios*, meaning "ancient"). Such bacteria would have lived without oxygen and gained their energy supplies by chemically transforming simple substances such as methane and hydrogen sulfide. This process, called chemosynthesis, releases energy that the organism uses to build the carbon-rich, complex substances to construct body parts. As the organisms consumed methane and hydrogen sulfide and released other gases such as carbon dioxide, they began to alter their environment. The mixture of gases in the atmosphere, for example, gradually changed.

For nearly 3 billion years all Earth's organisms were microscopic. Nevertheless, during this vast expanse of time, major changes were under way. By about 2.5 billion years ago some bacteria were trapping sunlight to gain energy in the process called photosynthesis, an alternative to chemosynthesis. Soon photosynthetic bacteria were flourishing. Photosynthesis produces oxygen as a by-product. At first, chemicals in rocks and water reacted with and removed this "waste" oxygen, but eventually levels of oxygen in the atmosphere began to rise.

By 1.2 billion years ago the fossil record reveals the presence of more complex types of cell called *eukaryotic cells*; the organisms themselves are called *eukaryotes* (from the Greek *eu* for "good" and *karyon* for "nut" or "kernel"). Bacterial cells, with their simpler structure, are called *prokaryotic cells* or *prokaryotes* (from the Greek *pro* for "before"). Eukaryotic cells probably arose when some bacteria survived *inside* other kinds of bacteria, and the two came to depend upon one another. This relationship is called *mutualism,* which is a type of *symbiosis* (see "Close associations," page 155).

Eukaryotic cells differ from bacterial cells in having membrane-bound structures (organelles) and a nucleus that contains the cell's DNA. Two of these organelles, mitochondria (which carry out respiration using oxygen) and chloroplasts (for photosynthesis), are similar in structure and have comparable DNA to bacteria. Such similarities suggest these organelles evolved from symbiotic bacteria.

By 850 million years ago some complex-celled organisms were no longer single celled. They had come together as clusters of cells—the first multicelled (many-celled) organisms. By 600 million years ago oxygen levels in the atmosphere had reached about 1 percent of today's levels. At about this time, the ancient supercontinent called Rodinia began to break apart. Shallow seas formed around its broken edges, creating ideal conditions to support a wide variety of marine organisms. The stage was now set for an evolutionary explosion of life. Those organisms that could harness oxygen for respiration (aerobic respiration) could obtain energy quickly, and this made possible the evolution of larger, faster-moving creatures. By 600 million years ago soft-bodied animals resembling jellyfish appeared. By 550 million years ago members of all the major animal groups (phyla) we know today had evolved. They all seem to have originated in the oceans.

The diversity and distribution of marine life

Today, the world ocean is home both to the largest animal that has ever lived—the 200-ton (180-tonne) blue whale—and to many of Earth's smallest organisms. Cyanobacteria (blue-green algae) teem in the surface waters, and several hundred of their smaller members could sit comfortably on the point of a needle.

Marine scientists estimate that there are at least 2 million species of microbes, plants, and animals living in the oceans. Some scientists believe there is several times this number. As of now they have identified only about 300,000 of them.

Scientists compare sampling the oceans to dragging a butterfly net through the leaf canopy of a forest. What they catch is a small and selective sample of what actually lives there, and this gives a false impression of the life of the forest. So it is with the oceans.

Until a decade or so ago, marine biologists were convinced that more species lived on land than in the sea. Now they are less sure. In the 1990s, when some marine scientists were dredging up sediment samples from the deep seabed of the North Atlantic, they found, on average, one new species of animal in each sample. When the numbers of small organisms in sediments and in coral reefs are taken into account, the number of marine species may be found to exceed those on land.

Marine life is not spread evenly throughout the oceans— far from it. Life is usually abundant in the shallow waters above continental shelves and on seashores. In the open ocean life is plentiful within the top 660 feet (about 200 m) of the water column, the depth to which enough sunlight penetrates to power photosynthesis. Life is also concentrated on and near the seabed and in the layer of sediment just beneath. Between the surface waters and the seabed, across a vertical extent reaching several miles, the water column is quite sparsely populated.

Even in the places where marine life is most abundant, its distribution is patchy. Across the surface waters "living hot spots" include regions of upwelling where cool, nutrient-rich water rises to the surface, encouraging the growth of phytoplankton and marine creatures that consume phytoplankton or eat other creatures. On the deep seabed oases of life flourish around hydrothermal vents amid hundreds of miles of comparative desert (see "Hot vents and cold seeps," pages 157–158).

Settlers, swimmers, and drifters

Scientists divide marine organisms into two main categories, based on where they live. Pelagic organisms (from the Greek *pelagos* for "open sea") swim or float in the water column. Benthic organisms, also called benthos (the Greek *benthos* meaning "depth"), live on the seabed or in the sediment.

Among pelagic organisms, those that are strong swimmers and can make headway in currents are called nekton (from the Greek *nektos* for "swimming"). They include squid, fishes, and marine mammals. Pelagic organisms that drift with ocean currents, and swim weakly or not at all, are called plankton (from the Greek *planktos* for "wandering"). They range in size from microscopic bacteria to large jellyfish and floating seaweed that are many feet long. Those plankton that are plants are called phytoplankton (Greek *phyton* for "plant") and those that are animals, zooplankton (Greek *zoon* for "animal").

Although plankton exist in many shapes and sizes, most are small—less than a quarter of an inch (6 mm) across. Being small has advantages if an organism needs to avoid sinking out of the surface waters. A small size and complex shape—often adorned with spiny outgrowths—increases the creature's surface area relative to its volume or mass. This adds to its friction with the surrounding water and makes it less likely to sink. Some zooplankton, salps and comb jellies among them, pump heavy ions (electrically charged atoms and molecules) out of their bodies while keeping lighter ones. This lowers their density so they float better. Some phytoplankton and zooplankton contain oil droplets or gas spaces that increase their buoyancy. By changing their chemical balance and altering their buoyancy, some zooplankton rise and fall in the water column in a vertical migration over a 24-hour period (see "Marine migrations," pages 146–149).

All living organisms need food. Most plants make their own by trapping sunlight in the process of photosynthesis. Most animals gain theirs by eating microbes, plants, or other animals. In any case, the food animals eat was originally made by plants or by chemosynthetic or photosynthetic microbes.

In the open ocean, phytoplankton, like plants on land, make their food by trapping sunlight and combining water and carbon dioxide with other simple substances to make carbohydrates (sugars and starches), fats, and proteins—the chemical building blocks of cells. Plants also break down carbohydrates and fats in the process of respiration to release energy to power living processes such as cell growth and cell division. Animals, too, need these complex substances. They cannot make them from scratch, so they obtain them from other organisms—by consuming them. They digest (break down) the food constituents—carbohydrates, fats, proteins, and so on—and reassemble the components in new ways to make body parts or respire them for energy to power movement and other life processes.

All the microscopic phytoplankton floating in the surface waters of the oceans weigh several billion tons in all, the equivalent of about 1 billion African elephants. As they photosynthesize, marine phytoplankton release about the same amount of oxygen as all the plants on land.

Bacteria and cyanobacteria

Within the last 30 years marine scientists have changed their view about the nature of feeding relationships in the open ocean's surface waters. Before then they saw feeding relationships as fairly straightforward, with phytoplankton making food, and zooplankton and larger marine creatures consuming food in a series of stages, with one animal eating another. They summarized the relationships in simple charts called food chains and food webs (see "Food chains and food webs," pages 135–138). This simple view became modified as biologists came to realize that many marine organisms, notably various forms of bacteria, had been slipping through their nets.

Most bacteria are tiny—less than two microns (two-thousandths of a millimeter) across, which is equivalent to less than 0.05 inch across. This minute size is easily small enough to pass through conventional sampling nets. Scientists use fine filters with microscopic pore sizes to extract bacteria from seawater. They can then grow bacteria in special cultures and study how they process chemicals to work out what roles they play in food chains and food webs.

Cyanobacteria and some other bacteria photosynthesize; they trap sunlight to make food. Tiny photosynthetic bacteria called prochlorophytes, together with cyanobacteria, account for 80 percent of photosynthesis in some parts of the ocean. Cyanobacteria have an advantage over other photosynthetic organisms: They can trap and use nitrogen gas, the major gas in air. This is their source of the element nitrogen (N) that they need to make proteins, DNA, and other important complex chemicals. Other photosynthetic organisms need to absorb nitrogen in the form of nutrients, such as nitrate, which can be scarce. Dissolved nitrogen gas is almost always abundant in surface waters.

Some marine bacteria feed on organic substances that leak out of phytoplankton, or else they feed on the dead remains of larger plankton. Either way, they are playing important roles in the recycling of chemicals in the sea— roles that scientists left out of traditional food chains and food webs.

Phytoplankton

Phytoplankton include photosynthetic bacteria and cyanobacteria at one extreme and floating seaweed such as *Sargassum* weed at the other. But most marine scientists, when they think of phytoplankton, think of protists (single-celled organisms with complex cell structure) that can photo-synthesize. Many have beautifully sculpted skeletons with geometric shapes: spheres, spirals, boxes, and cylinders. Among the largest are diatoms and dinoflagellates.

Diatoms have a two-part outer skeleton, hence their name (derived from the Greek *diatoma* for "cut in half"). The skeleton is made of silica, which is also the major ingredient in sand and glass. The diatom's boxlike structure is called a test (a microscopic shell), and it is perforated with holes to allow chemicals to enter and leave. The test varies in shape from an old-fashioned pillbox to a spiny sphere or tube, depending on species. In late summer diatoms multiply to become the commonest of the larger phytoplankton found in most temperate and polar waters.

Most dinoflagellates are smaller than diatoms. They have some animal-like features, such as two flagella (hairlike structures) that they use to row through the water, and from which they gain their name (*dino* for "whirling" and *flagellum* for "whip"). In tropical and subtropical waters dinoflagellates replace diatoms as the most numerous of the larger phytoplankton.

Coccolithophores are tiny phytoplankton covered in chalky plates, hence their name (*coccus* for "berry," *lithos* for "stone," and *phorid* for "carrying"). Coccolithophores are often common in the open ocean outside polar waters. When they die, their calcium carbonate skeletons settle on the seafloor, and eventually, over millions of years, this "snowfall" may

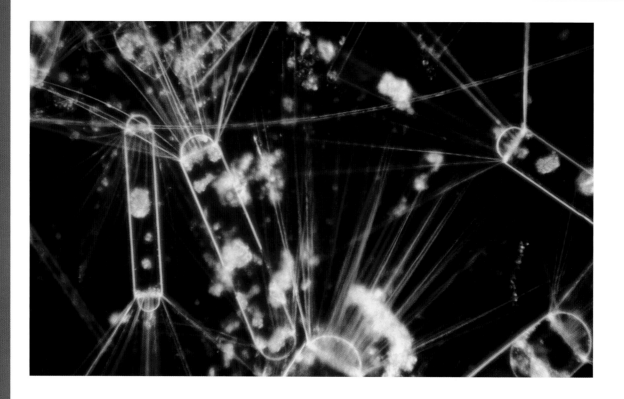

A selection of Southern Ocean diatoms, types of phytoplankton, viewed at high magnification (Courtesy of Flip Nicklin/ Minden Pictures)

compact to form chalk deposits tens of yards thick (see "Seafloor sediments," pages 42–44).

Phytoplankton thrive in surface waters where nutrients and sunlight are in abundance, and most marine food chains depend on phytoplankton as the primary producers.

Zooplankton

The smallest zooplankton are visible only with a microscope. These miniature forms include animal-like protists such as foraminiferans (with a calcium carbonate skeleton) and radiolarians (with an elaborate skeleton of silica). Both types of protist trap their food supply of bacteria and phytoplankton by extending sticky projections through holes in their armor.

Two kinds of crustaceans—the shrimplike copepods, and their larger relatives, the krill—are the most abundant of the larger zooplankton. Together, they are probably the most plentiful animals on Earth, outnumbering even individual insects on land.

Different species of copepods target various foods and employ distinct feeding strategies. For example, some copepods have especially hairy limbs that sweep phytoplankton and smaller zooplankton toward the mouth. Others use stabbing legs and mouthparts to capture and consume medium-sized zooplankton. Most copepods have long antennae that they use both to chemically "taste" the water and to detect disturbances in the water. The antennae help them find food and give warning of advancing predators.

Many of the larger zooplankton, including arrow worms, salps, comb jellies, and jellyfish, are semitransparent. This can act as camouflage, making them difficult to spot from below against the sunlight streaming through the surface waters.

Arrow worms, looking like feathered darts, are armed with grasping spines around the mouth that they use to stab unsuspecting prey. Jellyfish and comb jellies employ tentacles armed with stinging cells to capture their prey. Any small animal that brushes against the tentacles is impaled by dozens of tiny paralyzing poison darts. Once the victim is immobilized, the predator's tentacles pull it to the mouth.

Barrel-shaped salps and tadpolelike larvaceans filter the seawater for small plankton and edible fragments using nets of jelly. When the net is laden with food, they eat it. Larvaceans gain their name from their similarity to the tadpole-like larval (preadult) stage of the sea squirt. Despite their primitive appearance, larvaceans and salps have a strengthening rod called a notochord at some stage in their life cycle. This feature, among others, shows they belong to a group of chordates that are quite closely related to vertebrates (animals with backbones).

The zooplankton described so far spend their entire lives in the plankton community. Biologists classify them as *holoplankton* (from the Greek *holo* for "whole"). However, at certain times of the year, particularly in coastal waters, the surface waters teem with plankton that are the larvae of bottom-living creatures. These are the temporary plankton, or *meroplankton* (from the Greek *mero* for "a part"). Familiar creatures from the shore or seabed—barnacles, clams, crabs, lobsters, starfish, and flatfish among them—have larvae that drift among the plankton and bear little resemblance to the adults into which they will grow. For bottom-living animals, a plankton phase in the life cycle disperses the offspring so they can colonize new habitats some distance from the parents.

Zooplankton form the vital food connection between phytoplankton and the larger sea creatures of the surface waters. Small- and medium-size zooplankton eat phytoplankton, and they in turn are consumed by larger zooplankton. Some fish, squid, seabirds, and most baleen whales—the largest creatures in the sea—consume zooplankton.

Zooplankton also provide a vital link in food chains and food webs in midwater and on the seafloor. When zooplankton produce solid waste (feces), and when they die, the remains sink through the water column as marine snow. Animals in midwater consume this as food, then void the waste in their feces. Eventually, zooplankton fragments find their way to the deep-sea floor, sometimes having passed through several digestive systems on the way. Their remains then provide food for the bottom-living community.

Seaweeds

On almost any rocky seashore in a temperate part of the world, seaweeds are evident. They are the slippery fronds draped over the shore in assorted shades of brown, green, or red. You can also find seaweeds growing abundantly in shallow water attached to hard surfaces.

Seaweeds are large algae. They have a much simpler structure than the trees and grasses on land. Seaweeds lack true leaves, stems, and roots, but they have structures that perform similar functions. Instead of leaves for trapping sunlight, seaweeds have fronds. In some species the fronds contain air sacs that make them float up toward the sunlight, their source of energy for photosynthesis. Instead of roots, most seaweed have a holdfast that anchors the plant. Instead of a stem, seaweeds have a stalk that, like their fronds, flexes. Bending absorbs the force of waves and currents rather than resisting them, which would risk breakage.

Seaweeds are classified according to overall color—red, green, or brown—that, itself, is an indication of the pigments they contain. The largest seaweeds are brown algae called kelp, and the biggest of these is the giant kelp of the North Pacific. From holdfast to frond tip, giant kelp grow to 330

The view looking upward through an underwater forest of giant kelp (Macrocystis pyrifera) *in Channel Islands National Park, California* (Courtesy of Flip Nicklin/Minden Pictures)

feet (100 m). Their fronds can grow by a superfast 24 inches (60 cm) in a single day. With buoyant fronds floating up to the surface, a thick bed of kelp forms an underwater forest, a kelp forest.

Relatively few creatures actually eat living seaweed. Among those that do are sea urchins, some sea snails and sea slugs, and sea cows (types of marine mammals). Nevertheless, seaweeds provide a platform or safe haven for a host of animals and other plants. Microscopic algae grow on the surface of the fronds. So do animals such as hydroids and segmented worms that filter the seawater for plankton. These attached plants and animals serve as food for snails and shrimp. Worms, brittle stars (related to sea stars), and crabs live on and around the holdfasts. They filter the water for food, sift the sediment, or hunt other creatures. Fish thrive in the kelp forest. They find the forest of fronds a fairly safe refuge to hide from hunters such as seals and sharks.

People harvest seaweeds as a useful source of food, food additives, and agricultural fertilizer (see "Chemicals from marine life," page 195). The annual harvest of North American kelp weighs some 22,000 U.S. tons (20,000 tonnes), the equivalent of 10,000 Indian elephants.

Sea grasses

Sea grasses grow on shallow sandy or muddy seabeds. They are related to lilies, not grasses, and they are the only land plants that have fully adapted to life under the sea. They grow submerged, and their flowers produce pollen grains that drift through the water to reach and pollinate other flowers. They release their seeds underwater, too.

Like the land plants from which sea grasses evolved, they have true stems, leaves, and roots. Their roots enable them to anchor in soft sediment, which seaweeds are unable to do. Sea-grass roots also enable these plants to absorb nutrients from the sediment, which puts them at an advantage compared with phytoplankton and seaweeds, which have to obtain their nutrients from the seawater itself. Sea grasses can grow well in nutrient-poor waters.

Sea-grass roots help bind the particles of sediment in which they grow, and their leaves bend in the water, helping to reduce water turbulence from waves and currents. Together, these effects serve to reduce local coastal erosion.

Like grass meadows on land, sea grass meadows offer food and shelter for a host of animals. Among those that eat sea grass leaves or roots are sea urchins, parrot fish, green turtles, the marine mammals called sea cows (see "Other sea mammals," pages 131–134), and some migratory ducks and geese. Microscopic algae grow on the leaves of sea grasses. The algae, in turn, provide food for various small grazers, including sea snails and small fish. Many tiny animals, including sea squirts and segmented worms, attach to sea-grass leaves and filter the seawater for microscopic plankton. When sea grasses decay, their remains and the decomposers that feed on them provide food for bottom-living worms, clams, and sea cucumbers. Sea-grass meadows are nurseries for the

A healthy bed of sea grass in the Florida Keys National Marine Sanctuary (Courtesy of Paige Gill, Department of Commerce/ National Oceanic and Atmospheric Administration)

young of many fishes, mollusks, and crustaceans. In the late 1990s a substantial part of the North Australian prawn fishery, worth U.S. $70 million annually, depended upon sea-grass beds for the growth of juveniles.

Unfortunately, sea grasses are under attack from human activities. During the second half of the 20th century, many sea-grass meadows in Europe and North America died, and some are now a fraction of their original size. A variety of factors are implicated, including pollution by oils and heavy metals, and increased water cloudiness (turbidity) that blocks sunlight needed for photosynthesis (see "Pollution," page 200). Such factors have weakened some sea-grass meadows, making the plants more liable to die from disease.

Marine invertebrates

More than 95 percent of marine animal species do not have backbones; they are invertebrates. They range in size from the miniature meiofauna living in the seabed sediment and tiny zooplankton drifting in surface waters, to giant squid that reach 60 feet (18 m) long. Marine invertebrates belong to about 30 different groups called phyla (singular phylum), with each phylum-containing species sharing many features in common.

Sponges (phylum Porifera) are the simplest many-celled invertebrates. In structure a sponge is little more than a sac with pores. Inside, lining a central cavity, are cells with beating hairlike structures called cilia that create miniature water currents. These draw food particles into the sac through the pores. The traditional bath sponge is the skeleton of one type of sponge, now threatened because of overharvesting.

Cnidarians (phylum Cnidaria) include corals, sea anemones, and jellyfish. They have a rubbery or jellylike body with a central cavity for digesting food, and they capture prey using stinging tentacles. The 30-foot (9-m)-long tentacles of the Portuguese man-of-war jellyfish carry enough venom to cause a person paralysis and agonizing pain, which can be life-threatening for someone swimming in the sea. Box jellyfish, of some tropical and subtropical waters, are the most venomous creatures in the sea. Multiple stings can halt a human's breathing and heart beat within minutes.

Most cnidarians exist in one of two forms. The polyp form, found in sea anemones and corals, is essentially a tube, with a base at one end and a ring of tentacles around a mouth at the other. The other form is the medusa (named after the snake-haired monster of Greek mythology), which is a jellyfish.

Tens of thousands of marine invertebrate species are worms. Most live in or on the seafloor, but a few, such as the arrow worms (phylum Chaetognatha), float in the plankton (see "Settlers, swimmers, and drifters," pages 100–102). The bottom-living worms include simple flatworms (phylum Platyhelminthes), ribbon worms (Nemertea), smooth round-worms (Nematoda), and segmented worms (Annelida).

Arthropods (phylum Arthropoda), with some 40,000 sea-living species described so far, are among the most successful marine invertebrates. Like terrestrial arthropods such as insects, marine arthropods have jointed limbs and a hard outer skeleton. More than 95 percent of marine arthropods are crustaceans. They often occupy several levels of marine food webs as grazers, scavengers, and predators (see "Food chains and food webs," pages 135–138).

Among marine crustaceans are about 10,000 species of shrimp, lobster, and crab. Copepods and krill are shrimplike crustaceans that live among the plankton. Isopods (related to pill bugs) and small, shrimplike amphipods live on the seafloor or on the beach. Barnacles are sessile, that is, stationary and fixed. They hide their jointed bodies beneath thick, chalky plates, which makes them unlikely looking crustaceans.

Mollusks (phylum Molluska) are soft-bodied, and with about 75,000 marine species, they are arguably the most diverse marine invertebrate group. A hollow region, called the visceral mass, contains a mollusk's major internal organs. A muscular part, the foot, is used for crawling, swimming, or burrowing. Some mollusks, such as snails and clams, have a protective, chalky shell on the outside. Others have an internal chalky support, such as the cuttlefish's cuttlebone.

Bivalve mollusks (*bivalve* meaning "two half shells") include oysters, mussels, and clams. Most are suspension feeders, creating currents of water and filtering out suspended food items with their gills. Gastropod mollusks—sea snails, sea slugs, and limpets—most with a mouth armed with a rasping device, are mainly grazers or scavengers, but some, such as the dog whelks, are predators. Cephalopod mollusks—octopuses, squid, and cuttlefish—have sophisticated nervous systems and are fast-moving predators.

Echinoderms are members of the phylum Echinodermata (from the Greek for "spiny-skinned animals"). Their name refers to the chalky spines or plates that are embedded in their skin and act as a skeleton. Their circular body plan is usually based on five parts (think of a sea star, or starfish, with its five arms). Brittle stars, sea urchins, and sea cucumbers are also members of the group. Echinoderms have a unique feature: rows of water-filled tube feet that they extend and shorten for walking or burrowing. Some sea stars use their tube feet as suckers for prying open clam shells. Many sea urchins graze on algae, while sea cucumbers are important deposit feeders on the seabed.

Marine fishes

In terms of abundance and variety, fishes are the most successful vertebrates (animals with backbones). The 24,500 or so species of fish make up about 48 percent of all vertebrates.

All fish have a backbone or a similar structure made of bone or cartilage. They all have fins, and nearly all have gills for extracting oxygen from water. A few, such as some freshwater lungfish, have more or less abandoned gills in favor of lungs for breathing air.

The 14,700 or so species of marine fish have exploited most marine environments, from tide pools to ocean depths of more than 19,700 feet (6,000 m). Fishes range in size from gobies less than 0.4 inches (1 cm) long to the whale shark, which some experts estimate reaches about 60 feet (18 m) in length. As a technical point, the correct plural form to describe fish of more than one species is "fishes"; "fish" is the singular form, or the plural form where only one species is involved.

The ancestor of all of today's fishes was probably a creature called a heterostrocan, a small, primitive fish with a gaping

Life among lobster bristles

Entirely new groups of invertebrates turn up in unlikely places. In 1995 scientists described a new phylum, Cycliophora, based on a single species that lives in the bristles around a lobster's mouth. The species' name, *Symbion pandora,* refers to the animal's symbiotic relationship with the lobster (see "Close associations," page 155) and Pandora's box of Greek mythology, which, when opened, allowed all human ills to escape. In *Symbion*'s case, the pregnant mother bursts open to bear young, sacrificing herself in the process.

oval for its mouth and bony plates for body armor. This creature swam in shallow seas some 500 million years ago, sucking up small particles from the seabed.

Jawless fishes

Nowadays, the closest relatives of early fish such as the heterostracan are the eel-like hagfishes and lampreys. Like the heterostrocan, they lack the jaws and paired fins that more advanced fishes share. Instead of jaws to chew, hagfishes and lampreys have a roughened or toothed tongue that rasps away flesh.

Although hagfishes and lampreys look similar, hagfishes probably evolved more than 100 million years before lampreys, and recent research suggests that lampreys may be quite closely related to later, jawed fishes.

Hagfishes are possibly the most revolting fishes in the sea. Place a hagfish in a bucket of seawater, and the water soon turns to the consistency of wallpaper paste. Hagfishes produce enormous quantities of sticky slime, which is a deterrent to anything that wants to eat them.

Hagfishes have other unpleasant habits. Hagfish scent rotting carcasses or dying fish using sensitive tentacles around the mouth. Once located, a hagfish enters its victim through mouth, anus, or wound, and often consumes the dead or dying prey from the inside. Without teeth and jaws to tear chunks of flesh away, a hagfish ties its body into a knot that it slides down the body to the head. The knot levers the hagfish's anchored head away from the carcass, taking flesh with it.

Hagfishes are survivors. Ancient hagfishes probably swam in oceans more than 400 million years ago. While many kinds of fish have died out, and more advanced fish with complex jaws and fins have evolved, the hagfishes have carved out a successful life in the deep ocean.

Unlike hagfishes, which live only in the sea, with most species favoring deep water, lampreys are found in shallow seawater and in freshwater too. Some species of lamprey hatch from eggs in freshwater but migrate to the sea to mature and then return to rivers and streams to spawn. Other species (including landlocked forms of the marine lamprey in the United States) spend their entire life cycle in freshwater.

The adults of most lamprey species are parasites. They have a large sucker surrounding the mouth that they anchor to their fish victims. Then lampreys use their toothed tongue to rasp away flesh. This draws blood and damages tissues that they consume as a nutritious soup. The lamprey releases chemicals called anticoagulants into the wound, which stops the victim's blood from clotting. When lampreys have taken their fill, they release their quarry. Often the damage inflicted is enough to kill the victim.

Jaws and paired fins

Two major groups of fish dominate the oceans today. The members of one group, the cartilaginous fishes, have a skeleton made entirely of cartilage; those of the other group, bony fishes, have a skeleton of bone and cartilage. Both groups have true jaws.

The evolution of jaws was a major advance in fish design. Sometime between 500 and 410 million years ago, parts of the skeleton that supported the gills of some primitive fishes moved forward and formed structures that supported the mouth. Bone-supported jaws made fish better predators able to handle larger prey. Jawed fishes could bite or chew properly rather than simply suck or filter. By 250 million years ago 30-foot (9-m)-long sharks were traveling the seas, biting into other fish with their powerful jaws.

Major differences between cartilaginous and bony fishes

	Cartilaginous fishes (e.g., shark or ray)	Advanced bony fishes (teleosts) (e.g., herring or sea bass)
Skeleton	Made of cartilage	Made of bone and cartilage
Fins	Paired fins have limited range of movement. The upper part (lobe) of the tail fin is usually larger than the lower, to drive the head upward	Paired fins are highly maneuverable. The upper and lower lobes of the tail fin are usually the same size
Gills	Usually five pairs of gill slits	Usually a single pair of gill flaps
Buoyancy	Swim bladder absent. A fat-filled liver creates buoyancy. Fins generate lift	Swim bladder usually present
Skin	Covering of toothlike placoid scales	Covering typically of bony scales
Reproduction	Produce live young or lay a few large eggs, which are fertilized internally	Most lay many eggs, which are fertilized externally

Paired fins were another major advance. Almost all fishes, ancient and modern, have a dorsal (back) fin and a tail (caudal) fin. The tail fin, when moved side to side, drives the fish forward. The dorsal fin helps in steering and prevents rolling. But most modern fishes also have at least two pairs of fins, one pair at the shoulder (pectoral fins) and another pair farther back on the underside (pelvic fins). These fins offer better control when swimming. With paired fins, fish could more easily hunt their prey and escape their predators.

Cartilaginous fishes

About 820 species of cartilaginous fish swim the seas today. They include sharks and dogfishes (about 330 species) and flattened skates and rays (about 450 species). Cartilaginous fishes have a skeleton made entirely of cartilage familiar to people as the hard, shiny gristle normally found at the joint at the end of a bone. The gristly skeleton may be a way of lightening the load because cartilaginous fishes do not have an air-filled swim bladder as a buoyancy aid, as bony fishes do (see "Bony fishes," pages 119–120). Sharks and their relatives store oil in their liver to make them more buoyant, and their fins are airfoil-shaped, like the wings of an aircraft. When a shark swims forward, its fins generate lift.

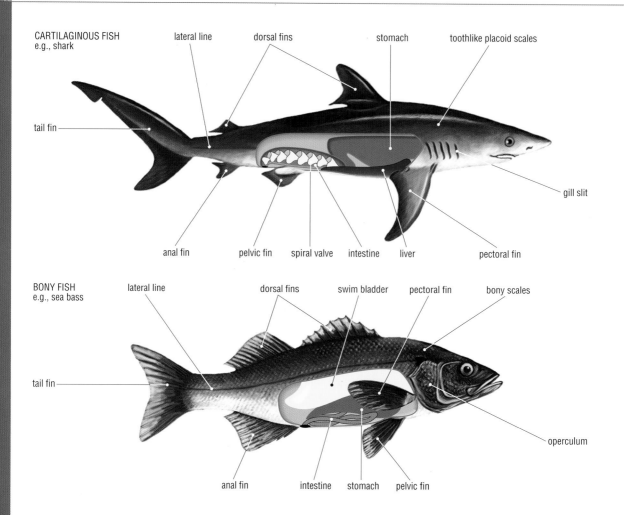

CARTILAGINOUS FISH
e.g., shark

lateral line — dorsal fins — stomach — toothlike placoid scales — gill slit

tail fin

anal fin — pelvic fin — spiral valve — intestine — liver — pectoral fin

BONY FISH
e.g., sea bass

lateral line — dorsal fins — swim bladder — pectoral fin — bony scales — operculum

tail fin

anal fin — intestine — stomach — pelvic fin

Similarities and differences between cartilaginous and bony fishes

Skates and rays are essentially flattened versions of sharks. Skates lay eggs that later hatch, while rays give birth to miniature young. The flattened body of skates and rays is an adaptation to living on or near the seafloor, although not all species do so today. Their pectoral fins are enlarged, almost like wings, and these fish flap them to swim.

The skin of most cartilaginous fishes is covered in sharp, toothlike placoid scales that feel rough to the touch. Gristly fish obtain oxygen by extracting it from water using blood-rich, feathery gills. They breathe in water through the mouth or through spiracles (openings similar to nostrils). The water crosses the gills and exits through gill slits. Skates and rays have gill slits on the underside and take in water through spiracles on top of the head. This way, when they breathe on the sea bottom, they do not choke their gills with sediment.

Most skates and rays have flattened teeth, which are adapted for crushing the bottom-living crustaceans, mollusks, and echinoderms on which they feed. Most sharks are primarily fish-eaters and scavengers. However, the largest sharks (the whale shark and the basking shark) and the largest ray (the manta) are plankton-feeders.

Some skates and rays have unusually powerful defenses. Stingrays harbor one or two poisonous barbs in the tail, which they lash forward to stab any threat. Some electric rays have rows of muscles along their backs that work like batteries. They can generate an electric current strong enough to stun small fish and discourage attacking predators.

Sharks have remarkable senses. Some species can smell blood at levels of one part per billion—equivalent to a drop of blood in about 26,000 U.S. gallons (100,000 L) of water. They also have a well-developed lateral line system along the

A great white shark (Carcharodon carcharias) off Neptune Islands, South Australia (Mike Parry/Minden Pictures)

Sharks attacking people

Sharks have an exaggerated reputation for attacking people. Most of us are much more likely to be struck by lightning than bitten by a shark.

Of about 330 species, about 40 are known to bite people. For about half of these species, the attack came because people provoked the shark by grabbing or prodding it. Even mild-mannered sharks will bite to defend themselves.

Most shark experts agree that three species—the great white, the tiger, and the bull shark—are probably responsible for most attacks. However, when ships capsize at sea, and people are attacked in the water, other species may be involved. There is no simple, straightforward explanation as to why sharks attack people. In some great white shark attacks, it is probably a case of mistaken identity. A person's silhouette on a surfboard can be confused for a seal or sea lion, the shark's normal prey. In some cases the shark is simply curious, mouthing potential prey to test its edibility. In the case of the great white, only rarely does an attacked person become a wholesome meal.

flanks that is sensitive to vibrations in the water, such as the ripples from a thrashing prey. Sharks track by smell and vibration at a distance and then use eyesight and an electrical sense as they approach. Jelly-filled pores on the shark's head pick up weak electrical fields produced by a prey's muscles. With this electrical sense, sharks and rays can even find flatfish and crabs buried in sandy seabeds.

Sharks, skates, and rays grow slowly and produce relatively few young. This means that if a population is heavily fished, the stock may take many years to recover or may not recover at all.

By June 2005 the International Shark Attack File (ISAF) had recorded 61 unprovoked shark attacks on people for the year 2004. Seven of the attacked people died as a result. In that same year people killed millions of sharks. In many cases living sharks had their fins cut off—to provide fins for the shark-fin soup trade—and the still-living, de-finned shark was thrown back into the water. In 2000 the U.S. House of Representatives passed legislation banning shark de-finning in U.S. waters. Some other countries are now introducing similar laws.

Bony fishes

There are about 23,500 species of bony fish. Most are advanced forms of fish called *teleosts* (from the Greek *teleios* for "perfect" and *osteon* for "bone"). These fish have fins supported by thin bony rays, and a body covered in lightweight, flexible scales. Most of the familiar food fish—cod, salmon, sea bass, and tuna, for example—are teleosts.

The flexible fins of teleost fishes are a major clue to their success. Their paired fins can rotate, enabling the fish to turn almost on a dime, hover in the water, or even swim backward. This maneuverability is increased by another feature that most bony fishes possess, a swim bladder—an air-filled sac. By altering the amount of air in the sac, most bony fishes can control their buoyancy so they do not rise or sink in the water. They can stop swimming and still float, thus saving energy. Their gills are also more efficient than those of cartilaginous fishes at extracting oxygen from seawater to power muscles. The marlin, perhaps the fastest fish of all, can swim at speeds of about 50 mph (80 km/h).

Different species of bony fish employ various kinds of mouth- or throat-teeth and gill devices to capture and process their food. Such adaptability is another key to their success. Barracudas have daggerlike teeth, and garfishes a needlelike array; both are adapted to grab and retain their fish prey. Parrotfishes have a horny beak that they use to bite off pieces of coral or to nibble at algal turf. At the back of the throat their grinding teeth reduce coral or algae to a digestible pulp. Herring, sardines, and anchovies, by contrast, are plankton feeders and use bony extensions of their gills—gill rakers—to strain small zooplankton from swallowed seawater.

Some species of bony fish swim in tightly packed shoals called schools. So closely synchronized are their movements that hundreds of fish seem to behave like a single giant creature. How are the fish able to stay in tight formation and yet change direction at high speed? The fish's lateral line—the sensory system that detects vibrations in the water—plays a key role. As the fish swims, it creates a V-shaped wake underwater, rather like the wave spreading out from the bow of a moving ship. Nearby objects, including other fish in the school, reflect this wave back. This array of vibrations provides the fish with a highly detailed "picture" of its surroundings and the movement of objects nearby.

The great advantage of schooling is probably to reduce predation. It is more difficult for a predator to find a single school, rather than hundreds of widely scattered individuals. When a predator attacks a school, the fish scatter, making it difficult for the hunter to single out one individual. Living in a school, each fish has slightly improved chances of survival.

Bony fishes reproduce in a wide variety of ways. Unlike cartilaginous fishes, which lay few eggs or bear live young, many bony fishes release thousands of eggs at a single spawning. The male then fertilizes the eggs in the water. A female North Atlantic cod typically produces about 10 million eggs a year. The eggs of cod and other oceanic species float up to the surface waters and form part of the plankton community. Zooplankton and fish eat the eggs and fish larvae, so from the original millions few survive to maturity.

Those species that live in coastal waters, on the seabed, or among floating seaweed tend to produce fewer eggs and spend more time and energy in their care. Several species of coral-reef cardinal fish are mouth-breeders. Males keep the fertilized eggs in the mouth to protect them until they hatch. In seahorses the pregnant female places her eggs in a brood pouch on her partner's belly. The male incubates the eggs, and when they hatch, tiny seahorses wriggle out of his pouch opening; he gives birth.

Marine reptiles

Of about 8,000 living species of reptiles, only about 80 live in seawater or brackish water (diluted seawater). Marine reptiles include sea snakes, sea turtles, two species of crocodile, and a lizard.

Around 400 million years ago complex forms of life began to invade the land. Within the space of 80 million years water-living algae gave rise to land-living mosses and ferns, and some marine arthropods (joint-limbed invertebrates) evolved to become insects that not only walked across the landscape but learned to fly. Amid this eruption of life, certain fishes—related to present-day lungfishes—began to make forays across marshy ground. They walked on fleshy fins and breathed air using lungs. Some evolved to become amphibians such as frogs and toads. Most amphibians lead a double life, living on land in damp conditions but laying their eggs in water.

By about 340 million years ago reptiles—the first true land vertebrates—evolved. Reptiles lay leathery or chalky eggs that do not need to be bathed in water. The first reptiles probably looked similar to present-day salamanders, but by 145 million years ago, in the middle of the Age of Dinosaurs, some evolved to become the biggest animals ever to walk the Earth. At this time some reptiles had already returned to the sea, producing fierce predators such as the long-necked plesiosaur, the dolphinlike ichthyosaur, and, by 85 million years ago, the terrifying giant mosasaur, a 50-foot (15-m) monster that ate sharks, bony fishes, marine reptiles, and small land dinosaurs.

Few reptiles inhabit today's oceans. In most cases their body design and life cycle, previously adapted to life on land, impose strict limitations on an aquatic life. For example, all marine reptiles must return to the surface regularly to breathe air. With the exception of most sea snakes, marine reptiles come ashore to lay their eggs.

Of the seven species of sea turtle, all are threatened or endangered by a combination of factors, including pollution and habitat destruction (see chapter 9); human hunting for turtle shell, meat, or eggs; and accidental capture of turtles in nets set for fish. All marine turtles are protected by international law, but that is very difficult to enforce on the open sea.

Male sea turtles remain at sea, but females come ashore to lay eggs. After mating, a female makes landfall on a carefully chosen sandy beach—the one where she hatched many years before. A green turtle, for instance, drags herself up the shore and digs a hole in which she lays a clutch of 100 or so eggs. She scrapes sand over the eggs and smoothes the surface to hide their location before hauling herself back to sea. As the most prolific sea turtle, she repeats the process several times in one season.

Inside the green turtle nest, temperature governs the sex of hatchlings. Typically, cooler eggs (below 82°F or 28°C) develop into males, while warmer eggs (above 87°F or 30.5°C) hatch into females. Hatchlings make a perilous journey across the sand to reach the sea. On the way birds and crabs pick them off. In the water waiting sharks or crocodiles devour them. Less than one hatchling in a 1,000 survives to reach maturity.

Like sea turtles, sea snakes spend all or most of their time in seawater and are specially adapted to do so. They are related to land-living cobras and are found mainly in the warmer parts of the Indian and Pacific Oceans. The yellow-bellied sea snake may be the most abundant reptile on Earth. Its tail, like that of other sea snakes that are well adapted for swimming, is flattened into a paddle. When diving for prey, the snake can remain submerged on a single lung full of air for well over an hour.

Many sea snakes use highly potent venom to paralyze their fish prey quickly, so the victims do not have a chance to swim away and hide. Such venom can be lethal to humans. Fortunately most sea snakes have small mouths and rarely bite people. Southeast Asian fishers are occasionally bitten fatally when they try to extract sea snakes from nets.

A marine iguana (Amblyrhynchus cristatus), *underwater grazing on seaweed off Santa Cruz Island, Galápagos Islands* (Courtesy of Tui de Roy/ Minden Pictures)

Among crocodiles, only the Pacific saltwater crocodile lives in full-strength seawater. A small population of the American crocodile lives in brackish water (seawater mixed with freshwater) at the southern edge of the Florida Everglades and in parts of the Gulf of Mexico and Caribbean Sea. Both crocodile species are fierce predators. They eat mostly fish and invertebrates, but they can grab sizable mammals, even people, drowning them before consuming them underwater.

The marine iguana of the Galápagos Islands is the only lizard truly adapted for life in the sea. It eats seaweed and swims by undulating its body and flattened tail, but it spends much of its time basking on rocky shores where it warms itself after a swim.

Seabirds

Like reptiles and mammals, birds evolved on land, but some—the seabirds—have returned to exploit the watery environment of their ancient vertebrate ancestors. Of about 9,000 living species of birds, fewer than 350 (or 4 percent) are seabirds.

Seabirds have adaptations for marine life, such as webbed feet for swimming or paddling and salt glands that empty into the nostrils to expel excess salt. Seabirds spend part of their time feeding in, on, or above the sea, but all species nest on land.

Migrating shorebirds, ranging from flamingos, ducks, and geese to small waders such as plovers and sandpipers, visit lagoons and mudflats in the thousands to feed upon sea grasses, algae, and small animals. Although these birds have a major effect on local shores, they are not regarded as true seabirds because they lack specific marine adaptations.

Seabirds have a greater effect on underwater life than appears at first sight. All seabirds are, to a greater or lesser extent, predators of zooplankton, fish, or squid. Where seabirds are numerous in coastal waters, they are major consumers. Along Peru's coast, cormorants, boobies, and other seabirds catch about 2.75 million U.S. tons (2.5 million tonnes) of fish in some years—nearly one-third of the local catch taken by human fishers.

Seabirds belong to four distinct groups: penguins (order Sphenisciformes); tubenoses (Procellariiformes); pelicans and their relatives (Pelecaniformes); and a mixed group (Charadriiformes) containing gulls, terns, puffins, and auks. Seabird species vary greatly in their flying, diving, and swimming ability. They have evolved a wide range of hunting strategies to exploit the surface-water community while reducing competition with one another for food.

Among seabirds, the 17 species of penguin are the best adapted for diving and swimming. They no longer fly in air but "fly" underwater using their wings as flippers. The emperor penguin, the deepest diving bird of all, can dive to depths exceeding 1,640 feet (500 m) for as long as 20 minutes in search of its food of fish and squid.

All penguins live in the Southern Hemisphere, and all species, including the equatorial Galápagos penguin, dive in cold water. To combat the cold, they have an insulating layer of fat beneath the skin and dense, waterproof, oil-tipped feathers that trap a layer of warm air close to the skin.

Petrels, shearwaters, and albatrosses are called *tubenoses* because their nostrils join to form a salt-expelling tube that runs along the top of the bill. Tubenoses are superb fliers. The wandering albatross, with a wingspan of about 11 feet (3.5 m), glides on updrafts of air, rarely needing to flap its wings. The bird gains its name from the two-year-plus flights it makes around the Southern Hemisphere, only occasionally settling on the sea surface to take small fish or squid.

The smaller tubenoses, including petrels and shearwaters, show amazing ability to fly or hover just above the sea surface. Storm petrels, for example, patter their feet on the water surface while plucking zooplankton and small fish from below.

The group containing gulls, terns, and auks has more seabird species than any other. Terns plunge dive into the sea to snatch small fish. Most gulls, by contrast, are generalist predators and scavengers. Whether scavenging the discarded fish or scraps thrown into the water by commercial fishers or sorting through litter left by sunbathers, they have benefited from their close association with people. The gull-like jaegars and skuas are pirates among seabirds. They

Atlantic puffin
(Fratercula arctica)*, with*
freshly caught capelin
(Mallotus villosus) *in its*
beak (Courtesy of Yva
Momatiuk and John
Eastcott/Minden
Pictures)

chase other seabirds to rob them of their fish catch, and
they nest near colonies of other seabirds, looting their eggs
and young. Puffins, like most other members of the auk
family, have thick beaks, and they dive to pursue and catch
fish. They return to shore with several fish dangling from

the beak—a record 62 fish in one case. Like penguins, auks use their wings like flippers to steer themselves toward their prey.

The diverse group containing pelicans and their relatives has many successful seabirds of tropical waters. Although quite varied in appearance, characteristically all species have webbing between all four toes.

Pelicans, such as the familiar brown pelican of the United States, plunge onto the sea surface and scoop up fish, using the pouch that hangs below the bill. Cormorants, black and long-necked, sit on the water surface and dive and pursue individual fish. Frigate birds—the males with scarlet chests that they inflate like balloons in the breeding season to woo females—snatch items from the beaks of other seabirds or harass them so that they spit out food. Frigate bird plumage is not waterproof, and in diving to take food from the sea surface the bird avoids getting its feathers wet.

Whales, dolphins, and porpoises

Like mammals on land, marine mammals are warm-blooded, they breathe air, and mothers suckle their young with milk from mammary glands. Those mammals that are well adapted to life at sea are cetaceans (whales, dolphins, and porpoises), sea cows (manatees and the dugong), pinnipeds (seals, sea lions, and the walrus), and the sea otter.

Some 50 million years ago the ancestors of today's whales had legs and looked like hairy crocodiles. Through natural selection over thousands of generations their descendants eventually lost legs and hair as adaptations for streamlining. Within the last 40 million years, other groups of mammals have made the difficult transition from land to sea, and at different times. In general, those mammals that made the move more recently show less adaptation to a marine way of life.

Whales, dolphins, and porpoises are *cetaceans* (from the Latin *cetus*, meaning "large sea creature"). From the giant size and gentleness of the great whales to the apparent intelligence and sociable nature of dolphins, they inspire in many people feelings of awe and affection.

All cetaceans are whales, but people often use the term *whale* only for larger cetaceans. The term *dolphin,* used correctly, refers to several families of smaller cetaceans that have conical-shaped teeth. *Porpoise* refers to small cetaceans that have spade-shaped teeth and blunt snouts (family Phocoenidae).

Nowadays, cetaceans are so well adapted to life at sea that many look rather like fish. The body is streamlined, the front legs serve as paddlelike flippers for steering, and the hind limbs are absent. Cetaceans have a tapering tail, which is flattened horizontally into two blades or flukes. Up and down movement of the tail drives the whale forward.

Cetacean nostrils are positioned on top of the head, forming one blowhole (in toothed whales) or two blowholes (in baleen whales) for breathing. Except for sea cows (see "Other sea mammals," pages 131–134), cetaceans are the only marine mammals that give birth underwater.

Toothed whales

Of the 80 or so species of whale, about 70 are toothed. They include dolphins, porpoises, most of the small- to medium-size whales, and the sperm whale, which grows to 65 feet (20 m) long and weighs up to 55 U.S. tons (50 tonnes).

Although all toothed whales have teeth, narwhals only have two (and in males, one is modified to form a tusk) while some types of dolphins have more than 100. Most toothed whales hunt fish or squid, although some search for crabs, sea urchins, and other bottom-living invertebrates. Orcas (killer whales) will take seabirds, turtles, and other marine mammals, including seals and even quite large whales.

Toothed whales generate loud clicks in their nasal passages to communicate with one another and to echolocate. Echolocation involves directing a beam of sound and listening for echoes that give the animal a "sound picture" of the environment. This is a very sophisticated form of sonar and is more sensitive than any human-designed version. Researchers working in aquariums have discovered that dolphins can tell the difference between a small kernel of corn

The head of a sperm whale (Physeter catodon), *the largest species of toothed whale. Notice its flaking skin and the two remora* (Echeneis *species*) *attached to its underside.* (Courtesy of Flip Nicklin/ Minden Pictures)

and a lead shot of the same size, simply by using echolocation. Scientists have watched dolphins in the wild echolocate fish and invertebrates buried up to one foot (30 cm) beneath sand.

Some scientists speculate that toothed whales use loud pulses of sound to stun or confuse their prey. Evidence to confirm this is difficult to gather because whales do not make loud noises in captivity. In a small enclosure resounding echoes are painfully loud.

Many species of toothed whale live together in tightly knit family or friendship groups called pods. Members of orca pods often stay together for life and cooperate closely to hunt prey. Some pods in Alaska work together to trap schools of fish in small bays. In Norwegian waters orcas surround herring schools and stun fish with tail slaps. Off the Pacific coast of North America, members of a pod have been filmed forcing themselves between a female gray whale and her calf so that they can attack and eat the infant.

Some cetacean experts believe certain species show signs of intelligence equivalent to that of apes. Dolphins and some other toothed whales have brains that are large in relation to their body size. Much of the brain's processing power is concerned with decoding sounds, not visual images. When scientists carried out experiments with captive dolphins in the 1960s and 1970s, they usually found that these animals were no more intelligent than sea lions. However, the flexible behavior of dolphins in the wild, including the way they cooperate with and learn from one another, suggests that they may be more intelligent than we think. Recent experiments with bottlenose dolphins in captivity show they have considerable reasoning ability. They can nudge underwater sensors that represent words to construct sentences with meaning.

A killer whale or orca (Orcinus orca), *a toothed whale that commonly hunts marine mammals such as seals. This individual is "spyhopping," rising up out of the water to observe its surroundings, perhaps on the lookout for seals.* (Courtesy of National Oceanic and Atmospheric Administration)

Mass strandings

Some species of toothed whale strand themselves on the shore in large groups. Without help from people, most die. What causes whales to strand? There are several theories. Those species that strand most often—pilot whales, sperm whales, and false killer whales—are deep-water species that live in social groups. Such species may be poor at navigating in shallow water. Once a whale strands, other individuals of the pod stay close by, and they, too, may run aground.

There is some evidence that certain species navigate by following natural magnetic fields in the seascape. Strandings may be more common where weak magnetic fields cross coastlines. Another possible explanation is that individuals may strand because their navigational system is damaged due to injury or disease. In some pilot whale strandings on the Massachusetts coast, individuals showed evidence of a harmful viral infection that might have damaged their hearing or other senses and caused them to become disoriented.

Baleen whales

Toothed whales have teeth. Baleen whales have baleen. The baleen is a filtering device made of long hairlike structures, known as whalebone. Whalebone bristles are fused together in a giant, many-layered comb that hangs down from either side of the upper jaw.

The 14 species of baleen whale include most of the larger whales. The blue whale, reaching 100 feet (30 m) long and weighing up to 200 U.S. tons (180 tonnes), is probably the largest creature that has ever lived.

Most baleen whales feed by taking in water and then partially closing the mouth, raising the tongue, and squeezing the water out through the baleen. The baleen traps zooplankton and small fish or squid, which the whale swallows. Only the gray whale has a very different diet from other baleen whales. It shovels up sediment from the shallow seabed and strains off disturbed amphipod crustaceans, mollusks, and worms with its baleen.

Nine species of baleen whale, including the blue whale and humpback whale, are rorqual whales. These whales have grooves, or pleats, along the throat and belly that allow the

Whale song

Baleen whales communicate with one another using a wide range of sounds, from deep bellows, grunts, and moans to high-pitched squawks, sighs, whines, and whistles. In male humpback whales this musical ability is taken to new heights. During the breeding season adult male humpbacks float almost vertically underwater, head uppermost, and sing. The singing probably attracts females and warns off other males. The male's complex song can last more than 15 minutes, and each male sings a different song, although whales in the same locality usually share a similar "dialect." The very deepest notes of baleen whales can travel hundreds of miles across the oceans through the sofar channel (see "Temperature and seawater," pages 54–57).

throat to expand, accommodating a vast volume of water. A blue whale, for example, can engulf more than 10 U.S. tons (9 tonnes) of water at a time, which contains many thousands of krill.

Other sea mammals

Sea cows (sirenians) look like a cross between a small whale and a walrus. Today only four species survive: three kinds of manatee and the dugong. They live in shallow, warm water, whether fresh, brackish, or full-strength seawater. In the sea sirenians browse, on sea grasses and seaweeds, and they are the only plant-eating marine mammals.

Like whales, sirenians almost entirely lack hair. They are less streamlined and less well adapted to diving than whales, with few sea cows able to hold their breath underwater for more than 10 minutes.

Sea cows are probably the source of the mermaid myth. Sailors may have mistaken female sea cows, lying on their backs suckling their young, for exotic creatures that were half woman, half fish.

Seals, sea lions, and the walrus are *pinnipeds* (from the Latin meaning "fin-footed"). Their closest land-living relatives are carnivores (order Carnivora), the group of mammals that includes dogs, cats, and bears. Pinnipeds belong to three

Bubble nets

Humpback whales have a remarkable hunting strategy that uses sheets of bubbles acting like nets. In cold waters two or more humpbacks may work together to blow streams of bubbles that form a curtain around a swarm of krill or a school of fish. The bubbles act as a net to herd the prey. Like human fishers adjusting the mesh size to match their target fish, the humpbacks can adjust the bubble size to the size of their quarry—small bubbles for krill, larger for herring. The whales spiral upward beneath the school or swarm, blowing bubbles to keep the prey tightly packed. Soon the whales push the ball of fish or krill close to the surface and then rise up together, with mouths open, engulfing as many of the quarry as they can. Common dolphins have been observed using a similar bubble-netting technique to herd fish into a tight ball.

A large species of baleen whale, a humpback whale (Megaptera novaengliae), *with its characteristically elongated flippers. Adult males of this species "sing."* (Courtesy of Mike Parry/Minden Pictures)

families: true or earless seals (19 species), sea lions and eared seals (14 species), and the walrus (one species).

Most seals hunt fish, but the walrus feeds on a variety of bottom-dwelling creatures, including worms and clams. For insulation, pinnipeds have a dense layer of short fur, and/or a thick layer of blubber beneath the skin. Some seals are supreme divers. The southern elephant seal can dive to a depth of more than 5,500 feet (1,675 m), staying submerged for an incredible two hours.

Certain features suggest that eared seals made the move from land to sea more recently than earless seals. For example, eared seals, such as the California sea lion and the northern fur seal, can move quite well on land. They swivel their hind flippers forward and walk or run on all four limbs. Their young will venture into water when only a few weeks or months old.

By contrast, earless seals, such as the harp seal and harbor seal, are more cumbersome on land. In most species the young can take to the water in a matter of hours or days. And further evidence of their long evolutionary history in seawater: Earless seals have lost their external ears, which makes them more streamlined underwater.

The sea otter belongs to the family Mustelidae, the group that includes land-living stoats and weasels, as well as freshwater otters. The sea otter inhabits coastal waters of the North Pacific and spends most of its life at sea, only coming ashore to give birth or to avoid violent storms. Despite this, the sea otter shows relatively few adaptations to a marine life. For example, it can hold its breath underwater only for a few minutes, and it lacks an insulating layer of blubber beneath the skin. Although its lush fur is very dense—one reason why it was popular with human hunters—the otter must groom its fur regularly to keep it waterproof and air-filled.

The sea otter is one of a very few tool-using animals. To break open hard-shelled invertebrates such as sea urchins, clams, and crabs, it floats on its back, balances a stone on its belly, and smashes the food item against the stone.

On some North American kelp beds the sea otter seems to be a "keystone" species, meaning that its presence or absence drastically alters a biological community. Historically, where fur hunters exterminated sea otters, the otters no longer kept sea urchin numbers in check. Sea urchins could multiply, consume most of the kelp, and then die off because of overcrowding, lack of food, and other factors such as disease. Then the kelp had a chance to grow back, the sea urchin numbers gradually built up again, and the "boom-and-bust" cycle repeated itself. Where otters are present, keeping sea urchin numbers in check, this boom-and-bust cycle is less likely to occur. In such cases sea otters help maintain the kelp beds.

CHAPTER 6

ECOLOGY OF THE OCEANS

When biologists study the environment, they break it down into manageable "chunks" to describe and analyze biological relationships and processes in a locality. The classic "chunk" is an ecosystem. Ecologists are biologists who study the populations of organisms within an ecosystem.

An ecosystem is a community of organisms (microbes, larger fungi, plants, and animals) and the locality (*habitat*) in which they live. Typically, an ecosystem has a more or less recognizable boundary. In the ocean the largest ecosystem is the entire global ocean. A body of water (such as the Red Sea, or the Persian Gulf) is a large ecosystem. Much smaller ecosystems include a stretch of shore, the vicinity of a deep-sea hydrothermal vent, or a single tide pool.

Food chains and food webs

With food so fundamental to life, in understanding how ecosystems work biologists usually begin by looking at feeding relationships. What eats what? They gather this data in many ways, such as observing feeding behavior, studying the gut contents of animals, or using radioactive tracers to track substances as they pass from one organism to another. They summarize their information as a food chain.

A food chain is a flowchart with arrows pointing from the organism that is eaten to the organism that eats it. Plants are usually the first step, or link, in the chain, because they make their own food and other creatures depend upon them. Because plants produce food, ecologists call them *producers*. In the open ocean the producers are phytoplankton. Close to hydrothermal (hot-water) vents, chemosynthetic bacteria are the producers (see "Hot vents and cold seeps," pages 157–158).

Animals—the second link in the food chain—eat the producers. Ecologists call these plant-eating animals *primary consumers*. In the surface waters of the ocean, most primary producers are zooplankton. However, some fish—including anchovies—also eat phytoplankton, as do some bottom-living invertebrates, such as sponges.

Larger animals eat the primary consumers, and they form the third link in the chain, *secondary consumers*. In the pelagic world they include the larger zooplankton such as jellyfish, arrow worms, and comb jellies (see "Zooplankton," pages 104–106). They also include plankton-eating fish, such as herring, and small predatory fish, such as mackerel.

At the fourth level of a food chain, larger predators, called *tertiary consumers,* eat secondary consumers. Among these are squid, tuna, marlin, and fish-eating marine mammals, such as dolphins.

Organisms that break down the dead remains of microbes, plants, and animals are a vital ingredient in biological communities. In the surface waters these *decomposers* include bacteria and protists (single-celled organisms with complex cell structure). To keep matters simple, biologists often leave decomposers out of food chains, but they are an important omission.

When drawing a food chain, an ecologist often uses a single species to represent each level, or link, in the food chain. Each level in the chain is a *trophic* (feeding) *level*.

A food chain is a simple version of a complex real-life situation. In the surface waters of the North Atlantic, for example, hundreds or thousands of different types of organisms occupy each trophic level. And at higher trophic levels, one species may consume items from more than one trophic level. For example, adult herring eat secondary consumers such as arrow worms and sand eels, but they also eat primary consumers, such as plant-eating copepods. Thus a herring is both a secondary and a tertiary consumer. Some zooplankton are omnivores (they eat both plants and animals), so they are both primary and secondary consumers.

To show feeding relationships more realistically, biologists draw complex flowcharts called food webs that incorporate

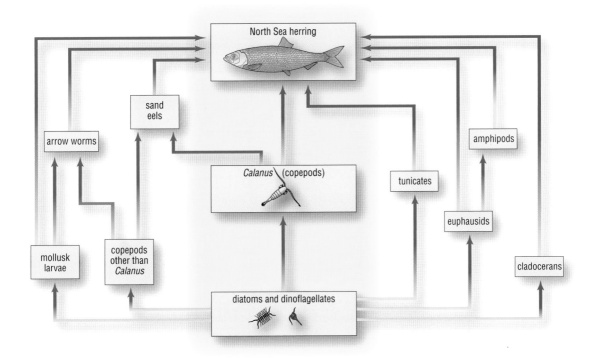

A North Atlantic food web. A food chain is shown highlighted.

many food chains. Even these, however, are a simplification. Herring, for example, eat different kinds of zooplankton at different stages in their lives.

The number of feeding levels in a marine community varies with locality. In clear tropical waters nutrients tend to be in short supply and the mass of organisms in open water is low. Here, zooplankton are small and food chains are long, with up to six trophic levels. In temperate or polar regions where upwelling occurs (nutrient-rich deep water rises near the surface), food chains are shorter, with three or four trophic levels, and the zooplankton tend to be larger.

Six trophic levels is a general upper limit for a marine food chain because of the poor energy transfer from one trophic level to the next. For example, phytoplankton use up some of their food supplies in respiration to keep their life processes running. And zooplankton often find phytoplankton skeletons indigestible. For reasons such as these, only about 10 percent of the energy trapped by phytoplankton (producers) is passed on to zooplankton in the next trophic level (primary consumers). The same applies for energy transfers between other trophic levels: On average, only about 10 percent of the energy in one trophic level is passed on to the next. This loss of energy limits the number of levels to six or fewer. There is simply not enough energy transfer to sustain more.

Working out the links in a food web, and calculating the efficiency of energy transfer from one trophic level to the next, is of great importance to those who wish to manage or conserve ecosystems, or specific populations within them (see "Managing fishing," pages 220–221). For example, knowing the efficiency of energy transfer from phytoplankton to sardines or anchovies enables fish scientists to calculate the likely yield of these fish in a given year. Knowing the food web and energy transfers for North Atlantic herring, marine scientists can work out what other food resources herring might exploit if their food supply of sand eels was decimated by overfishing.

The intertidal zone

The intertidal ("between tides") zone is the true meeting place of land and sea. It is the shore between the levels of the highest and lowest tides plus that narrow strip of land that is splashed by waves and soaked by sea spray. Because the intertidal zone is often accessible to people on land, it is the most intensively studied part of the ocean.

The intertidal community of plants and animals varies according to the nature of the seabed (whether hard or soft, for example), water quality (such as whether the water is clear or cloudy), the degree of exposure to wave action, and the climate of the locality. In temperate waters, for example, seaweeds grow on rocky shores while sea grasses favor soft sediments. In polar waters winter ice smothers or scrapes off shore animals and plants. The best shore survivors are those that move into deeper water, as Antarctic limpets do in winter, or into crevices out of the way of moving ice, as in the case of arctic periwinkles (small snails). In tropical waters fringing coral reefs develop in the lower intertidal where the seabed is rocky and the water clear. Where the seabed is soft, mangroves often grow on the middle and upper shore, and sea grasses in the lower intertidal and subtidal zones.

Within a particular locality the intertidal community of animals and plants also varies with height on the shore. Tides rise and fall once or twice a day, and the biggest and smallest tidal ranges peak in a cycle over about two weeks (see "Tides," pages 81–84). Those organisms that live toward the upper shore are left high and dry for more of the time than those living on the lower shore. When exposed to the air, shore animals must be able to withstand drying out (desiccation), and if they feed underwater, they must manage for long periods without food. Those organisms that live in the middle of an exposed rocky shore tend to be battered by waves for more of the time than those living on the upper or lower shore.

Rocky shores

Rocky shores vary from smooth, near-vertical cliff edges to boulder-strewn, gently sloping beaches. Observed closely, many rocky shores reveal a series of bands or "zones" of different color at distinct levels on the shore. The zones develop because various communities of plants and animals survive best at different levels. A combination of physical factors (such as ability to withstand drying out) and biological factors (such as competing with other organisms for space and food) determines the species' upper limit on the shore. Biological factors (such as shore animals being eaten by marine predators, or seaweeds competing with one another for sunlight) often govern the species' lower limit of distribution.

Many marine scientists divide the intertidal zone into the upper, middle, and lower intertidal zone based on the conditions in each and the community of organisms that live there.

Between high tides the upper intertidal goes for long periods without being covered or splashed in seawater. Organisms that live here must be able to withstand drying out. The conditions are demanding, and only a few species thrive.

On temperate shores it is quite common to see two or more colored bands, from yellow or white through to black, at the top of the intertidal. Rock-hugging lichens of various kinds create the bands. Lichens are partnerships of algae and fungi that eke out a living on bare rock. Patches or tufts of green algae grow between the lichen and slightly lower on the shore, and they provide food for grazing periwinkles (a type of sea snail) and limpets. Periwinkles avoid drying out by retreating to moist crevices in the heat of the day. Limpets keep moist by being covered in a thick shell and anchoring very firmly to the rock with a tight seal around their base. Crabs are among the few marine scavengers and predators that venture into the upper intertidal.

Regularly submerged and uncovered by the tides, the middle intertidal is the widest vertical extent of the shore. On most temperate rocky shores of North America and elsewhere there are two distinct bands within this zone. Barnacles usually dominate the upper band. These unusual crustaceans (which look more like mollusks; see "Marine invertebrates," pages 110–112) can close their chalky shells when the tide falls. When submerged on the rising tide, they open their shells and kick their feathery legs in the water to catch plankton. Marine snails called dog whelks feed on barnacles, but they like to be regularly submerged in water, and to bore a hole in a barnacle shell takes them time. This limits dog whelks from feeding on barnacles on higher levels of the shore.

Mussels and brown seaweeds dominate the lower band of the middle intertidal. Scattered among them grow sea anemones and barnacles. Topshell snails graze the short turf of green algae that grows on rocks and seaweeds alike. On the rising tide marine predators such as crabs, sea stars, and dog whelks roam over the middle intertidal, scavenging morsels or breaking into mussel and barnacle shells. At low tide most of the predators retreat under the seaweed, or into crevices or tide pools, to hide from shorebirds and to avoid drying out.

The lower intertidal is covered in seawater most of the time. Red, green, and brown seaweeds thrive here and compete for sunlight. Sea urchins graze the seaweeds, and sea stars and dog whelks have plenty of opportunity to consume the barnacles and mussels that grow here. At extreme low tide the seaweeds still trap plenty of moisture beneath their fronds, where they offer a safe haven for sea anemones, crabs, and small predatory fish such as gobies and blennies.

The lower boundary of the intertidal zone merges with the subtidal zone—the shallow waters next to the shore that are rarely, if ever, exposed by tides or storm waves. In general, there is a gradient in mass of living material (biomass) and variety (biodiversity) from the top of the shore to the bottom. The variety and overall mass of organisms tends to increase going down the shore, as conditions become more favorable for a wider variety of marine life. The subtidal is typically among the most biodiverse and most productive parts of the ocean realm.

Sandy shores

Sandy shores lack a firm, hard surface onto which seaweeds and sessile (fixed and stationary) animals can attach. At low tide a sandy shore can seem remarkably devoid of life. You may see scuttling crabs and beach hoppers or beach fleas (types of amphipod crustacean) along the strandline. The surface of a sandy shore is a hostile place at low tide. In summer the Sun bakes its surface; in winter the cool air chills it. Predators such as shorebirds patrol its surface for tasty morsels. Most shore inhabitants stay beneath the sand to hide from surface predators and avoid drying out, but when the rising tide covers the sand, the hidden sand-dwellers burst into action.

The surface layers of the sand contain microscopic photosynthesizers such as cyanobacteria (blue-green algae), diatoms, and dinoflagellates. But most of the community's food arrives from elsewhere. Plankton, fragments of seaweed, and the carcasses of marine animals arrive on the rising tide.

Among the larger animals, several groups of invertebrates (animals without backbones) dominate the sand-dwelling community: segmented worms, bivalve mollusks, marine snails, crustaceans, and echinoderms (see "Marine invertebrates," pages 110–112). Segmented worms such as fanworms extend their feathery tentacles to capture suspended particles that settle on the sandy surface. Many of the bivalve mollusks are suspension feeders, filtering the seawater for plankton.

Under the shell bivalves have miniature hairlike structures, called cilia, which draw in water through a tube called a siphon. The bivalve's gills trap plankton before expelling the seawater through another siphon.

Clams and cockles burrow through the sand by narrowing and extending their muscular foot, widening it to anchor it into the sand, and then shortening the foot to drag the body forward. Worms, such as lugworms, use a similar method, extending the front end, widening it as an anchor, and then pulling the rest of the body up behind. Crustaceans, such as crabs and shrimps, use claws and legs to dig.

Among the sandy-shore echinoderms, heart urchins and sand dollars use spines and tube feet to burrow through the sediment. They are deposit feeders, scraping off and consuming the organic matter that coats sand grains. Sea cucumbers swallow sand as they burrow, digest what is useful, and then expel the "cleaned" sand as pellets. Sea stars attack and eat mollusks, crustaceans, and other echinoderms.

Microworld

The seashore harbors hidden life. A sample of wet seashore sand or mud easily demonstrates this if placed in a container and left for an hour. In this time the tiny animals that live between the sand or mud particles use up their oxygen supplies. They rise to the top layer to get more. Collected with a small dropper, placed on a glass slide, and observed under a low-power microscope, the surface liquid reveals a magical world.

The spaces between sediment particles are home to a community of miniature animals. They are called the *meiofauna* (from the Greek *meio,* meaning "lesser," and *fauna* for "animal"). Ranging in size from 0.004 to 0.08 inches (0.1 to 2 mm), they include hydroid cnidarians with snakelike tentacles and protists that flow into ever-changing shapes. There are also tiny versions of familiar larger animals, such as segmented worms, roundworms, and bivalve mollusks. The worms of this world often sport strange suction devices to anchor to sand grains, for sucking up food particles, or to grab hold of other animals. Like the larger animal world of the sandy shore, the meiofauna includes plant-eaters, meat-eaters, and omnivores (those that consume plants and animals). Because the meiofauna move about by squeezing between sand grains, many are flattened or shaped like worms.

Similar meiofauna live among the sediments at the sea bottom, and together with the microbes that live there, they represent a rich variety of life that marine biologists have only recently begun to study.

Depth zones

Oceanographers divide the open ocean into layers, or zones, based on depth. The deeper in the water column a location is, the darker, cooler, and higher-pressure this underwater world becomes. Distinct communities of organisms live in the different layers. The zones described here are those of the pelagic (open-water) environment. Marine scientists also describe a similar zonation for the benthic (seabed) environment, extending from the subtidal zone to the bottom of ocean trenches.

The topmost layer of the open ocean is the sunlit or epipelagic zone, (from the Greek *epi* for "top"). In clear tropical water this zone extends down to about 660 feet (200 m), the deepest at which there is sufficient sunlight penetration for phytoplankton to photosynthesize. For a person at this depth using a pressure-resistant diving suit, the water is several degrees cooler than at the surface, the water pressure is nearly 20 times greater, and what little sunlight remains has been filtered to a faint blue.

The sunlit zone is where much of the sea's biological activity takes place. Most of the sea's biomass is concentrated here. It is here that phytoplankton make food and zooplankton come to graze upon them. Squid and fish eat the zooplankton, and most of the seafood that humans eat comes from this zone.

In clear tropical waters a twilight world extends from the bottom of the sunlit zone to about 3,300 feet (1,000 m), the depth by which all sunlight has been absorbed. This gray world of the mesopelagic zone (from the Greek *meso* for "middle") is interrupted by blue and green flashes of light. This is bioluminescence—natural light created by some of the creatures of this zone.

Bioluminescence serves different purposes in different species. Twilight-zone squid squirt a cloud of bioluminescent ink to dazzle and confuse predators. Hatchetfishes, so called because they look like shiny hatchet blades, use light spots on their undersides to break up their outline when seen from below. This makes them much less visible to predators. Lanternfishes can recognize the light-spot patterns of their own species and detect those of the opposite sex as potential mates. Twilight-zone anglerfishes dangle a luminous lure from the top of their heads to attract inquisitive prey such as shrimp and fish.

Beyond depths of 3,300 feet (1,000 m) is a world of utter darkness, interrupted only by sporadic flashes of bioluminescent light. This is the dark zone. Most of the zone extends downward to the abyssal plain at depths between 2.5 and four miles (4 and 6 km). In places the dark zone reaches down into trenches, the deepest of which are more than six miles (about 9 km) beneath the sea surface. Dark-zone water is a chilling 32 to 39°F (0 to 4°C), with water pressure at 100 times to 1,000 times surface pressure.

The dark zone is Earth's largest near-uniform habitat. It holds more than three-quarters of the ocean's water. Food is scarce here. Of the food produced in sunlit and twilight zones, only about 5 percent reaches the dark zone.

Most animals of the dark zone are nightmares in miniature. Few of the fish are longer than three feet (about 1 m), but most are brutish and ugly. Most dark-zone animals are predators. Many cruise slowly in search of prey, or they adopt a "float and wait" strategy. With so little food available, creatures of the dark zone save their energy. They have weak muscles and skeletons, relying on their giant mouths to overcome prey. Most dark-zone fish lack a swim bladder (an air-filled buoyancy sac) because this organ is difficult or impossible to maintain at such high pressures. To float level in the water, most pack their flabby bodies with water and fat. With a distended head, a giant mouth often armed with long teeth, and a curiously shrunken body, the fish of the

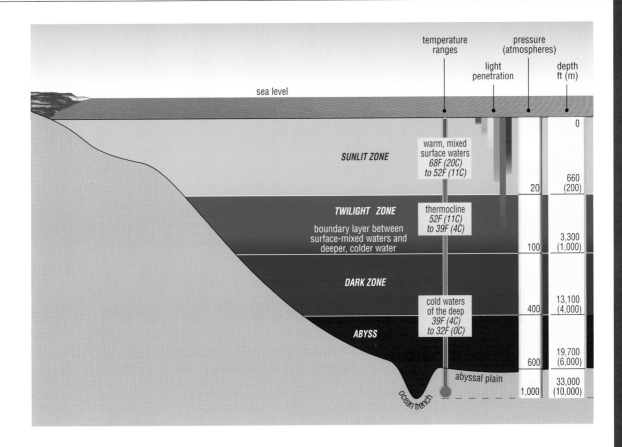

temperature ranges

pressure (atmospheres)

light penetration

depth ft (m)

sea level

SUNLIT ZONE

warm, mixed surface waters
*68F (20C)
to 52F (11C)*

0

20

660 (200)

TWILIGHT ZONE

boundary layer between surface-mixed waters and deeper, colder water

thermocline
*52F (11C)
to 39F (4C)*

100

3,300 (1,000)

DARK ZONE

400

13,100 (4,000)

ABYSS

cold waters of the deep
*39F (4C)
to 32F (0C)*

600

19,700 (6,000)

abyssal plain

1,000

33,000 (10,000)

ocean trench

dark zone eat almost anything they can swallow. In the case of the gulper eel, with its expanding stomach and enormously wide mouth, this includes fish larger than itself.

Most animals in the dark zone are black, dark brown, or red. These colors do not show up well in the blue or green bioluminescent light that most fish use at these depths. In the darkness senses other than vision come to the fore. In most species eyes are small; in some they are absent.

Most dark-zone fish have a highly developed lateral line system, a system of sensitive cells along the flanks that detects vibrations in the water. Many supplement this with vibration-sensitive hairs or antennae. Some deep-sea shrimp have enormously long, touch-sensitive antennae that detect potential hunters or victims venturing near. Most dark-zone creatures have a refined sense of smell. They can detect succulent prey, the odor of detritus, or the fragrance of a potential mate.

Depth zones based on the biological communities adapted to the different physical and chemical conditions in each zone

Deep encounter

Studying dark-zone animals is challenging. When raised from the depths, these creatures usually die from the pressure change. Occasionally, researchers bring live creatures to the surface in pressurized containers. But the best way to observe deep-sea creatures is from the safety of a piloted submersible, using a camera mounted on a robot vehicle, or using bait anchored near a camera on the seabed. There is no substitute for seeing the live animal in its natural environment. The deep-sea mollusk *Vampyroteuthis* (its name means "vampire squid from hell") looks like a cross between a squid and an octopus. Based on study of dead specimens, scientists thought *Vampyroteuthis* was a poor swimmer until they observed one alive in the deep sea. It was looping-the-loop at high speed.

If finding food in the deep ocean is a problem, finding a mate can be harder still. To help ensure breeding success, some species have resorted to extreme strategies to make the most of encounters. A few deep-sea crustaceans and fish are hermaphroditic, meaning individuals have both male and female sex organs. Any adult can mate with any other of the same species, and they can both become pregnant.

In most deep-water fish species, mates probably locate each other using smell. They release chemicals called pheromones that attract the opposite sex. Male anglerfish track down females by smell but at closer range they rely on sight.

In some anglerfish species the male is a parasite of the female. Having found her, he bites into her underside. His mouth fuses with her body and he gains nourishment from her blood. He breathes oxygen with gills, but otherwise becomes a reproductive appendage of the female, always available to fertilize her eggs.

Marine migrations

Some fish, squid, and crustaceans make regular journeys up and down in the water column every day (see "Depth zones," pages 143–146). Many marine animals travel long distances across the oceans, along regular routes, to feed or breed. Both kinds of mass movement are migrations.

Using sensitive echo sounders, researchers often find sonar traces showing echoes from "false" seabeds in the top half of the water column. Stranger still, these bogus seabeds seem to rise and fall with time of day. Marine biologists now know that these *deep scattering layers* (DSLs), as they are called, betray the presence of living organisms. When shrimp, krill, or small fish gather at a particular level in the water, their hard parts, air spaces, or oil droplets reflect sound waves and can show up on the sonar trace.

Deep scattering layers rise and fall as the organisms that produce them move up and down in the water column, a phenomenon known as vertical migration. A DSL indicating krill, for example, may rise near the surface at dusk, and then descend to the twilight or dark zones near dawn. It seems that krill take advantage of cover of darkness to feed on phytoplankton while reducing the chances of being seen and eaten by predators themselves. During the day krill sink out of the sunlit zone to avoid predators, but also perhaps to conserve energy by slowing their metabolism (the body's chemical reactions) in cooler water. Another possibility is that by sinking to a different level, they hitch a ride on currents that will take them to a new food supply when they ascend the next day. Some krill and shrimp rise and fall distances of 3,300 feet (1,000 m) over a 24-hour period. Size for size, this is roughly equivalent to a daily 60-mile (100-km) swim for a human.

Many larger marine creatures migrate across the ocean, rather than—or as well as—up and down in the water column. Young Atlantic cod, for example, hatch from eggs floating in the plankton, and the larvae feed upon zooplankton. When older, cod swim close to the seabed and feed on fish and squid. Thus, those regions of the ocean that make good feeding grounds for young cod tend to be quite different from those suitable for adults. For adult fish, breeding grounds may be quite separate from feeding grounds, and fish migrate between the two. Many other kinds of animal migrate, too, and for the same reasons—to find food or the right place to breed.

To migrate successfully, animals must set out at the right time and know in which direction to travel. They do so instinctively, or they learn by following other individuals. Environmental changes, such as increasing daylight hours in spring, can act as a trigger for migration.

Some fish species make marathon migrations between freshwater and seawater. The larvae of European and American freshwater eels hatch from eggs in the Sargasso Sea. The larvae travel on ocean currents for two years or more to reach rivers in Europe and North and Central America. The young eels, called elvers, swim upriver. For 10 years or so, until fully grown, they live in freshwater. Then they migrate downstream, enter the sea, and swim to the deep waters of the Sargasso Sea where they spawn and die.

Salmon of Atlantic and Pacific Oceans spawn in rivers but grow to maturity in the sea, the reverse situation of that of eels. As adults salmon usually return to spawn in the very same river where they hatched. Scientists suspect that salmon follow familiar ocean currents, navigate by local magnetic fields, and then recognize the scent of their home river when they approach its estuary.

In the South Atlantic some adult green turtles that feed on sea grass near the Brazilian coast migrate to breed at Ascension Island in the middle of the Atlantic, some 1,300 miles (2,100 km) away. Ascension Island is only five miles (8 km) wide—a tiny destination in a big expanse of ocean. Like fishes, turtles probably use a variety of environmental clues—smell, ocean currents, and local magnetic fields—to find their way.

The longest-distance migrator of all is a seabird, the arctic tern. Breeding birds travel up to 20,000 miles (32,000 km) in a year. By crossing the equator and experiencing the summer in both Northern and Southern Hemispheres, they probably encounter more hours of daylight each year than any other creature.

Adult arctic terns begin their journey at breeding and feeding grounds along northern coasts of Europe and North America. In the northern autumn they fly south, crossing the equator, to arrive at feeding grounds in the Southern Ocean and the far south of the Pacific, Indian, and Atlantic Oceans. Their arrival, during the southern summer, is timed to coincide with the productive time of the year for the plankton and small fish on which they feed. In the late southern summer the terns migrate northward, arriving back at their northern grounds in spring.

How do birds find their way? More experienced birds in a flock act as guides for younger ones. During the day birds navigate by observing visual cues such as sea wave patterns and coastline shapes, and by orienting themselves by the moving path of the Sun as it travels from east to west. At night some species navigate by the stars. The Earth's local magnetic field may also act as a guide.

Among marine mammals, gray whales and humpback whales are long-distance migrators that follow regular routes. In the past, whalers only had to wait for the right time of year to intercept them on their migration run (see "Hunting," pages 182–185).

Both gray whales and humpbacks feed in polar or subpolar waters in summer. They travel to tropical and subtropical waters in winter to breed. Adult eastern Pacific gray whales migrate annually between their feeding grounds in the Bering Sea and their breeding grounds off Baja California. It is a 10,000-mile (16,000-km) round trip.

Why do whales migrate in this way? Whale calves probably have a better chance of survival in warm water, where a thick layer of blubber is not necessary for insulation. Also, adults may use less energy by moving to warmer water, rather than staying in polar waters during the cold and lean winter.

Life on shallow seabeds

About 8 percent of ocean area is occupied by shallow waters covering continental shelves (the submerged, sloping edges of continents). The depth here is rarely greater than 650 feet (200 m). These waters include the most productive in the oceans. Waves, currents, and tides stir the water column, ensuring that nutrients are distributed to all levels. Rivers add nutrients, and the combination of nutrient-rich water and sunlight penetration ensures that phytoplankton thrive. This yields, in turn, plentiful zooplankton and detritus for bottom-dwellers to feed upon.

The seabed habitat extending from the bottom of the inter-tidal zone to the edge of the continental shelf is the subtidal zone. As in the intertidal community, the type of underlying surface—hard or soft, and if soft, the size of particles—is a major factor that determines the nature of the subtidal community. Because of the high levels of sediment that settle out in shallow water, many near-shore seabeds are sandy or muddy.

On sandy seabeds the subtidal community of invertebrates is similar to that on nearby sandy shores. However, the variety of animals tends to be greater because the physical conditions in the subtidal are less demanding than those on the shore.

Across the world, sea-grass communities develop on many shallow, soft seabeds (see "Sea grasses," pages 108–110). Seaweeds flourish on hard surfaces in cooler waters (see "Seaweeds," pages 106–108).

As on sandy or muddy shores, soft seabeds support a rich meiofauna (tiny animals that live within the bottom sediment). Among the macrofauna (larger animals) are those that feed on particles drifting in the water (suspension feeders) and those that consume particles that settle on the bottom (deposit feeders).

Suspension feeders consume plankton and drifting detritus. Among those that live in the bottom sediment (infauna), many create water currents from which they filter suspended particles. They include various types of bivalve, such as the soft-shelled clam and razor clam. Sea pens and sea pansies extend feeding structures into overlying water. Formed from colonies of tens or hundreds of cnidarian polyps, their feeding fans make them look like delicate plants. At night the sea pen unfurls its fan—looking like an old-fashioned quill pen—into the water to catch zooplankton.

Deposit feeders eat organic matter, dead or living, that settles as particles in or on the bottom sediment. The lugworm is common in the muddy subtidal and consumes the sediment as it burrows, expelling the processed mud as a pile, called a worm cast, near the exit of the worm's U-shaped burrow. Deposit feeders that roam over the sea bottom (epifauna) include various types of amphipod crustaceans, small crabs and shrimp, and brittle stars.

Preying upon the suspension and deposit feeders are a range of active predators: sea stars, marine snails such as whelks and moon snails, crabs, lobsters, larger shrimp, octopuses, and fishes such as skates, rays, and flatfishes.

In cooler waters, where the seabed is hard and bathed in sunlight, seaweeds grow. In clear, unpolluted, warmer waters, coral reefs develop (see "The living reef," pages 151–154).

In seaweed communities the grazers include sea urchins and a range of mollusks, such as snails, chitons, and limpets. They consume the more fragile parts of seaweeds and graze the fine turf of green algae that grows over many surfaces. Some seaweed have defenses to combat grazing. Many brown algae are tough and leathery, while some red and green algae—the coralline algae—contain chalky granules to discourage grazers.

Attached to seaweed fronds live various barnacles, cnidarians, sea squirts, sponges, and tube-dwelling annelid worms. They ply their trade as suspension feeders. Active predators of these animals include a range of species similar to those found on nearby soft-bottom habitats, and predators often move between the two.

The living reef

A reef is a massive limestone structure produced underwater by living organisms. There are several kinds of reefs in the world's oceans, but the most important—for people and for other life-forms—are coral reefs.

Coral reefs take up only 0.2 percent of the world's ocean area, yet they contain one-quarter of all marine fish species. Reef habitats contain at least half as many types of animals and plants as rain forests do on land.

Coral reefs become large and spectacular because of the successful partnership between reef-building coral polyps and the algae they contain. The primary producer is contained within an animal. It is as though two steps in a food chain are contained in one organism, and this makes for a very efficient transfer of energy from plant to animal. Coral reefs are among the most productive biological communities in the ocean, despite growing in clear, nutrient-sparse waters.

Coral reefs, like rain forests on land, owe their biological diversity, at least in part, to their complex, three-dimensional shape. The coral reef is full of holes, chambers, and channels, ranging in size from microscopic to many yards across. This provides a multiplicity of different places for microbes, plants, and animals to live.

To the casual observer, corals and fishes seem to dominate the living reef. Look closely, however, and you can see algae of various colors and kinds growing as a thin cover on parts of the reef, or sprouting in clumps. Plant-eating fishes and invertebrates graze the algae, and everywhere, in the nooks and crannies, small creatures live. Almost every major group (phylum) of invertebrates has living members on a coral reef.

The fishes we see on a coral reef are so spectacular in color and pattern it is difficult to imagine how such colors might evolve. For an animal survival depends on finding food, not being eaten, and breeding successfully. Being camouflaged can be beneficial if a fish aims to stalk its prey or avoid a predator, but if it wants to find a mate, being hidden could be a disadvantage.

Some fish are brightly colored as a warning. The lionfish, for example, is boldly striped in red and white to broadcast that its spines are venomous. Butterfly fishes have strong stripes of color that break up their outline, making them less visible against the background of the reef. Blotches and bands hide the position of the butterfly fish's eye and in many cases create a false eye on the dorsal fin. Such features probably direct predator attacks away from the fish's vulnerable head and gills. Undoubtedly, some fishes have vivid colors and bold patterns to identify themselves to others of the same species. But why this should not attract predators as well is not known. Perhaps predatory fish see light, shade, and color in a very different way than humans do.

On a coral reef the competition for space is so intense that stationary (sessile) organisms have evolved strategies to prevent being overgrown by neighbors. One of the most successful strategies is chemical defense. Many sessile animals

Coral atolls

Hard corals can form coral reefs in clear, warm, sunlit waters. Under the right conditions a fringing reef forms alongside the shore. If the land should sink (or sea level rise), the reef may grow offshore as a barrier reef, separated from the shore by a lagoon. Should this happen around an island, then the island may sink completely beneath the waves due to subsidence (sinking of the ground) or sea-level rise. Then a ring of coral—a coral atoll—may be all that remains at the sea surface.

Stages in the formation of a coral atoll. 1. A volcanic island rises and a fringing reef forms. 2. The volcanic island subsides (or sea level rises) and a barrier reef develops. 3. The volcanic island further subsides (or sea level continues to rise) and a coral atoll forms.

Coral snowstorm

One of the most spectacular biological events on Earth happens annually several days after a full Moon. On coral reefs thousands of coral colonies release pale packets of eggs or sperm. The water fills with tiny spheres, looking like an upside-down snowstorm drifting upward from the reef. Corals synchronize their spawning to maximize the chances of egg and sperm meeting successfully. Also, by overwhelming predators with a superabundance of food, synchronized spawning helps ensure that some fertilized eggs survive to hatch into larvae.

Soft coral (Dendronephthya *species) growing on a coral reef in the Red Sea* (Courtesy of Chris Newbert/Minden Pictures)

produce toxins that not only prevent their being eaten but also ward off other creatures that grow too close. Scientists have found some of these chemicals to be medically valuable (see "Chemicals from marine life," page 195).

Close associations

Many marine organisms have close relationships with other species that do not involve one killing and eating the other. Such associations are kinds of symbiosis (from the Greek *syn,* meaning "with," and *bios* for "life"). Symbiosis covers a range of relationships, from those that are definitely harmful to one individual to those that are beneficial to both. A coral reef is a good place to study them.

Reef-building coral polyps and the algae that live inside them are an obvious example of symbiosis. Here, the symbiotic relationship is beneficial to both. This form of association is called *mutualism* and the partners are called *symbionts.*

In the second type of symbiosis, called *commensalism,* one member of the association, the *commensal,* gains an advantage. The other, the host, does not appear to benefit, but neither is it harmed. Sharks that visit the coral reef at night are often accompanied by remoras—smaller fish that loosely attach to the shark with a sucker and hitch a ride. Remoras gain some protection by staying with the shark and also secure leftover scraps of food when the shark feeds. The sharks are not harmed by this behavior; neither do they appear to benefit.

In the third form of symbiosis, *parasitism,* the parasite clearly benefits at the expense of its host. In most cases the parasite consumes its host's tissues as food and lives in or on the host, which provides home and protection. The fish louse, for example, is a parasitic copepod that attaches to the surface of many types of fish. It consumes its host's body fluids and tissues, and in large numbers it can seriously weaken its host (see "Farming the sea," pages 188–191).

Most parasites are small, and they are easily overlooked. However, more than one-half of the major animal groups (phyla) have members that are parasites. One scientist studying parasites among fish on the Great Barrier Reef in Australia estimated that among the 1,000 local fish species, each probably harbored an average of two species of monogenean flatworm, along with 18 other species of parasite.

Cleaning stations

Diving on a coral reef, it is quite common to find places where medium- and large-size fish appear to be lining up for the attention of smaller fish or shrimp. These places are cleaning stations, where smaller creatures can be seen grooming the skin of their clients. In the case of the cleaner wrasse, this small fish even enters the mouth and gills of its customer. This arrangement seems to benefit both parties. The cleaner fish gains a food supply in the form of the client's external parasites and any damaged or diseased tissue. In return, the client has its parasites removed and its wounds cleaned.

The deep seabed

Much of the deep-ocean floor—the abyssal plain—is an expanse of mud. Observing it in the powerful beam of a deep-water submersible, one can see a circle of light only a few yards across. Mounds, craters, and tracks suggest life, but the creatures responsible are not visible. Occasionally, a ghostly pale sea cucumber trudges past, its internal organs visible through its semitransparent body wall. It feeds by sucking up seabed deposits. The sediment seethes with invisible life, with microscopic animal-like foraminiferans feeding on bacteria, and the foraminiferans, in turn, being devoured by meiofauna, especially miniature roundworms.

Until the 1980s most deep-sea biologists assumed the ocean floor altered little from season to season. Now they know this is not so. In the North Atlantic, for instance, the spring bloom of phytoplankton brings a "snowfall" of detritus to the deep seabed several weeks later. This marine snow contains dead phytoplankton, the carcasses of small zooplankton, and fecal pellets (zooplankton's solid waste). The mixture gathers as a green-brown sludge in hollows on the seabed, where it provides a welcome seasonal feast for bottom-living creatures.

One way to find out what lives on the deep-ocean floor is to leave a carcass as bait close to a remotely operated camera. Within hours, large amphipod crustaceans, ghostly pale galatheid crabs, hagfishes, six-gilled sharks, and rattail fishes (a type of cartilaginous fish) will gather and start to devour

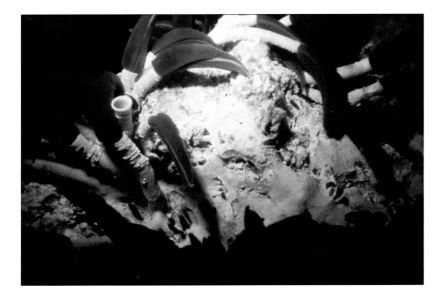

Vestimentiferan tube worms (Riftia pachyptila) *at a Pacific hydrothermal vent* (Courtesy of C. Van Dover/OAR/National Undersea Research Program [NURP])

the carcass. Slower-moving crustaceans, snails, and echinoderms arrive later to join the banquet. Within a matter of weeks, even a whale carcass can be reduced to a heap of bones. The deep-ocean scavenging community wastes little time in taking advantage of such bounty.

Hot vents and cold seeps

Most communities of marine organisms rely upon food that is produced by the photosynthesis of plants, ranging from microscopic phytoplankton to giant seaweeds. But there are exceptions.

In 1977 scientists in the submersible *Alvin* were exploring hydrothermal (hot-water) vents along the Galápagos Ridge, a section of spreading ridge in the eastern Pacific Ocean (see "Pacific Ocean," pages 10–12). At depths greater than 7,300 feet (2,225 m) they stumbled across an astoundingly rich community of animals. Close to the vents were dense beds of three-foot (1-m)-long tubeworms and mussels and clams about 10 inches (25 cm) long—much larger specimens than their cousins in shallower water. Crabs and shrimp clambered over the worms, and the rocks nearby were smothered with sea anemones. Further investigation showed that more than 90 percent of the species scientists found here were new to science. Since then, similar hydrothermal vent communities—with various combinations of animals—have been found at more than 100 deep-water sites across the Pacific, Atlantic, and Indian Oceans.

Without energy from the photosynthesis of plants, what was sustaining such bountiful animal communities? The answer lay in the vent water. Bacteria were using the hydrogen sulfide from vent water to make their food by chemosynthesis (see "Life's beginnings," pages 94–98). In turn, the vent community of plants and animals was relying on the chemosynthetic bacteria as their primary food source. Many of the chemosynthetic bacteria are free-living, but some live symbiotically inside vent animals. The tubeworms, for example, have plumelike gills that trap hydrogen sulfide for the bacteria. The bacteria grow in a special chamber inside the worm and make up about half of the tubeworm's mass. This is all the more surprising because hydrogen sulfide is a deadly poison to most forms of life. The worms have found a way of protecting themselves from its harmful effects while supplying it to their symbiotic partners.

In 1984 deep-sea biologists exploring the ocean floor in the Gulf of Mexico came across animal communities similarly abundant and diverse as those at hydrothermal vents. In this case, however, a spreading ridge and hydrothermal vents were nowhere nearby. Instead, the main fuel for these communities was cool methane gas. Gas seeping from the seafloor was fuel for chemosynthetic bacteria living inside mussels. The mussels were part of a food web that included crabs, isopod crustaceans, and fishes, with chemosynthetic bacteria as the primary producers. In other parallels with hydrothermal-vent communities, biologists later discovered giant tubeworms nearby. They were of a different species from the vent worms, but they too were absorbing hydrogen sulfide for their chemosynthetic bacteria.

CHAPTER 7

HISTORY AND EXPLORATION OF THE OCEANS

Ancient voyages of discovery

The earliest evidence that people crossed the sea beyond sight of land dates back some 70,000 years. Evidence from studies of past climates, archaeology (using recovered artifacts to shed light on history), and genetics (the study of inherited characteristics) suggest that all of today's people descended from those living in Africa some 150,000 years ago. Since then, their descendants have migrated to different parts of the globe and evolved to become the different racial groups we see today. Some early people moved southward from the Asian mainland through Indonesia about 80,000 years ago. Stone tools point to the existence of aboriginal communities in Australia around 70,000 years ago. To get there, the aboriginal people crossed the 100-mile (160-km) gap between Timor (the southernmost part of Indonesia) and Australia. To do so, they must have crossed in boats and sailed beyond view of land. Today, this gap is about 300 miles (500 km) wide, but about 70,000 years ago a mini ice age had lowered sea levels by some 260 feet (80 m), so narrowing the gap.

Evidence from archaeology shows that people from New Guinea colonized the nearby Pacific islands of Melanesia (the name means "black islands") by 4000 B.C.E. By 1500 B.C.E. their descendants had reached the South Pacific islands of Tonga and Samoa more than 1,550 miles (2,500 km) to the east of New Guinea. To reach these islands, the colonizers must have sailed across gaps hundreds of miles wide.

The earliest seagoing craft were powered by sails and/or oars and included dugout canoes, log rafts, skin-covered frames, and reed boats. Carvings from Egypt and Mesopotamia (the region between the rivers Tigris and Euphrates, which is now in Iraq) show reed boats of various designs that are at least 5,000 years old. Some South American

Testing a theory

An ancient legend from Tahiti, a Polynesian island in the South Pacific, tells of the first Polynesians arriving from the east (the Americas), not from the west (Asia) as most scholars believe. In the 1940s Thor Heyerdahl (1914–2002), a Norwegian anthropologist (someone who studies the development of human cultures), decided to test whether this ancient legend could be based on fact. He built a balsa-wood raft of similar design to that used by the ancient Incas of Peru. He called the craft *Kon-Tiki* after an Inca Sun god. In 1947 Heyerdahl and his crew set sail from Peru, heading for the South Pacific islands in their fragile craft. They arrived 101 days later, having traveled 4,350 miles (7,000 km) and proving that such a trip was possible in ancient times. Despite this demonstration, today the balance of evidence supports the view that Polynesians arrived from the west, not the east.

peoples still make reed boats from bundles lashed together in the shape of a hull, and some South Pacific islanders use traditional outrigger canoes to this day.

Colonizers and traders

There are several reasons why people might have wished to cross the oceans thousands of years ago and face uncharted waters. Then, as now, some people feel the urge to explore. For others, there are practical reasons, such as finding new fishing grounds, creating new opportunities for trade, or colonizing new lands.

Egyptian accounts dating back to about 2000 B.C.E. tell of expeditions traveling down the Red Sea and into the Indian Ocean to bring back spices and herbs from Punt (present-day Somalia). At about the same time, Egyptian traders in the Mediterranean were sailing northeast to Lebanon to pick up cedar wood to build boats. Egypt lacked large trees with high-quality wood for use in building boats.

The Greek historian Herodotus, writing in about 460 B.C.E., talks of the Egyptian pharaoh Necho II sponsoring a Phoenician expedition in the seventh century B.C.E. The expedition aimed to find a sea route from the Red Sea to the Mediterranean around the southern tip of Africa. Luckily, in sailing this route, the Phoenicians were pushed along by favorable winds and currents, and they completed the voyage successfully. Herodotus also wrote of tin and amber being brought back from "the ends of the Earth." He was referring to the cold lands of Britain and Ireland and the countries and islands of northern Europe. Long before this, traders from the Middle East and Far East were sailing widely across the Indian Ocean. Certainly, by 2000 B.C.E., sea trade between the Persian Gulf and the Indus Valley (in present-day Pakistan) was well established.

Early navigation

Today, navigators at sea can rely on radar, sonar, the global positioning system (GPS), and other electronic devices to precisely plot their position and direction of travel. For thousands of years, however, seafarers had to read clues in their environment to find their way.

Within sight of land, coastal features such as headlands and estuaries provide reliable guides. The ancient Greeks and Egyptians built lighthouses to help steer seafarers safely to port. Beyond sight of land, the Sun's movement and the position of stars in the sky are trusty guides. The Sun rises in the east and sets in the west, thus allowing an observer to estimate the approximate direction of the four points of the compass (north, south, east, west). In the Northern Hemisphere the North Star (Polaris) shows north. In the Southern Hemisphere the cluster of stars called the Southern Cross (Crux Australis) marks south.

The best navigators also read the signs in the air and water around them. Cloud clusters on the horizon, and landbirds or shorebirds flying past, can be signs of nearby land. Muddy water indicates a near estuary. Experienced navigators can tell by the taste and color of seawater, and the objects floating in it, where an ocean current has come from.

In the 12th century C.E. European seafarers brought back magnetic compasses from China, where they had been in use for hundreds of years. A magnetic compass, with a pointer made of magnetic material such as the mineral lodestone, indicates magnetic north (lying in the general direction of true north, but sometimes as much as 20–30 degrees to one side). Using a compass, navigators could estimate their direction of travel even when clouds obscured the Sun and stars.

In addition to these methods, navigators kept a check on progress by the technique of "dead reckoning." This involves estimating speed and direction of travel taking into account factors such as winds and currents, and then plotting the ship's position on some form of map. This method gave a rough estimate of distance and direction of travel, which could be checked when more information became available. Estimating speed has given rise to two seafaring terms still used today. A wooden *log* with a knotted rope attached was thrown overboard to estimate the boat's speed. The rate at which the rope was pulled from the hand gave the boat's speed in *knots* (today, equivalent to one nautical mile an hour, which is 1.15 miles an hour, or 1.85 km/h). The measurement was recorded in the *logbook,* the journal in which seafarers still record measurements and observations.

Viking, Arab, and Chinese exploration

By the eighth century C.E. the Vikings (seafaring inhabitants of Scandinavia) were leaving their overcrowded homelands to find new lands to pillage or settle. The exploratory seafaring vessels of the Vikings were longships with a single sail and a line of rowers on each side. Shipbuilders formed the longship's elegantly curved hull from overlapping planks of wood nailed to a central wooden keel. Viking trading vessels were made wider and deeper than warships to accommodate cargo.

By 1000 C.E. Vikings had sailed through the rivers of Russia and extended their trading empire as far as the Black Sea to the east. Others ventured along the Atlantic coast of Europe and entered the Mediterranean, reaching as far south as Crete. But most impressive of all, some sailed across the North Atlantic via Iceland and Greenland. A few reached the Americas nearly 500 years before Christopher Columbus did.

Around 1000 C.E. Leif Eriksson (ca. 975–1020), son of the Viking chieftain Erik the Red, sailed from Greenland in search of western lands glimpsed in previous voyages by other Vikings. After sailing across the Davis Strait to Baffin Island and then south to Labrador, Eriksson's expedition finally landed in a place they called Vinland ("land of the vine") because of the abundance of berry-bearing plants they found there. In the 1960s archaeologists excavated the remains of a Viking settlement on Newfoundland. This was probably Leif Eriksson's Vinland settlement.

At the time of the European Middle Ages, the design of sailing ships and the skill of Chinese and Arab seafarers were far in advance of those of their European counterparts. Arabs were sailing ships called *boums,* which had triangular (lateen) sails slung from two or more masts. These ships were more maneuverable than the European vessels of the time, called *cogs,* which usually had a single square sail hung from a mast. Meanwhile, the Chinese were sailing massive ships called *junks*. These craft were flat-bottomed, with several masts and multiple squarish sails. The biggest junks were 180 feet (55 m) long and 30 feet (9 m) across and contained 60 cabins. They incorporated advanced design features, such as watertight compartments. If a hole broke through the hull, only part of the vessel would flood, and the ship could remain afloat. In craft such as these, the Chinese admiral Zheng (Cheng) Ho (ca. 1371–1434) sailed widely across the Indian Ocean and beyond between 1405 and 1433. He reached as far as East Africa to the southwest and almost as far as Japan to the northeast.

The Portuguese explorers

Historians called the 30-year time span 1492–1522 the Western Age of Discovery. At the beginning of this period, the Italian-born navigator Christopher Columbus (1451–1506) crossed the Atlantic. By the end, Ferdinand Magellan's expedition had sailed right around the world.

Three developments helped spearhead this burst of sea exploration. In 1416 Prince Henry of Portugal (1394–1460) founded a school to train seafarers in the most up-to-date methods of navigation (determining position and course to travel to a destination) and charting (using maps). His navigators were quickly pressed into service to find and colonize new lands and develop trade routes. In 1453 the Ottoman sultan Mehmed II captured Constantinople and denied Europeans access to the main overland trade route to Asia. Trade between Europe and the Far East was almost halted, and Europe became starved of silks, spices, jewels, and porcelain from the Far East. European navigators began searching in earnest for sea routes to the Far East. The third factor was an agreement signed by the pope in 1514. This gave Portugal the right to establish colonies east of Europe with Spain having rights to set up colonies to the west.

In the mid-15th century European navigators were still guided by charts dating from the days of ancient Rome. These charts showed no sea route south of Africa. However, as Portuguese navigators sailed farther and farther down the west coast of Africa, it was only a matter of time before they reached its southern tip. Portuguese navigator Bartholomeu Dias (ca. 1450–1500) did so in 1487–88, and he was perhaps the first European to sail around the Cape of Good Hope from the Atlantic into the Indian Ocean. In 1497–98, Vasco da Gama (1460–1524) sailed across the Indian Ocean to Calicut, India, opening up a new sea route to Asia (then known as the Indies).

Meanwhile, in 1492, Christopher Columbus was sailing under a Spanish flag to reach the Indies by the westward route. By crossing the Atlantic Ocean, he believed he would reach Asia within a few thousand miles. What he did not know was that the Americas (later to be known as the New World) lay between Europe and Asia. After sailing west from the Canary Islands, Columbus's expedition arrived in the Bahamas on September 6, 1492 after five weeks without sight of land. Thinking he had arrived in Asia (the Indies) he dubbed the local inhabitants "Indians."

After the papal agreement of 1514, the Portuguese nobleman Ferdinand Magellan (1480–1524) gained backing from the Spanish for a voyage to the Spice Islands (today the Moluccas in Indonesia). He believed he could sail west beyond the New World to reach the Indies. Like Columbus before him, he underestimated the distance. His expedition of five small vessels set out from Spain in September 1519. After crossing the Atlantic Ocean and sailing around South

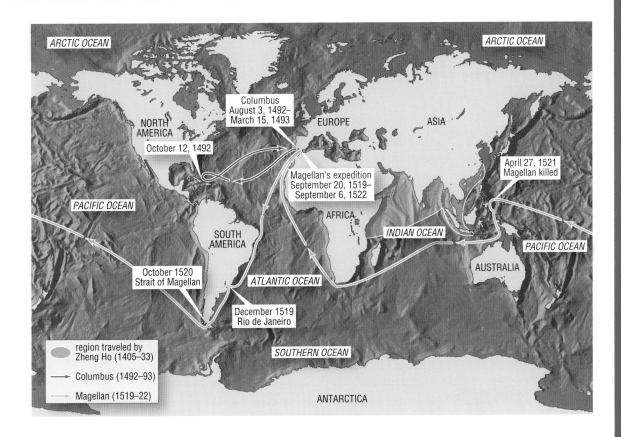

America, they had to cross the vast Pacific Ocean, which took 100 days. During the crossing the crews were reduced to eating rats and mice, chewing leather for food, and drinking soup made from wood shavings. They reached the Indies, but Magellan was killed in a skirmish with Philippine islanders in 1521. Only 18 of the expedition force of 237 completed the round-the-world voyage by sailing across the Indian Ocean to arrive back in Spain in September 1522. They had completed an incredible 43,500-mile (70,000-km) journey—the first round-the-world voyage.

Voyages of Zheng Ho (1405–33), Christopher Columbus (1492–93), and Ferdinand Magellan (1519–22)

The Northwest Passage

Magellan's expedition took a southern sea route to reach the Pacific Ocean from the Atlantic. By the mid-16th century European seafarers knew that a northern sea passage around North America would be a much shorter route to Asia, if such a passage existed. They began to search for this Northwest Passage.

The British seafarer Martin Frobisher (ca. 1535–94) searched for the passage on three voyages between 1576 and 1578. He reached as far as the islands north of Canada—claiming several for Elizabeth I of England—but failed to find a way through the icy seas. So began more than 300 years of searching, with seafaring heroes such as the Dane Vitus Bering (1681–1741), and the English explorers Henry Hudson (ca. 1570–1611) and William Baffin (ca. 1584–1622) charting more and more of this northerly region. Their exploits are recorded in the names of the northerly landscape and seascape: Bering Strait, Hudson Bay, Baffin Island. The fateful 1845–47 expedition of Englishman John Franklin (1786–1847) led to the final discovery of the Northwest Passage. His two vessels became ice-locked, and the entire expedition perished when, after surviving a winter in freezing conditions, they tried to walk to safety. Their remains, found by later expeditions, included written evidence that Franklin's expedition had found a passage through the islands of northern Canada. An English expedition led by Robert McClure (1807–73), in searching for the remains of Franklin's expedition, entered the Northwest Passage in 1851, when their ship became locked fast in the ice. Finally, in 1903–06, the Norwegian polar explorer Roald Amundsen (1872–1928) led the first successful sea voyage through the Northwest Passage in the steam sailing ship *Gjöa*. Even today, this route is safely passable by only a few ice-breaking ships and submarines.

The southern continent

The English navigator Captain James Cook (1728–79) was an unusual man of his time. While other seafarers were exploring uncharted seas and islands to make their fortune, Cook was more interested in mapping uncharted seas and shores and making scientific discoveries. These interests led him to make three groundbreaking voyages to the Pacific Ocean.

In his first Pacific voyage (1768–71) Cook searched for the great southern land called Terra Australis—what we know today as Antarctica. In Cook's time geographers believed a large, as yet undiscovered, landmass lay in the Southern Hemisphere to balance the landmasses of the Northern Hemisphere. Cook did not find Antarctica, but he did map the coastlines of New Zealand and New Guinea. He also established that the land Dutch seafarers called New Holland was a continental landmass (we now call it Australia, meaning "southern land"). He landed on the east coast of Australia and claimed the land as a British colony.

On his second Pacific expedition (1772–75) Cook sailed right around Antarctica, reaching within 100 miles (160 km) of its coast before being turned back by ice. But he never saw the continent and concluded it did not exist. It was left to the Russian navigator Fabian von Bellingshausen (1778–1852) to discover Antarctica during his 1819–21 expedition. Meanwhile, Cook undertook a third Pacific voyage (1776–79), this time to find a route through the Northwest Passage from the

Harrison's chronometers

John Harrison (1693–1776), an English cabinetmaker and clocksmith, revolutionized navigation at sea. In 1707 four British warships were shipwrecked with the loss of 2,000 lives when they ran aground because navigators had miscalculated longitude (east-west location). In 1714 the British government offered a large reward to anyone who could devise a means of measuring longitude accurately at sea. One approach involves accurately measuring local time relative to standard time.

The Earth revolves on its axis once (360°) every 24 hours, so one degree of longitude is equivalent to four minutes of time ([24 × 60] ÷ 360). Zero degrees longitude lies at Greenwich, London. Suppose a ship's clock is set to Greenwich Mean Time (GMT), and the vessel is sailing westward. If the crew discovers that at local midday (when the Sun is highest in the sky) their clock reads 12:20, then the ship's position is longitude 5°W. This approach is effective—but only with a highly accurate clock. Early clocks were affected by the pitch and sway of the ship and were notoriously inaccurate. Between 1735 and 1770, however, Harrison designed a revolutionary series of accurate timepieces, called chronometers, that did the job. The judges responsible for deciding the prizewinner wanted a scientist to win and unfairly withheld prize money from Harrison until 1773, when he was 80.

Pacific Ocean side. Sailing through the North Pacific, he discovered the Hawaiian Islands and mapped much of the coastline of the Pacific coast of North America. He failed to find the Northwest Passage, and on his return to Hawaii in 1779, he was killed in a dispute with islanders.

Cook's Pacific legacy included highly accurate charts of previously unmapped coastlines and undiscovered islands. He pioneered a scientific approach to taking accurate measurements of seawater temperature, wind speed, sea currents, and water depth. And the naturalists he took on his expeditions brought back specimens and drawings of exotic plants and animals that encouraged other European explorers to travel to the Pacific.

The beginnings of oceanography

The birth of oceanography (the science of the sea) was slow in coming. The biggest problem, then as now, is that the oceans are so vast, so deep, and so difficult to probe. The Greek philosopher Aristotle of the fourth century B.C.E. was among the first to study the sea and its marine life in a systematic way. He identified about 180 types of marine animals and suggested why the sea was salty. But it was not until nearly 2,000 years later, in the 1660s C.E., that European researchers began to take interest in the scientific study of the oceans. Fellows of the Royal Society in London wrote a practical guide to encourage seafarers to make scientific measurements at sea, such as taking sea-temperature readings and depth soundings, and using nets to catch tiny marine creatures. However, the biggest problem was that, beyond sight of land, seafarers could not work out their exact position. Using devices such as the astrolabe, quarterstaff, or back staff, they could measure the height (elevation) of the Sun or certain stars above the horizon and so calculate their latitude (north-south location). But they did not have accurate timepieces that they would need to measure longitude (east-west location). With the development of accurate timepieces—chronometers—in the 18th century, longitude suddenly became measurable and seafarers could plot their precise location at sea. James Cook took one of John Harrison's state-of-the-art chronometers to sea with him on his second Pacific expedition (1772–75). Using the chronometer and sextant to find his ship's precise position, Cook produced the finest charts of his time.

By the early 1800s the governments of several seafaring nations were producing accurate sea charts. Safe passage at sea—for example, avoiding hidden reefs that could sink a ship—could be vital to a country's fishing industry, sea trade, and naval success. Explorers were beginning to study creatures hauled up from the ocean depths. In 1817–18 the Scottish explorer John Ross (1777–1856) dragged up worms and starfish from a depth of more than 4,100 feet (about 1,250 m) in Canada's Baffin Bay. Some 20 years later, his nephew, James Clark Ross (1800–62), captured similar animals from more than 13,100 feet (4,000 m) deep near Antarctica. James Clark Ross concluded that similar species must live in the cold depths in many parts of the world. However, the British naturalist Edward Forbes (1815–54), who in the 1840s was towing fine-mesh nets behind a ship to capture small marine organisms, was coming to a very different conclusion. He noted that the deeper the tow, the

Matthew Fontaine Maury—"The Father of Oceanography"

Matthew Fontaine Maury (1806–73), an officer in the U.S. Navy, had his active service cut short by a stagecoach accident that left him lame. Forced to work in a naval office rather than at sea, he began compiling data on winds and currents from a wide range of sources. He encouraged seafarers of different nationalities to gather wind and current data in a systematic way, and he compiled the information in charts. He was also instrumental in organizing the first International Meteorological Conference, held in Brussels in 1853. In 1855 he published his international best seller, *The Physical Geography of the Sea.* This book incorporated a wide range of information about the physical and chemical nature of the sea and its inhabitants. It also included the world's first depth map of an ocean basin (the North Atlantic). Many marine scientists regard Maury's book as the first classic work of oceanography and dub Maury "The Father of Oceanography."

fewer creatures he collected. He estimated that beyond depths of 300 fathoms (1,800 feet or about 550 m) there would be no marine life at all. Of course, his conclusions flew in the face of the Ross's earlier findings, but his ideas sounded reasonable because few people could imagine there was enough warmth, food, or oxygen to keep creatures alive in the deep ocean. It was arguments such as this that prompted some naturalists to launch expeditions in the mid-19th century to study the life, if any, of the deep ocean.

The *Challenger* expedition

Following successful oceanographic expeditions in British warships in 1868–69, British scientists William Benjamin Carpenter (1813–85) and Charles Wyville Thomson (1830–82) convinced the British government to pay for the conversion of a warship into a floating research laboratory. Thus, the world's first oceanographic vessel, HMS *Challenger,* was born. Equipped with hundreds of miles of rope and piano wire for taking soundings (depth readings) and some 12 miles (20 km) of cable for hauling dredges and sampling nets, the ship carried a crew of 240 plus nine scientists.

The *Challenger* expedition set out in 1872 with the aim of "exploring all aspects of the deep sea." The expedition returned three and a half years later, having crossed the Atlantic, Indian, and Pacific Oceans and completed a 79,000-mile (127,500-km) voyage of discovery. That single voyage yielded more information about the undersea world than the combined results of all expeditions that had gone before. Among the remarkable count of the expedition's scientific measurements were 133 dredge hauls of the seabed, 151 trawls of midwater using a bag-shaped net, and 492 depth readings. The scientists identified more than 4,000 new species, discovered strange potato-size lumps of metal (manganese nodules) on the deep seabed, and plumbed the deepest part of the world's ocean—the Mariana Trench—to a depth of more than five miles (8 km) using piano wire. It took dozens of scientists, from Britain and elsewhere, more than 20 years to examine all the expedition's specimens and analyze all the results. The expedi-

HMS Challenger *of the* Challenger *expedition (1872–76). This sail-and steam-driven vessel was the world's first ship to be adapted specifically for oceanographic exploration.*

tion's findings, published in 50 thick volumes, laid the foundations of oceanography.

International cooperation

Matthew Fontaine Maury had been encouraging cooperation between seafarers and scientists from different nationalities as early as the 1830s. Sharing information gave hope that knowledge of the oceans could be pieced together, despite the ocean's formidable size. In any case, people from different nations had shared problems. As early as the 1870s Scandinavian scientists suspected that stocks of North Sea cod and herring were being overfished—that fish were being caught in larger numbers than could be replaced by natural breeding. If so, this would be a concern for all nations that fished the North Sea. Such shared interests led to the establishment of the first international marine research organization, the International Council for the Exploration of the Sea (ICES), in 1902.

Prince Albert I of Monaco (1848–1922) developed a strong interest in oceanography, and he sponsored and led international oceanographic expeditions into the Mediterranean Sea and the North Atlantic between the mid-1880s and 1915. In

The first marine laboratories

In 1872, the year HMS *Challenger* began its expedition, the German biologist Anton Dohrn (1840–1909) set up the world's first successful marine laboratory, where researchers could study marine organisms under experimental conditions. Matthew Maury, having sided with the Confederates in the American Civil War, had fallen out of favor with the U.S. government, and times were lean for marine science in the United States. In the 1870s, against this background, the Swiss zoologist Alexander Agassiz (1835–1910) and other zoologists with marine interest began coastal investigations in the locality of Woods Hole, Massachusetts. Ultimately, the existence of marine laboratories in this area led to the establishment of the Woods Hole Oceanographic Institution (WHOI) in 1930. In 1903 William Ritter, a former student of Alexander Agassiz, set up a marine research laboratory on the U.S. west coast. In 1912 it became the Scripps Institution for Biological Research, which is now the Scripps Institution of Oceanography, based in La Jolla, California. Marine laboratories such as Scripps and Woods Hole explain marine life to the public, but their primary role is to act as research centers. Expeditions are sent out from these centers and then return to examine their samples, analyze their data, and publish their findings.

1905 he published the first depth charts of all the oceans of the world.

Modern oceanography

The development of modern oceanography began with the introduction of new technologies based on electronics. Electronic equipment such as sonar enables scientists to "see" beneath the waves. In 1925–27 the German oceanographic expedition of the South Atlantic in the research vessel *Meteor* was the first large survey to use echo sounding to map the contours of an ocean basin.

After 1945, when World War II ended, the navies of the United States and several European countries put many of their smaller warships up for sale. This gave oceanographic research centers the opportunity to buy vessels cheaply, and with electronic equipment already fitted. The late 1940s and early 1950s saw much of the deep-ocean floor being mapped using sonar and seismic techniques. In the mid-1950s a team of scientists at the Lamont-Doherty Geological Observatory in New York compiled this data to produce maps of the world's ocean floors. Their findings revealed the mid-ocean ridge system that snakes through the world's oceans. This, in turn, led other scientists to propose the seafloor-spreading hypothesis (see "Seafloor spreading," pages 34–35) by which new seafloor forms at mid-ocean ridges and spreads outward. In 1968 the U.S. deep-sea drilling ship *Glomar Challenger* began taking cores of seafloor sediment and crust. The expedition's findings showed that crust and sediment close to mid-ocean ridges was younger than that farther away. This evidence supported the idea of seafloor spreading, which in turn helped confirm the theory of plate tectonics—the idea that the Earth's surface is made up of a number of giant, slowly moving plates (see "Moving plates," pages 35–38).

Today marine researchers lower electronic sensors into the sea to measure seawater's temperature and its ability to conduct electricity (a measure of salinity). The information is relayed back to the ship and compiled and analyzed using computers. This way, readings can be taken at different depths and from many locations in a single day. Before the age of electronics, scientists had to take readings one at a time, using pressure-proof thermometers and taking water samples that they analyzed chemically back on board ship. Today oceanographic data can be gathered much more quickly, and with less effort and cost. Even so, an oceanographic research vessel costs upward of $50,000 a day to operate. The ship's position for each sample is logged precisely using the satellite-based global positioning system (GPS). Remote-sensing satellites monitor the sea surface from space and gather additional information (see "Satellites," pages 176–178).

Diving

Diving beneath the sea surface is always a challenge for a human. As air-breathing, land-living mammals, people need to take an air supply with them to stay underwater for more than a few minutes. People also need protection and insulation to prevent precious body heat from rapidly leaking into the surrounding water.

In the 1690s the English scientist Edmond Halley (1656–1742) designed and tested a diving bell. Called a bell because of its shape, this wooden, cone-shaped device, closed at the top and open at the bottom, was lowered into the water with trapped air inside. Free divers (divers without masks or breathing equipment) could enter the bell from beneath and breathe the air inside before swimming out again. As the air inside the bell became stale, fresh air in barrels was emptied into the bell from below. Divers using such bells could work underwater to build or repair bridge supports and harbor walls.

During the mid-1800s the German inventor Augustus Siebe (1788–1872) designed a diving helmet and suit combination that became the standard gear in common use until the mid-1900s. The suit protected divers from the cold, and the brass helmet resisted water pressure. Fresh air pumped from the surface provided oxygen. Divers using the rig could stay underwater at depths of more than 165 feet (50 m) for an hour or more. Moving clumsily in lead-weighted boots and a heavy helmet, however, they could not swim.

By the late 1800s inventors were developing various designs of scuba (self-contained underwater breathing apparatus) that enabled a diver to carry the air supply on his back. But it was not until 1943 that the French diving pioneer Jacques Cousteau (1910–97) and engineer Émile Gagnan developed a new type of breathing valve that revolutionized shallow-water diving. Their invention, called the demand valve, enabled the user to breathe air at the same pressure as their underwater surroundings. The air was supplied from a high-pressure air tank on the diver's back, and the air they exhaled rose to the surface as bubbles. This equipment—dubbed the *aqualung*—was safer and easier to use than earlier scuba designs. In combination with a rubber diving suit, mask, and fins, the aqualung gave the diver new freedom to swim underwater for an hour or more.

Today most shallow-water divers use some form of aqualung. At greater depths, down to about 2,000 feet (600 m), divers use an atmospheric suit that encloses the body in a pressure-resistant shell and inside which they breathe air at atmospheric pressure.

Underwater diving vehicles

Submarines are cigar-shaped diving vessels. Navies use them for military purposes, although increasingly commercial organizations are developing shallow-water submarines as underwater-viewing platforms for tourists. Submersibles are smaller diving vehicles of various designs, often used for underwater research and exploration.

Navies keep secret how deep their submarines can dive, but the most sophisticated submarines probably dive to little more than 3,300 feet (1,000 m). One solution to withstanding the high pressures of the deep ocean is to design craft based on a sphere, which resists the pressure equally on all sides.

In 1934 the zoologist William Beebe and engineer Otis Barton made a record-breaking dive in a hollow steel ball with viewing ports called the *bathysphere* ("deep sphere"). This vessel was lowered from a ship to a depth of 3,028 feet (923 m). Beebe and Barton became the first people to view deep-sea creatures in their natural environment. The Swiss engineer Auguste Piccard (1884–1962) extended the bathysphere design in 1948, when he produced a bathyscaphe ("deep boat"). This was essentially a bathysphere slung beneath a submarine-shaped buoyancy and propulsion unit. In 1960 Piccard's son Jacques and U.S. naval officer Don Walsh descended 35,802 feet (10,912 m) to the bottom of the Mariana Trench in the bathyscaphe *Trieste*. This is the deepest descent by any diving vehicle before or since.

Today, only a dozen or so underwater craft can descend beyond about 13,000 feet (roughly 4,000 m), and only about half that number are designed to reach the deepest parts of the abyssal plain at about 20,000 feet (approximately 6,000 m). Taking people to such depths is hazardous and expensive, and because of human needs for food, oxygen, regular sleep, and so on, carrying people severely limits the length of dives. Increasingly, scientists are looking to robot vehicles to gather information from the deep ocean.

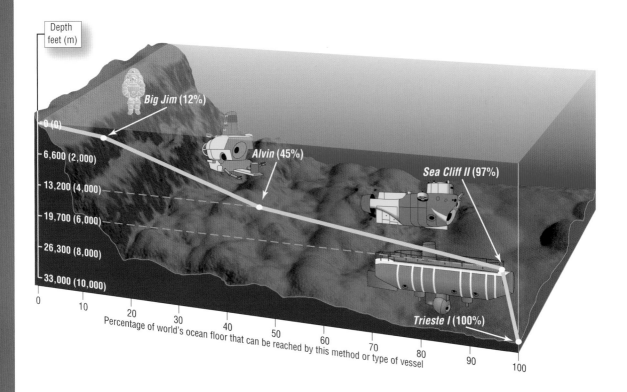

The depths reached by different diving methods and vehicles and the percentage of the world's seafloor accessible to them

Remotely operated vehicles (ROVs) are robotic vehicles that are connected to a manned surface or underwater craft. About 200 ROVs are in operation—many in the offshore oil and gas industry—with most operating at depths of less than 3,300 feet (1,000 m). Autonomous underwater vehicles (AUVs) are programmed to operate without any physical connection to another craft. Research institutions use AUVs that can operate for days or weeks gathering physical, chemical, and biological data from the seabed before returning to the surface to download their discoveries.

Satellites

Satellites orbiting Earth are among the most useful research tools in the armory of today's oceanographers. Specialized remote-sensing satellites such as *Seasat*, *SeaWiFS*, *Nimbus-7*, and *ENVISAT* are mounted with combinations of two types of sensors to monitor the sea surface and the near-surface waters.

The submersible Alvin

Alvin is a three-person submersible operated by the Woods Hole Oceanographic Institution and designed to dive to depths up to 14,765 feet (4,500 m). Launched in 1964, in 1966 it located a hydrogen bomb lost in the Mediterranean. In 1977 its crew discovered remarkable animal communities close to the Galápagos Islands at a depth of about 7,300 feet (2,225 m). In 1986 *Alvin* explored the wreck of the *Titanic. Alvin* is overhauled every three years, when many of its parts are replaced and updated. Since 1964 the various versions of *Alvin* have accounted for more than 3,500 dives. In 2001–02 scientists and filmmakers fixed an IMAX-format movie camera in *Alvin*. The camera filmed the creatures at hydrothermal vents for the large-format feature film *Voyage into the Abyss.*

Active sensors beam down radio waves that bounce off the sea surface and return to the satellite. The time it takes for the radio waves to return and the way they are scattered by the sea surface reveal information about height of sea level, surface slope, and surface roughness. This provides scientists with information on the size of sea waves, the direction and strength of surface winds, and the dips and bulges created by ocean currents. The sea surface also follows the rises and hollows on the seabed, so mapping the sea surface can help scientists work out the contours of the seabed. In the 1990s U.S. scientists Walter Smith and David Sandwell combined satellite data with existing data from depth soundings and sonar surveys to update maps of the ocean floor.

Passive sensors mounted on oceanographic satellites detect temperature (in the form of infrared radiation emitted from the sea surface) and colors reflected naturally from the top few tens of yards of the water column. Browns reveal the presence of mud particles emptied into the sea from nearby rivers. Greens can show blooms of phytoplankton. Black can reveal oil spills. In many cases, scientists check the source of the coloration by taking water samples from boats, but as scientists gather more data, they are more confident about what causes the different color tones. Satellite remote sensing is proving invaluable in helping scientists to monitor pollution incidents (see "Managing pollution," pages 218–220), spot ships that are breaking fishing regulations (see "Managing fishing," pages 220–221), and estimate the biological productivity of different parts of the ocean based on the presence of plankton blooms.

CHAPTER 8

THE USES OF THE OCEANS

The value of water

Water itself is a valuable resource and one many people take for granted. In the mid-1990s each person in the United States used, on average, about 177 U.S. gallons (670 L) of water a day for their immediate needs such as washing, drinking, cooking, and waste disposal. People in Mozambique, Africa, had to make do with about three U.S. gallons (11 L) a day. Above and beyond these basic needs, people need water to grow crops and feed livestock. In more developed countries water also has a wide range of industrial uses.

Most of the salts can be removed from seawater to provide freshwater. However, to do so is expensive. Some desalination (desalting) plants use the Sun's energy to heat seawater. The water evaporates leaving most of the salt behind. The water vapor is then condensed to an almost salt-free liquid. More sophisticated desalination plants use a reverse-osmosis process in which pressurized seawater pushes out pure water across a membrane. Hot, freshwater-starved countries with long coastlines are coming to rely heavily on desalination plants. Worldwide, there are more than 12,000 large desalination plants, with some of the biggest in California and the Middle East.

Icebergs floating in the sea are another source of freshwater. In the 1970s U.S. scientists made calculations to show that it was possible to tow icebergs from the Arctic and Southern Oceans to water-starved regions in warm parts of the world. No one has yet put these ideas into practice.

Ports and shipping

The development of jet airliners in the late 1950s and early 1960s meant that passenger travel by sea became less fashionable. Over long distances, air travel was cheaper and quicker. Today ferries carry millions of passengers across short stretches of seawater, but long-distance sea travel is largely restricted to holiday cruise ships and cargo vessels. About 90 percent of imported heavy goods travel by sea at some point in their journey.

Historically, ports have developed where there was safe anchorage for ships and good access for transporting people and goods inland. Because of the importance of seaports in trade and commerce, it is not surprising that some of the world's largest cities—New York, London, Tokyo, and Hong Kong among them—developed from ports.

During the late 1800s steel hulls and engine-powered propellers began to replace the wooden hulls and cloth sails of the ships that went before. Today's cargo ships are many times larger than those of a 100 years ago. The largest oil-carrying supertankers are about 1,640 feet (500 m) long and carry more than 550,000 U.S. tons (500,000 tonnes) of petroleum oil.

In the 1960s shipping engineers introduced the standard-size, metal-box container for carrying loose cargo. Containers enable goods to be transported with speed and efficiency. The container is loaded—with anything from frozen meat or chilled fruit and vegetables to electrical goods—and then sealed. Each container is readily loaded and stored on ship and then unloaded onto road or rail for transport to its final destination. Some modern ships carry more than 7,000 containers.

As ships have gotten larger, so have ports. More than 100 container ships enter the port of Singapore daily. The port's computer-controlled cranes help it handle more than 45,000 containers a day.

With today's ships and ports being so large, there is great potential for environmental damage. More shoreline is now taken up by dockside facilities. Deep-water channels are kept open by dredging to allow large supertankers to dock at the harbor. When one of today's tankers spills oil, the local environmental impact can be devastating (see "Oil," pages 203–204).

The sea's military importance

Since the time of the great civilizations of ancient Egypt, Greece, and Rome in the first millennium B.C.E., the ocean

Flags of convenience

The United States is the greatest international sea trader. Yet its name does not appear among the top six list of merchant fleets (fleets of trading ships). The top six fleets are registered with small countries: Panama, Liberia, the Bahamas, Malta, Greece, and Cyprus. Companies in the United States register their ships in these countries because they have less strict safety regulations and their crews receive lower wages. It is cheaper for U.S. companies to operate through these "flags of convenience."

has been a highway for naval fleets. Warships can intercept merchant ships of other countries, so crippling their trade and starving them of supplies. The sea is often the best way, or only way, to invade another country. Even today, ships are still the most effective means of delivering military forces, plus their equipment and supplies, to many parts of the world.

The United States, United Kingdom, Russia, France, and China operate the biggest navies. Each country's vessels roam over much of the ocean, protecting their nation's interests. Sometimes their ships move into position to threaten other nations when talks between governments are floundering. Governments sometimes use "gunboat diplomacy" to speed up talks by threatening naval action. Navies can menace without entering another country's territory. When China's fleet goes on maneuvers in the Straits of Taiwan—perhaps to threaten the independence of their neighbor Taiwan—U.S. naval vessels sail to the region to counter the potential threat.

Governments with the largest navies operate a policy of "deterrence" with potential enemies. The aim is to persuade an enemy not to attack because to do so would result in a devastating counterstrike. These navies are part of a two-tier approach to deterrence. At the first level, a government makes it clear that a nonnuclear military attack against them would be followed by a precision counterattack using nonnuclear weapons. At the second level, a nuclear attack or an attack with biological or chemical weapons could be met with a nuclear counterstrike. Nuclear weapons are so destructive that if unleashed in large numbers they could wipe out most of a country's population. Many military experts believe it is the threat of nuclear retaliation that has kept an uneasy peace over much of the world for more than 50 years.

The two-tier approach to deterrence means that large modern fleets carry both nuclear and nonnuclear weapons. Some modern submarines carry nuclear weapons called ballistic missiles that can strike targets on land. Nuclear-powered submarines can stay submerged for months at a time, keeping an "underwater eye" on what is happening on the sea surface.

The nonnuclear capability of the largest naval fleets is centered on aircraft carriers. The largest carriers are called super-carriers, and each of these, such as the USS *Kitty Hawk,* has more than 5,000 crew and carries airstrips for at least 85 warplanes. Smaller warships, such as cruisers and destroyers, help protect the supercarriers and also offer other types of firepower, such as guided missiles and cannon-fired shells.

Modern naval fleets can launch attacks on targets on land, in the sea, or in the air. Fleets use strike-at-a-distance weaponry such as carrier-based attack aircraft and ship-launched missiles. Their use was demonstrated in 2003, when U.S. and British forces attacked Iraq. Warships launched nonnuclear, GPS-guided cruise missiles against Iraqi targets, while carrier-launched aircraft carried out precision attacks using cruise missiles and laser-guided "smart bombs."

Hunting

People have hunted marine mammals for thousands of years. They can provide a rich harvest of meat, fat, oil, fur, and other valuable products. Marine mammals are long-lived and slow to breed, and so it is quite possible to hunt them to extinction.

In 1741 European seafarers sailed into the Bering Sea and discovered massive sea cows (see "Other sea mammals," pages 131–134), which look like giant walruses, swimming slowly through the chilly Arctic waters. Weighing up to 11

U.S. tons (10 tonnes) and with meat "as good as the best cuts of beef," the slow-swimming Steller's sea cow was so attractive as a food source that within 30 years sailors had hunted it to extinction.

Moving forward two centuries, by the 1970s intensive whale-hunting had brought several species to the brink of extinction. Even today, northern right whales are endangered, meaning they are classified by the World Conservation Union (IUCN) as facing a very high risk of extinction in the wild in the near future (see "Overhunting," page 210).

Until the mid-1800s, being a whaler (whale-hunter) was one of the world's most dangerous occupations. Most whalers set out in small, open boats and harpooned the whales by hand. Some whales fought back and sank the hunters' fragile craft. It could take a whale hours to die from blood loss and fatigue.

Early whalers were prepared to take risks because the rewards were so great. Each whale carcass contained many tons of meat. Whalers also boiled down blubber to produce whale oil, which had many uses. People burned the oil as fuel to light lamps and used it as a major ingredient in soap. In the 1800s, before chemists worked out how to process petroleum oil, whale oil was the main lubricant keeping the wheels of industry turning. Clothiers used the whalebone from baleen whales as supports in women's underclothes. Perfume makers used spermaceti, a waxy substance from the head of sperm whales, as a fixative in perfumes. Whaling was a profitable business.

By the late 1600s European whalers had exhausted local stocks of slow-swimming whales. The whalers turned their attention to the whaling grounds off the east coast of North America. By 1700 hunting had reduced the population of North Atlantic right whales to a fraction of their former numbers. (They were called right whales because they were the "right" whales to catch: They migrated along the coast, were slow-swimming, and floated when dead.) By the 1840s the hunted population of North Atlantic bowhead whales had plummeted, too.

In the 1860s Norwegian whalers introduced steel-hulled, steam-driven ships. These ships were armed with a new type

Russian whaling ship with captured minke whales (Balaenoptera acutorostrata) (Courtesy of Mitsuaki Iwago/Minden Pictures)

of harpoon that was fired from a cannon and exploded inside the whale. Whalers could now overpower their quarry much more quickly and with much greater ease. Whaling ships could travel farther and faster and catch even the largest and swiftest whales. Using the new technologies, European and North American whalers severely depleted all the stocks of larger North Atlantic whales by 1900. In the early 1900s they turned their attention to the whales of the Southern Ocean.

By the 1920s whaling companies began using giant factory ships to process the whales caught by several smaller hunting vessels. More time at sea could be spent hunting whales. By the 1970s the larger species of whale had been hunted to commercial extinction (there were too few animals left to make it worthwhile to target them). Whalers turned to smaller species such as the sei and the minke. Finally, in 1986, the international Whaling Commission (IWC), an organization set up in 1948 to regulate the whaling industry, called for a moratorium (a temporary ban) on commercial whaling. Most countries abide by this. However, Japan and Norway still catch several hundred whales a year. They say the catch is taken for scientific purposes; however, the meat and other products from these whales are often sold commercially.

Fishing

Today seafood makes up less than 10 percent of the world's diet. However, fish and shellfish flesh is rich in protein, which is an essential nutrient in the human diet. Fish and shellfish are the major source of protein for an estimated 1 billion people. Fish flesh is rich in vitamin D and certain B vitamins that are necessary for healthy body function. Fish with oily flesh, such as tuna and herring, contain oils that in a person's diet can help lower blood cholesterol, making them less likely to suffer heart disease and other circulatory problems.

Fishing means hunting for fish or shellfish using nets, traps, harpoons, or baited hooks. Several million fishers in developing countries catch fish on a small scale to feed themselves and their families. Any excess they sell at local markets. Fish are a vital source of food and cash in these communities.

Artisanal (small-scale) fishers catching tuna in the Red Sea (Courtesy of Ben Mieremet, Department of Commerce/National Oceanic and Atmospheric Administration)

Most of the world's catch of fish and shellfish is captured by fishing boats from richer countries. They take about half the world's catch of marine fish from shallow waters in the North Pacific, North Atlantic, and off the west coast of South America, where high levels of nutrients in surface waters encourage phytoplankton to grow rapidly. These microscopic plants form the base of rich food chains that include fish.

Commercial fishers sell most of their larger fish for human food. Most of their smaller fish and fish waste are ground into fish meal. The meal is used for animal feed and agricultural fertilizer and in a wide range of products from soaps to glues and paints.

Fishers use different fish-capture methods depending on the species they are targeting and where it lives in the water column. For fish that swim near the surface, some fishers use a curtain of net to encircle a shoal. The device is called a *purse seine,* because when it is pulled closed, it forms a giant bag or purse under the fish, trapping them. This method is popular for taking small pelagic fishes such as sardines, anchovies, and herring, but it can also be used for some larger species, such as yellowfin tuna.

For larger, near-surface species, some fishers set gill nets. These hang vertically in the water and fish swim into them, pushing their heads through the mesh and becoming ensnared by their gills. The drift net is a giant version of the gill net. Drift nets can be several miles long and fishers leave them for hours or days floating in the sea. They catch a wide range of species, including unintended quarry such as endangered species of shark, turtle, dolphin, and porpoise. Drift nets are banned in many parts of the world, but they are still used illegally.

Another approach to catching the larger, near-surface species is using long lines carrying hundreds of baited hooks. Although more environmentally "friendly" than drift nets, they too catch endangered species.

For catching mid-water or bottom-living fish, most fishers use a trawl net. This is a giant, funnel-shaped mesh bag towed behind a fishing boat called a trawler. Trawlers catch bottom-living fishes, such as cod and haddock, and flatfishes such as plaice, sole, and turbot. Some trawlers use small-

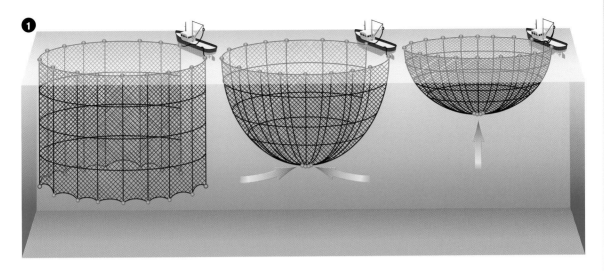

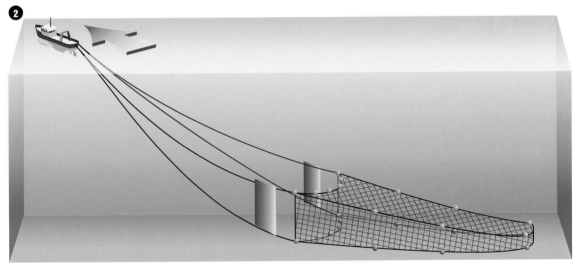

meshed nets in midwater to catch shrimp, or they trawl along the seabed to catch crab, clams, and other kinds of shellfish.

The biggest trawlers, supertrawlers, haul a trawl net that is big enough to swallow a jumbo jet. The net can capture more than 110 U.S. tons (100 tonnes) of fish at a time, which are immediately gutted, filleted, frozen, and packaged onboard ship to keep fresh. The supertrawler can stay at sea for weeks on end, processing 660 U.S. tons (600 tonnes) of fish a day and only returning to port when its hold is full of fish.

Two fishing methods that account for most of the world's marine fish catch: (1) the purse seine and (2) the otter trawl

Finding fish

The splashes of hunting dolphins, seals, tuna, and diving birds can betray the presence of fish schools near the surface. Fishers use their knowledge of ocean currents and the shape of the sea floor to predict where deeper-swimming fish are likely to gather. Using sensitive sonars called fish finders, they can see the outline of the seabed and spot schools of fish at various levels in the water column. The ship's global positioning system (GPS) allows the captain to pinpoint the exact location of the find so he can return to the same place at another time.

Farming the sea

Natural stocks of fish and shellfish are declining because of overharvesting, habitat loss, marine pollution, and other factors (see "Overfishing," pages 207–210). Meanwhile, mariculture—the farming of marine organisms—is gaining in importance. Today, about 10 percent by weight of the seafood people eat is farmed. Farmed produce are mostly high-value items and probably account for about 25 percent of the money U.S. consumers spend on seafood.

Mariculture is not new. The Chinese have been farming seaweeds, fish, and shellfish for food for at least 3,000 years. Asian oyster farmers have a long history of raising oysters for pearls.

In traditional mariculture, farmers rear fish in ponds on coastal land or in cages in shallow water. They rely on the

Bycatch

Trawling captures not only the targeted species but unwanted species as well, including immature fish. These unwanted fishes are called bycatch. Unfortunately, by the time they are hauled aboard the ship and separated from the wanted catch, the fishes in the bycatch are usually dead. Often it is illegal to take the bycatch back to port and sell it. Instead, it is wastefully thrown overboard.

natural productivity of the seawater to feed the fish, or they might add agricultural waste such as rice or wheat husks to fatten their stock. Another approach is to grow shellfish such as mussels and oysters in baskets hanging in shallow water, or on submerged ropes, wooden frames, or fences. Such low-tech methods usually rely on farmers getting their supply of young fish or shellfish from natural populations.

Modern, intensive mariculture, on the other hand, involves the farmer growing selected strains of marine animals under carefully controlled conditions. The farmer uses costly equipment to monitor and control the cleanliness, salinity, and temperature of the seawater in ponds or tanks. This is costly, and to make it worthwhile, the seafood needs to be of premium value or grow very quickly—preferably both. The farmer gives the stock nutrient-rich food. Under crowded conditions, diseases can spread rapidly among the farmed animals, and the farmer often introduces antibiotics into the feed to prevent bacterial diseases from breaking out. In many countries bordering the Pacific and Atlantic Oceans, farmers raise young salmon in freshwater ponds or tanks and then transfer them to floating seawater pens or cages to grow them to market size. American and Asian farmers intensively raise shrimp and lobsters in saltwater tanks and ponds.

Nowadays, scientists and commercial breeders are beginning to use genetic engineering (the process of manipulating genes using sophisticated techniques) to produce new strains of fish and shellfish that would never occur in the wild. Breeders have created sterile strains of food animals that channel their energy into gaining weight, not breeding. Breeders are developing disease–resistant and better-tasting strains. They hope to produce animals with flesh that will stay fresh longer after harvesting.

Some people object to breeders altering the genetic characteristics of animals in this way. They argue that genetically engineered strains, accidentally released into the wild, might interbreed with natural strains and weaken them. People also fear that the technology will benefit only those in the richest countries, although others argue that given time the technology will serve those in developing countries and will help to meet shortfalls in protein supplies.

Major factors limit the growth of mariculture. Only a few marine species can be farmed intensively. For example, many open-water species cannot survive in pens or cages. Another constraint is that the bays, lagoons, and estuaries suitable for mariculture occupy only a limited area of the ocean. Moreover, to be productive and to provide food that is safe for human consumption, these coastal waters need to be relatively pollution-free.

Mariculture creates its own problems of pollution and disease. In Scotland, for example, some scientists and environmentalists are alarmed that ammonia and solid wastes released from salmon farms are poisoning or smothering natural communities of organisms in lochs (marine lagoons and bays in Scotland). Fish lice (external parasites that feed on the salmon's tissues) are present in high numbers in many farmed salmon. The lice release their larvae directly into the water, and the larvae then infect wild stocks of salmon. Scientists suspect that the lice may be killing wild salmon or, at the very least, reducing their breeding success. The lice may

Aerial view of a shrimp farm carved out of a mangrove forest in Borneo. Many such farms have proved unsustainable. (Courtesy of Frans Lanting/ Minden Pictures)

be a major cause of the decline of some North Atlantic salmon stocks.

Mining

Sand and gravel lie on many shores and in shallow water on many continental shelves. Many deposits were laid down during recent ice ages and have since been covered by the sea. The sand and gravel (called aggregates) are valuable resources for the building industry. As onshore and near-shore aggregate reserves are used up, prospectors dredge in deeper water of the continental shelves. There is environmental concern about the effects of this dredging. It disrupts seabed organisms and changes current and wave patterns, causing greater erosion on nearby shores. The United States and many European countries have strict controls on most dredging operations, but this is not the same the world over.

The action of waves and tides erodes the shore and sifts and sorts dislodged particles. This natural sorting action is rather like a gold prospector panning for gold. It concentrates valuable metals eroded from nearby rocks in hollows on the seabed. Such concentrations of minerals are called *placer deposits* because they are "placed" there by moving water.

Around the world, prospectors are excavating many placer deposits both onshore and in waters less than 165 feet (50 m) deep. Beaches in Alaska and Oregon yield gold, while some Oregon shores provide chromite (a mineral containing chromium). Namibian beaches and offshore deposits yield diamonds.

Offshore placer deposits of tin, in the form of the mineral cassiterite, account for more than 10 percent of the world tin trade. Many other minerals could be extracted from beneath the sea if it were financially worthwhile to do so. Technical know-how exists to mine minerals from the seabed at depths of 13,000 feet (4,000 m) or more.

As land reserves of minerals become exhausted, so mining for them may move offshore. For example, phosphorite—a mineral rich in phosphate used in agricultural fertilizers—is currently mined from the land. But massive

Chemicals in seawater

Although traces of most substances are dissolved in seawater, only a very few are present in sufficient amounts to make extraction worthwhile. First and foremost is sodium chloride (common salt), the main ingredient in seawater apart from water itself. Salt is a popular food additive. People sprinkle it on foods to enhance flavor, and salting is a traditional way of preserving meat and fish. Many warm countries produce table salt by evaporating seawater in natural or artificial ponds. Other valuable chemicals in seawater, such as the metal magnesium and the gas bromine, are extracted by carefully controlled chemical reactions in industrial facilities.

deposits lie in ocean sediment at depths beyond 330 feet (100 m), and these may become worth exploiting within the next 100 years.

Fist-size manganese or polymetallic (many-metal) nodules lie on the seafloor at depths greater than 13,000 feet (4,000 m). One day they could be swept into piles for raising to the surface. The nodules appear to have formed over thousands of years from the activities of deep-sea bacteria. Many marine scientists and environmentalists are concerned because people do not understand what part these nodules play in maintaining biological communities in the ocean. They suggest that people should not try to remove the nodules until they know what role they play. Environmental pressure groups are also troubled that deep-sea mining operations could disturb sediments that will swamp deep-water animal communities.

Energy sources

Oil and natural gas are the lifeblood of modern societies. Burning them powers ships, cars, and aircraft; heats homes and offices; and generates electricity. Oil lubricates industry's machines, and it is a raw material in a vast range of products, from plastics to pharmaceuticals.

As land-based oil reserves become used up, tapping oil and gas from beneath the ocean is becoming increasingly attractive to prospectors. By the late 1990s more than 30 percent of the world's oil was being extracted from beneath the sea. Most of the world's undiscovered oil and gas reserves probably lie beneath continental shelves and continental slopes.

Within 30 years' time it is possible that supplies of fossil fuels, such as petroleum oil and natural gas, will begin running out. Alternative forms of energy supply will need to be found. The oceans are a good place to look.

Fossil fuels are nonrenewable sources of energy, meaning that when they are used they are not rapidly replaced. It takes millions of years for new oil and gas reserves to form. Fossil fuels have other disadvantages. When people burn them, they produce carbon dioxide, a greenhouse gas that is probably contributing to global warming. Oxides of sulfur and nitrogen may be released, which dissolve in water vapor to produce potentially harmful acid rain.

Nuclear power is an alternative to burning fossil fuels. But the nuclear reactor disaster in 1986 at Chernobyl, in Ukraine (then part of the Soviet Union), demonstrates the potential dangers associated with the technology. Dozens, perhaps hundreds, of people died when the reactor released high levels of radiation into the environment. Land thousands of miles away from the site became contaminated by Chernobyl's nuclear fallout. Even without such disasters, disposing of radioactive waste safely is still a problem challenging engineers.

Renewable energy, on the other hand, replaces itself naturally. In the oceans, tides, waves, currents, winds, and even temperature differences are renewable energy sources. They are "cleaner" sources of energy because, once renewable-energy plants are constructed, their operation generates little or no air pollution.

Tidal power stations harness the rise and fall of tides to generate electricity. Water flowing through sluices (gated channels) in a barrage (barrier) turns a turbine (a wheel with paddles or vanes) that generates electricity. An early tidal power scheme, the Rance Estuary Barrage in France, built in 1966, generates enough electricity to power tens of thousands of homes. Tidal power stations work well where the tidal range—the difference between high and low tides—is regularly greater than 33 feet (10 m). Currently, large schemes operate in Canada, China, and the former Soviet Union, with new projects being considered in the United States and Britain.

Sea waves contain plenty of energy, but it is tricky to harness. Waves vary in height and direction, so it difficult to design a device that captures their energy efficiently. One successful wave-power design works when waves force air in and out of a chamber, creating a flow of air that turns a turbine to generate electricity. Small-scale wave power stations could be built at many sites around the world where wave heights do not vary too much and tidal ranges are small.

Fast-flowing ocean currents carry massive amounts of kinetic energy (energy of movement). According to one plan, underwater turbines near Florida's coastline could capture enough of the Gulf Stream's kinetic energy to meet up to 10 percent of Florida's electricity needs. The fast-flowing Kuroshio Current in the western Pacific is also being considered for ocean-current schemes. Technical challenges need to be overcome, and environmental effects assessed, before such schemes could enter operation.

In some tropical seas there is a temperature difference of 36°F (20°C) between water at the sea surface and that at 3,300 feet (1,000 m) depth. This temperature difference is enough to operate OTEC (Ocean Thermal Energy Conversion) schemes.

OTEC plants work in a similar manner to conventional fossil-fueled or nuclear power stations in that liquid is heated to a vapor and used to rotate a turbine to generate electricity. In conventional power stations the liquid is water and the vapor steam; in OTEC plants the liquid is ammonia, propane, or some other liquid that readily turns to gas.

OTEC plants usually use warm surface water to vaporize the liquid and cool water raised from the deep to condense the vapor. One by-product is warm, nutrient-rich water that could be used in OTEC-linked fish or shellfish farms. Various OTEC devices are being tested, but the building and running costs of current designs are too high to be commercially viable. This situation could change in the near future.

Chemicals from marine life

Aside from food, marine plants and animals yield a range of valuable products. Kelp, for example, contain the substance algin. Food and drug manufacturers use algin to help mix fats and oils with water and to bind and thicken other substances. Algin is found in products as diverse as bread, ice cream, salad dressing, and in the coatings of drug capsules.

Many marine organisms—especially those that live on crowded coral reefs—have developed chemical defenses to prevent their neighbors from overgrowing them. Many species produce chemicals to prevent attack by predators, parasites, or other disease-causing organisms. Some species can counter chemical attack by destroying poisons. Drug companies can harness some of these chemicals to make medically useful products.

Pharmaceutical companies are currently testing thousands of marine species to see whether they might contain chemicals that could be used to combat medical conditions such as AIDS and cancer. In the last 20 years more than two dozen medically useful drugs have been obtained from marine organisms. Avarol, obtained from a sponge, is active against HIV, the virus that causes AIDS. Ecteinascidin, a chemical extracted from a Caribbean sea squirt, seems to be helpful in treating several kinds of cancer. Vinblastine and vincristine, extracted from the Madagascar periwinkle (a marine snail), are used in the treatment of Hodgkin's disease, which is a cancer affecting the human lymphatic system. Other drugs from marine sources include some that act against parasitic worms, some that are muscle relaxants, and others that are local anesthetics. Many more discoveries await.

Supplies of chemicals from marine organisms are limited by the abundance of the organism in the wild. To obtain a large, regular supply, organisms need to be farmed. Alternatively, the substance could be made artificially once its chemical nature is known. Chemicals from marine organisms provide "leads" to pharmaceutical companies in developing new classes of drug. The chemical richness of marine organisms is one of the arguments in favor of maintaining the rich biodiversity of marine ecosystems (see "Biodiversity," pages 199–200).

Recreation

Most people can appreciate the beauty of a sun-baked sandy beach, the ever-changing sea surface, and the hypnotic rhythm of waves on the shore. Surprisingly, it is only in the last century or two that seaside recreation has become fashionable for millions of people. Many ocean sports have an even shorter history. Today the oceans and their shores provide places to swim, to surf, to scuba dive, to snorkel, to sail, to fish, or simply to relax and sunbathe. In the United States nearly one-third of all the money spent on leisure activities is spent on water sports and other recreation based in and around the sea. Sandy shores and clear waters attract tourists like a magnet.

World travel organizations estimate that by 2010 about 1 billion people each year will be vacationing overseas, many by the sea. Marine tourism brings opportunities, but dangers, too. Opportunities include the income marine tourism can bring to island communities that have few land-based resources. This applies, for example, to some of the islands in the Caribbean and Mediterranean Seas, and to many of the oceanic islands in the Pacific and Indian Oceans. The danger is that unless tourism is properly managed, what brings tourists there in the first place could be destroyed.

At many vacation destinations tourist numbers are increasing to the point at which the local marine environment is suffering. In the Red Sea, for example, 20 years ago there were only a handful of hotels in the vicinity of Hurghada, Egypt. What was then a fishing village has now expanded to become a busy holiday resort with more than 100 hotels. Every day, dozens of boats take tourists diving and snorkeling on nearby coral reefs. Many of the larger fish species have been scared away, and the coral reefs now sustain physical damage from careless visitors.

Coastal resorts affect the marine environment in many ways. New airports, hotels, and roads alter the natural runoff from the land. Previously clear stretches of seawater may receive high levels of sediment-laden freshwater, which dilutes the seawater and alters the local marine community. Thousands of tourists visiting resorts can create problems of

A humpback whale (Megaptera novaengliae) breaching near a whale-watching boat in southeast Alaska (Courtesy of Flip Nicklin/Minden Pictures)

litter and of sewage disposal. And water sports, such as power-boating, jet-skiing, and scuba diving, can directly endanger wildlife. In Florida's coastal waters, for example, manatees have to contend with marine pollution. Moreover, every year dozens of manatees are struck and injured or killed by power boats.

One way governments can help preserve marine wildlife is by setting up and managing marine protected areas (see "Marine protected areas," pages 221–222). Tourists can be made to pay toward the costs of protection. In the Central American country of Belize, for example, visitors pay a small tax that goes toward wildlife conservation. Many tourism-dependent countries are adopting similar programs.

Today, the underwater world that was once the preserve of a few scientists is becoming available to thousands of people. Several dozen tourist submarines now operate at holiday destinations around the world, taking visitors to view marine life down to depths of 165 feet (50 m).

Marine wildlife cruises have blossomed within the last 20 years. They range from local day trips to view seabirds and marine mammals, to long cruises to demanding destinations such as the Arctic and Southern Oceans.

Building possibilities

Today seafront property is among the most sought after. In 20 years' time developers will probably be building on and under the sea on a large scale. Even today, property developers in Tokyo have created several artificial offshore islands to accommodate offices, leisure complexes, and high-value housing. Florida has an underwater hotel where visitors have an undersea view from their bedroom window. In Dubai in the United Arab Emirates, underwater hotels, vacation homes, and skyscraper hotels—due for completion in 2005—are being built on artificial islands. Within the next few decades it is likely that the world's most prestigious properties will be on floating islands, towed from one place to another to take advantage of the changing seasons.

Marine engineers are exploring the possibility of growing houses underwater. By trapping the Sun's rays to generate electrical energy, they believe it will be possible to pass electricity through submerged metal frames to attract chemicals in seawater. Walls and roofs could be grown in a manner similar to the way coral polyps create their own limestone skeletons.

Hundreds of public aquariums are on view around the world. The largest, such as California's Monterey Bay Aquarium and Japan's Osaka Aquarium, have giant displays holding thousands of marine creatures.

CHAPTER 9

THE HEALTH
OF THE OCEANS

Biodiversity

Scientists use the term *biological diversity,* or biodiversity, to describe the rich variety of life on Earth. The greater the biodiversity, the more species that thrive and the greater the variety of habitats in which they can live.

Why is biodiversity important? Many argue the moral case that people do not have the right to destroy habitats and endanger species in the pursuit of making money. Most would agree that reducing biodiversity reduces enjoyment of nature and the pleasure passed on to future generations. If people destroy a coral reef, children as yet unborn will not have the opportunity to experience its wonders.

More practically, marine ecosystems—communities of marine organisms in their habitats—provide many services. The ocean's phytoplankton play a vital role by removing carbon dioxide from the air and replacing it with oxygen. A salt marsh cleans the water that passes through it. When people drain salt marshes and other wetlands, the water quality in nearby estuaries often suffers. If people destroy ecosystems, they take away the services these natural systems provide.

Scientists rarely understand enough to know which organisms are most important for maintaining ecosystem services. Removing a single key species (such as the sea otter on Pacific kelp beds; see "Other sea mammals," pages 131–134) can drastically alter the balance of other organisms in a community.

Finally, the living oceans are a storehouse of chemical riches. In the last 20 years dozens of useful substances have been recovered from marine organisms, ranging from anticancer drugs to natural pesticides. If human actions make species extinct, valuable substances may be lost forever.

In 1995 the U.S. Committee on Biological Diversity in Marine Ecosystems decided that there were five major threats to marine biodiversity:

- fishing operations
- chemical pollution
- invasions by "exotic" species
- physical alteration of marine habitats
- global climate change

How people respond to these threats will have a great effect on the health of the world's oceans.

Pollution

In 1970, when the Norwegian explorer Thor Heyerdahl crossed the Atlantic Ocean in *Ra II,* he saw litter floating past his boat every day. The world's waters have become much more polluted since then. Even the deepest, most remote parts of the seabed contain fragments of litter dumped from ships.

Oil spills and broken sewage pipes make dramatic news stories. But most pollution of the sea goes unnoticed. Every day, the world's rivers unload thousands of tons of harmful chemicals into coastal waters. Every day, factory chimneys and vehicle exhausts belch thousands of tons of polluting chemicals into the atmosphere that dissolve in water droplets and fall to Earth in rain. Most marine pollution enters the sea from the land. A relatively small proportion—less than a quarter—is discharged from ships at sea.

Pollutants are chemicals that can cause environmental damage: An enormous variety enter the sea. They include oils, human sewage, heavy metals, and artificial chemicals such as plastics and synthetic pesticides. Added to this are radioactive wastes, particles from mining operations, and agricultural runoff. Even the heat from power stations is a pollutant when it raises the temperature of seawater and alters the local community of marine organisms.

Sewage

Sewage, or general wastewater, may be the most ancient pollutant. Today sewage from towns and cities includes mostly organic (carbon-containing) matter, such as the solid waste (feces) people produce. But added to this can be oils, heavy metals, plastics, and so on, from local industries.

High levels of organic matter in sewage produce three polluting effects. First, the nutrients in sewage act as a fertilizer,

A black rat (Rattus rattus) *escaping on floating debris from a sinking cargo vessel at Santa Cruz Island, Galápagos Islands. The rat is an unwanted visitor to the islands.* (Courtesy of Tui de Roy/ Minden Pictures)

Dead zone

In the Gulf of Mexico just beyond the Mississippi estuary, a "dead zone" forms each year when nutrients from the river fuel dense phytoplankton blooms in summer. In some years the dead zone covers an area of about 6,180 square miles (16,000 km^2)—about the size of New Jersey.

causing phytoplankton and seaweeds to grow in an uncontrolled way. Zooplankton and other grazers cannot check their growth. When large numbers of phytoplankton die and decay, bacteria multiply in the water and remove oxygen that other organisms depend upon. Those organisms that cannot swim away will die. On coral reefs too many nutrients cause an overgrowth of green algae that smothers the coral.

Second, some of the phytoplankton blooms triggered by high nutrient levels involve species that produce toxins. So-

Red tides

When phytoplankton multiply so quickly that they form dense blooms creating a scum on the sea surface, they are sometimes called red tides. Although these blooms are usually red or brown, they can be other colors. Some red tides contain poisonous chemicals released by certain species of phytoplankton, especially dinoflagellates. In many cases, the poisons do not harm invertebrates but do affect vertebrates. Shellfish can feed upon the algae unharmed; however, when people consume the shellfish, they may become ill and can even die. Some scientists suspect that red tides are becoming more common as agricultural and sewage pollution raises nutrient levels in coastal waters. Currently, authorities monitor U.S. coastal waters to check for harmful algae. Shellfish beds are closed to harvesting when there is a threat of algal poisoning. In spring 2005 a bloom of the dinoflagellate *Alexandrium fundyense* forced the temporary closure of New England shellfish beds. Such closures, and their associated scientific monitoring program, cost the United States at least $50 million a year.

called red tides can poison other creatures, and even people can be harmed if they consume animals that have eaten the poisonous phytoplankton.

Finally, disease-causing organisms, ranging from viruses and bacteria to the eggs and larvae of parasitic worms, are common in human sewage. People can become infected when they swallow fouled seawater or when they eat shellfish that have consumed the harmful organisms. As the world's population continues to increase, treating sewage to prevent its harmful effects becomes a costly but necessary process.

Oil

Petroleum oil is a valuable commodity. Crude (unprocessed) oil is usually a thick, dark, green-brown liquid. For the foreseeable future people will continue to depend upon this oil, which, when processed, provides fuel and is incorporated in a wide range of products, from plastics to fertilizers. For the moment we live with oil and the consequences of transporting it around the world in huge tankers.

Although major oil spills from shipwrecks gain the most publicity, every day some oil leaks into the sea from pipelines and from tankers that clean their tanks at sea. Such discharges are illegal, but authorities tend to prosecute only the worst offenders. Satellite remote sensing can spot ships that discharge oil. Chemists can analyze the oil in a spill, then tell by its precise mixture where the oil came from and which vessel must have been carrying it.

When crude oil is spilled at sea, it clogs the feathers of seabirds, making them unable to fly. It removes their insulation, and they die of cold. The oil also clogs the gills of fish and the hair of seals and otters. Swallowed oil can kill marine creatures by poisoning or by blocking air passages. Some of the chemicals in oil dissolve and can poison plankton in the surface waters. Eventually, however, bacteria and fungi break down oil by natural processes into harmless substances.

Major oil spills from tankers continue to occur. Oil-processing companies continue to use outdated, flag-of-convenience tankers to transport oil (see the sidebar "Flags of convenience," page 181). One such vessel, the

Crude oil from the Exxon Valdez floating on the sea surface in Prince William Sound, Alaska (Courtesy of Flip Nicklin/Minden Pictures)

Bahamas-registered *Prestige,* sank off the coast of Spain in November 2002, releasing fuel oil onto Spanish fish and shellfish grounds and polluting more than 185 miles (300 km) of coastline. The wreck has the potential to release twice as much oil as the *Exxon Valdez* spill of 1989.

Heavy metals

Domestic and industrial wastewater, and runoff from polluted land, may contain trace amounts of heavy metals such as mercury, lead, and cadmium that are poisonous to many forms of life.

The most dramatic case of heavy-metal pollution happened in Minamata Bay, Japan, in the mid-1950s. A local plastics factory began discharging mercury-contaminated

---

Exxon Valdez oil spill

On March 24, 1989, the supertanker *Exxon Valdez* struck a reef in Prince William Sound, Alaska. About 38,500 U.S. tons (35,000 tonnes) of oil spilled into the sea. The oil spill eventually covered more than 1,200 miles (1,950 km) of shore in an unsightly sludge that smothered or poisoned wildlife. Experts estimated that up to 300,000 seabirds, 5,000 sea otters, and 300 harbor seals died in the incident. The local herring- and salmon-fishing industry was devastated. However, the affected shores and coastal waters are slowly recovering. By 2000 the salmon were back and so were many seabirds, although harbor seals and herring had yet to return. Today safety vessels escort all tankers that enter Prince William Sound.

---

wastewater into the sea. The wastewater contained a particularly harmful mercury-based substance, methyl mercury. This substance enters the cells of organisms more readily than mercury itself. An unusually large number of local people began experiencing a range of symptoms: headaches, shaking, paralysis, and even blindness. It took about 10 years for the authorities to be convinced that the contaminated wastewater was the cause of the outbreak. By that time, several hundred people had "Minamata disease" and were disabled by it. Eventually, more than 100 people were to die as a direct result of the methyl-mercury poisoning.

Studies at Minamata showed that plankton were taking in methyl mercury and plankton-eating fish and shellfish were consuming the poison and concentrating it within their bodies. If organisms cannot break down or get rid of a poison, then it is passed to animals higher up the food chain that can accumulate large amounts of it. This process is called biomagnification. In Minamata Bay locals who ate plenty of seafood were consuming dangerously high levels of methyl mercury.

Today, most governments recognize the threat to human and environmental health posed by heavy-metal pollution. They impose laws to stop companies from discharging metal-contaminated wastewater.

Particles, plastics, pesticides, and PCBs

Particles of sediment may not be poisonous, but they can still be pollutants. They cloud the water and stop sunlight from penetrating, which starves marine plants of sunlight for photosynthesis. Settling sediment can also smother bottom-living creatures and clog the feeding apparatus of filter feeders. Coral reefs are particularly sensitive to smothering.

In 1990 UN experts estimated that the world's rivers carried three times more silt than they did before the growth of agriculture and industry. When people cut down forests for wood or to clear the land for agriculture or building developments, tree roots no longer bind the soil and more washes off the land. This extra silt enters rivers and eventually empties into the sea at estuaries.

Many artificial substances made by industrial processes are nonbiodegradable; they do not break down readily by the natural processes of decay. When such substances enter the environment, they can stay there unchanged for decades or more. Among such substances are most plastics and some pesticides. Worldwide, fishers lose or throw away more than 110,000 U.S. tons (100,000 tonnes) of nylon fishing lines and netting every year. These go on wastefully ensnaring fish and other sea life for months on end. An estimated 40,000 seals each year are killed by various kinds of plastic. They become entangled in nylon line, rope, or netting, or swallow plastic objects that block their digestive system. Either way, they die a painful, lingering death.

The synthetic pesticide DDT was widely used by farmers and health agencies until the late 1970s. Now many countries have banned it because of its cumulative affect on wildlife. For example, in the late 1960s and early 1970s studies of DDT pollution in the coastal waters of Los Angeles discovered high levels of DDT and its breakdown products in dead seagulls and cormorants in Los Angeles Zoo. DDT was also linked to breeding failure in local sea lions and brown pelicans. The DDT contamination was traced to wastewater from a nearby DDT manufacturing plant. DDT became passed along local food chains and accumulated in fish that gulls and cormorants then ate.

Polychlorinated biphenols (PCBs for short) are industrial chemicals that were once widely used in a range of products,

Radioactive substances

Radioactive substances are an invisible but highly dangerous form of pollution, causing mutations and cancers that disable or kill organisms. Until 1982, high-level radioactive waste from nuclear power stations and military uses was dumped into the sea in sealed containers. This practice is now banned internationally. However, low levels of radioactive substances are still emptied into coastal waters from nuclear-reprocessing plants such as Cap de la Hague in France and Sellafield in northern England. High-level sources of radiation include sunken nuclear-powered submarines, crashed planes and satellites, and leaking (pre-1982) containment vessels. Low-level radioactive waste, such as clothing and equipment contaminated with radioactive chemicals, is sealed in containers and dumped legally at sea. It is likely that some illegal dumping of high- and low-level waste takes place, too.

from plastics to paints. Now banned in most countries, PCBs do not degrade quickly. They find their way into the sea from products that have been dumped on land or at sea and degrade to release PCBs. High levels of PCBs have been found in the fatty tissues of dead seals, sea lions, and cetaceans (whales, dolphins, and porpoises). It is difficult to prove the link between PCBs and the cause of death. In some cases, the animals have died of disease, and it appears that the PCBs have disrupted the animals' immune (disease-fighting) systems. Some PCBs mimic biological chemicals involved in reproduction, and they may make marine mammals less fertile.

Overfishing

Humans are important predators in the marine environment. Fishers have a widespread effect on marine communities, whether fishing for high-value species that are predators near the top of food chains or fish species at lower levels in food chains. Fishers disrupt food chains by removing predators, such as cod and tuna, or by taking bait fish, such as anchovies, sardines, and herring, that would otherwise be available to marine mammals, seabirds, and larger fish. In addition, more than one-third of the fish that trawlers take is bycatch (unusable or illegal catch), which is wastefully thrown back into the sea, usually dead.

Many fish stocks are being overfished. Fishers are catching fish at a faster rate than can be replaced by natural breeding. In the late 1990s the United Nations' Food and Agricultural Organization (FAO) concluded that 13 of the world's 17 biggest fisheries were being fished to their limit or were overfished. How did this happen?

In the 1960s food and fisheries experts believed that catching more fish would be one way to meet the growing demand for protein from the world's human population. The global catch of seafood was about 44 million U.S. tons (40 million tonnes), and experts believed this could be increased by about 150 percent—to 110 million U.S. tons (100 million tonnes)—with the use of more efficient technology and if new fish stocks could be exploited. Already, some stocks of fish—notably Californian sardines, Peruvian anchovies, and North Atlantic herring—had shown catastrophic declines. However, most fisheries experts believed that these stocks would recover.

Governments and fishing companies listened to the experts and invested heavily in new fleets fitted with the latest fish-catching technology. The world's fish catch has increased since then, but at a heavy environmental cost. In addition, the early estimates were overly optimistic. The global catch of marine fish and shellfish peaked at about 98 million U.S. tons (89 million tonnes) in 1989, and it has not risen since. Meanwhile, fishers travel farther afield to catch their fish.

Fishing is sustainable (can continue year after year, without decline) if the fish being caught are replaced by young fish that grow to adult size. If the stock is being overfished, however, the caught fish are not replaced, and the number of fish in the population drops. If the overfishing continues, the average size of the fish gets smaller and there are fewer adults left to breed. It is possible for the breeding population to become so small that the species cannot breed successfully and the population dies out.

In the early 1990s cod and haddock fisheries in the Northwest Atlantic collapsed following years of overfishing. Some Canadian and U.S. fishing grounds had to be closed, which led to more than 40,000 fishers and other workers losing their jobs. In 1999 some limited fishing for cod began, but the fish population had not recovered as anticipated. Warming seas may have affected the cod's breeding success, and dogfish (types of small shark) seem to have replaced the role of cod in the food web. Dogfish are now eating the food that cod once consumed, and dogfish eat young cod too. Overfishing alters the structure of biological communities in the sea as well as threatening people's jobs.

To help prevent overfishing, scientists study fish populations to work out how many fish can be caught (and of what size) in a sustainable way. To make their calculations, scientists catch their own samples of fish and take samples from commercial fishers. By studying the growth rings in the scales and earbones of fish (the more rings, the older the fish), they can work out how quickly fish are growing. If the average size of fish in the catch goes down each year because fish do not live long enough to grow to adult size, this can be a sign of overfishing.

Unfortunately, calculating how many fish can be caught each year in a sustainable way is not easy. For example, the breeding success of a fish population varies from year to year depending on factors like the weather and the availability of food. Scientists try to estimate quotas—the numbers and sizes of fish that fishers can catch in a sustainable manner. However, even when scientists get their calculations right,

Going, going . . .

By 1996 the World Conservation Union (IUCN) listed more than 100 species of commercially caught fish and shellfish as vulnerable (facing a high risk of extinction in the wild in the medium-term future) or endangered. They included several species of salmon and sturgeon that migrate between freshwater and seawater. Overfishing, pollution, and damming of rivers were among the factors responsible for their decline.

the authorities that regulate fishing may not listen to their recommendations. Even if they do, setting fishing quotas is one thing, but making sure fishers obey them is another. Unless authorities regularly check fishing vessels and their catches, fishers may ignore the quotas. Unless regulated, fishers compete with one another to catch as many fish as possible.

Overhunting

Marine mammal populations, like fish populations, cannot withstand uncontrolled harvesting. In fact, because marine mammals mature slowly and produce few young, they are even more susceptible to overharvesting.

Intensive whaling resulted in the great whale populations of the Southern Ocean declining by an estimated 90 percent between 1900 and the late 1970s. The World Conservation Union (IUCN) has placed Southern Ocean blue, fin, humpback, and sei whales on the endangered species list. In 1986 the International Whaling Commission (IWC) brought in a worldwide temporary ban on commercial whaling. To give whales further protection, whale sanctuaries were set up in the Indian Ocean in 1979 and in the Southern Ocean in 1994.

Coastal marine mammals must bear the onslaught of marine pollution, of being accidentally entangled in fishing gear, and having their food supply removed by overfishing. Nevertheless, there are several success stories that show that when overhunted marine species are protected, some can make a comeback (see "Species protection," page 222).

Alien invasions

Ships carry an unwanted, often unseen cargo. Growing on their hulls and thriving in their ballast water (seawater that fills hull tanks to adjust the ship's buoyancy) are marine species picked up in one location, which ships inadvertently carry to other destinations. Many of these alien species die off at their new destinations. Some live more or less harmoniously with the creatures they meet in their new habitat.

However, in some cases the newly introduced species out-competes local species and may drastically alter the local marine community.

By the early 1980s ships from the East Coast of North America had arrived in the Black Sea, carrying a species of comb jelly in their ballast water. This animal escaped into the surrounding seawater and without its natural predators to curb its numbers, it multiplied unchecked. Within 10 years this aggressive predator had decimated the Black Sea's zoo-plankton population, including the eggs and larvae of impor-tant food fishes such as herring and anchovy. By 1990 some important Black Sea fisheries, including the Sea of Azov anchovy fishery, had collapsed.

In some cases, species introductions have been carried out purposely. For example, people tried to introduce an East Coast oyster species into San Francisco Bay. The experiment failed, but other species attached to the oyster's shell (or car-ried in the oyster's water) did make the transfer. Today, it is estimated that three-quarters of the larger bottom-living invertebrates of San Francisco Bay are nonnative species that have been introduced purposely or by accident.

The International Maritime Organization (IMO) is seeking to find ways that ships can treat their ballast water to kill hitchhiking marine organisms. Chemical treatment and irra-diation with ultraviolet light are being considered.

Habitat loss

Continental shelves occupy only 8 percent of the ocean's area. But it is in these waters that most of the world's fish catch is taken. The sea's most productive communities—coral reefs, seagrass meadows, kelp forests, and mangrove forests—are found here. It is these marine communities, along with estuaries and their salt marshes, that are most at risk from land-based pollution and from a wide range of damaging human activities.

About two-thirds of the world's population lives less than 100 miles (160 km) from the sea. Many of our largest cities are situated on or near the coast. When developers create or enlarge a coastal settlement, they build dams or seawalls to protect the land from the sea. They drain coastal wetland to provide firm, dry foundations for building upon. In so doing, they destroy the biological communities that live on sandy beaches, rocky shores, mudflats, and salt marshes. The effects are not just local. Building towns, cities, and industrial complexes creates marine pollution and alters the pattern of freshwater runoff. This can change the salinity, cloudiness, and temperature of coastal water, so altering the communities of animals and plants that live there.

Away from the coast, fishers rake the seabed with their dredges and trawl nets. They catch their targeted fish and shellfish, but in the process they cause wider disruption. Their fishing gear damages the burrows of bottom-living invertebrates, dislodges organisms, and raises sediment that smothers them. Trawling or dredging can almost wipe the seabed clean, and it can take months or years for the seabed community to recover.

In shallow warm waters mangrove forests and coral reefs are experiencing devastating losses. The global extent of these two biological communities has been surveyed in recent years with the help of satellite remote sensing.

Missing mangroves

A few hundred years ago, mangrove forests covered about three-quarters of tropical and subtropical coastlines. Today only about half the original area of mangroves remains. Mangroves are cleared to provide land for agriculture, mariculture, industry, and to build towns and cities. Mangroves are cut down to provide timber and firewood. Pollution in the form of heavy metals, oil, pesticides, and untreated sewage has also claimed mangroves. Damming rivers reduces the flow of freshwater needed to create the brackish water (diluted seawater) that some mangroves depend upon.

Mangroves are important communities because they support terrestrial (land-living), aerial (air-living), and aquatic (water-living) communities of animals and plants. Although the marine community associated with mangroves is not enormously diverse, it is highly productive. Mangroves also provide the nursery grounds for many commercially important species of fish and shellfish. When mangroves are removed, their roots no longer bind the sediment, and coastal erosion increases.

Environmental agencies (see "International cooperation and environmental treaties," pages 223–225) recognize the importance of mangrove communities and encourage both the sustainable harvesting of mangroves for timber and firewood and the replanting of mangroves in areas where they have been removed. At the time of writing, the loss of mangroves still outstrips the rate at which they are replaced.

Coral grief

Hard corals build reefs only under a fairly narrow range of conditions. First, the algae inside hard coral polyps need moderately strong sunlight to photosynthesize. Coral reefs will only grow in clear water near the sea surface. Second, reef-building corals need seawater of near-normal salinity and cannot grow in dilute seawater. Along a coastline coral reef systems have gaps where freshwater enters the sea. Third, coral reefs grow best where surface temperatures lie within the range 64 to 86°F (18 to 30°C). Such demands mean that corals are particularly sensitive to environmental change.

Human activities have had a profound negative effect on coral reefs in the last 30 years. It is sometimes difficult to know whether negative effects are caused by human actions, natural events, or a combination of both. For example, the crown-of-thorns, a coral-eating sea star, has multiplied in the western Pacific since the early 1960s. Plagues of the starfish have badly damaged 5 percent of coral reefs on the Great Barrier Reef in Australia and moderately affected a much larger area. Reef areas are stripped of live coral, and new coral species replace them. Researchers suspected that some human influence was the cause. However, in 1989, a study of the fossil record of the Great Barrier Reef region showed that crown-of-thorns starfish have undergone cycles of abundance in the last 80,000 years. The current plagues may be an entirely natural phenomenon.

In 2000 the Global Coral Reef Monitoring Network estimated that 11 percent of the world's coral reef area had been destroyed before 1998 by human causes. A further 16 percent was lost during the 1997–98 El Niño event. Various stresses from human activities combine to damage the health of coral populations. Such factors include:

- removing preferred fish species, such as Napoleon wrasse and coral cod, thus altering the balance of plant-eaters and predators on the reef
- using fishing methods that physically damage the reef, such as explosives, or using cyanide (which kills coral polyps) to stun fish for the aquarium trade
- removing live coral and shellfish for tourist souvenirs
- building shoreline developments that alter land runoff and change coastal current patterns; the related wastewater discharges dilute seawater, make it cloudy, and introduce chemical pollution
- direct damage to coral reefs from tourist activities such as boating, snorkeling, and scuba diving
- introducing alien species that compete with local species

Much can be achieved by encouraging the conservation and sustainable use of coral reef ecosystems (see "International cooperation and environmental treaties," pages 223–225). However, El Niño events, together with global warming, are probably the most serious short-term threat to coral reefs. During the strong El Niño of 1997–98, surface temperatures in some tropical seas rose 1.8 to 3.6°F (1 to 2°C) above normal for months on end. This was enough to trigger the most extensive coral-bleaching event on record: Stressed coral polyps ejected their colorful symbiotic algae, turning pale. Unless polyps regain their algae quickly, they die. On some Indian and Pacific Ocean reefs, bleaching killed more than two-thirds of the coral cover.

In 2001 the Intergovernmental Panel on Climate Change (IPCC) estimated that sea surface temperatures would proba-

bly rise by about 5.2°F (2.9°C) on average by the year 2100. Thus, coral bleaching is likely to become more frequent and more widespread. At the same time, climate change is making weather patterns more extreme. We can expect larger storms and unpredictable changes in ocean currents to further disrupt coral reefs.

Partially bleached hard coral (Porites *species*) *on an Indonesian coral reef* (Courtesy of Fred Bavendam/Minden Pictures)

CONCLUSION:
MANAGING THE OCEANS

The ocean is a three-dimensional environment much more than one mile deep beneath most of its surface. The geographical boundaries in an ocean are rarely as clear-cut as those on land. Boat traffic, sea life, and pollution move freely from one ocean region to another. This makes managing the oceans a great challenge.

In the early 1600s the Dutch statesman Hugo Grotius put forward the idea of "freedom of the high seas." According to this, the seas offshore were open to anyone who could reach them. This idea suited the purposes of powerful European nations of the time. They wanted easy access to the high seas to expand trade with other parts of the globe, especially the Far East.

In 1672 the British claimed a strip of water alongside their coastline as "territorial sea." The British territorial sea was three nautical miles (5.6 km) wide, the width people judged could be protected by cannonfire from the land. British people could fish these waters, but fishers of other nationalities would need to seek permission. Soon, other countries established territorial seas of similar width.

These two traditions—freedom of the high seas, and territorial seas—persisted largely unchallenged until 1945. Then U.S. president Harry Truman, in his "Truman Proclamation on the Continental Shelf," claimed U.S. control over the seabed of continental shelves alongside U.S. territories. The outer boundary of the continental shelf was taken to be a depth of 100 fathoms (600 feet or 183 m) and usually far beyond the limit of the territorial sea.

The Truman Declaration prompted other nations to begin claiming control over their continental shelves. Nations along the west coast of South America have a narrow continental shelf because of the presence of a nearby trench (see

"Moving plates," pages 35–38). A U.S.-style claim would not suit their situation. They declared control over a zone extending 200 nautical miles (370 km) from the shore. In addition, they claimed the resources of the water column within this zone, not just the seabed. They also asserted the right to control access to the zone by vessels of other nations.

In an effort to set up standard rules on claims of access to the sea and its resources, the United Nations called an international conference on the Law of the Sea. This group met many times between 1958 and 1982, when 130 nations finally signed a Law of the Sea Treaty. The treaty became international law in 1994 and has now been signed by more than 150 countries.

The Law of the Sea Treaty

The Law of the Sea Treaty seeks to be fair to nations of different sizes, so that those with large navies and fishing fleets do not plunder the marine resources of smaller nations. Several of the Law of the Sea's many rules govern control of coastal waters and access to the deep seabed.

The treaty gives countries sovereignty over territorial sea that extends 12 nautical miles (22 km) from their shores. They can also claim an exclusive economic zone (EEZ) that extends 200 nautical miles (370 km) from the coast. Within this zone they control commercial activities—fishing, drilling, and so on—both on the seabed and in the water column. The controlling nation is also expected to care for the living resources of their territorial waters and their EEZs.

In the Law of the Sea, the deep seabed beyond the continental rise is called "the Area." It is judged to be "the common heritage of humankind," and if anyone wishes to mine its mineral riches, they should gain permission from an organization called the International Seabed Authority (ISA). The intention of the treaty was to make income and technology from deep-sea mining operations available to developing nations, so that not only the most technologically advanced nations would benefit from deep-ocean resources. This part

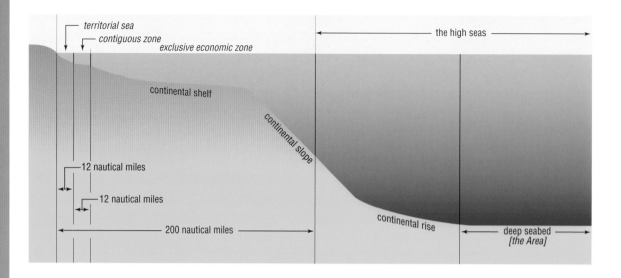

Law of the Sea Treaty zones. These zones are regions of the ocean that are subject to specified levels of access, control, and exploitation by different nations.

of the treaty is among the most controversial, and countries fail to agree on how it should be put into effect. At the moment, deep-sea mining is economically unprofitable. In the near future, however, those who wish to mine the deep-sea for minerals will test this part of the treaty.

Managing pollution

More than three-quarters (by volume) of marine pollution enters the sea from the land, from rivers, or through the air. To curb marine pollution, human activities on land need to be regulated as much as those at sea.

International law aims to prevent ships from dumping almost any kind of waste at sea. Several international treaties have rules governing pollution at sea, but these rules need to be enforced to be effective. In 1991 the U.S. General Accounting Office estimated that fewer than one-third of the member countries of MARPOL (the International Convention for the Prevention of Pollution from Ships) actually stuck to the treaty's rules. The situation has improved slightly since, but it is a tough battle to get member states to enforce the rules to which they have agreed.

The United Nations Environment Program (UNEP) is leading the way in monitoring the oceans for signs of pollution through its Regional Seas Program. UNEP highlights those

Boundary disputes

Small islands can claim a 200-nautical-mile exclusive economic zone (EEZ) around their shores. Many smaller nations have EEZs that are many times larger than their country's land area. Consequently, countries have a special interest in claiming small islands as their territories. In 1982 the Falklands War between Britain and Argentina was fought partly over disputed claims to the Falkland Islands' EEZ. Several nations—including China, Malaysia, the Philippines, Taiwan, and Vietnam—have laid claim to the Spratly Islands in the middle of the South China Sea. These otherwise insignificant islands have massive EEZs that hold significant fishing and mineral resources.

Because sea levels are rising as a result of global warming (see "Climate change," pages 91–93), some countries are concerned that their outlying islands may disappear beneath the waves. If so, these countries might lose their claim to the island's EEZ. Japan, for example, is building sea defenses around a remote, low-lying island in the Pacific to help make sure this does not happen.

regions worst affected by pollution, then seeks to get scientists, politicians, and planners from the countries affected to work together to tackle shared problems.

Seas that are almost entirely surrounded by heavily populated land are the most polluted of all. Such seas include the Caribbean, Mediterranean, and Baltic (see "Marginal seas of the North Atlantic," pages 18–22). The Mediterranean, for example, is bordered by at least 24 countries. The countries include developing countries of North Africa, wealthy countries of southwest Europe, and former Soviet Union countries to the east. Despite their political and economic differences, 16 of these countries met in 1975 to consider the pollution problems of the Mediterranean Sea. By 1985 the countries had agreed to a Mediterranean Action Plan (MAP). This aimed to reduce pollution from land, sea, and air, to protect endangered species, and to establish marine protected areas (MPAs). It also sought environmental impact assessments (scientific evaluation of how developments might affect the environment) for all new development projects. Progress has been relatively slow. By 1995, 10 major MAP objectives had not yet been achieved. Red tides and dolphin die-offs in the

Mediterranean continue to occur. Each year, more than 440 million U.S. tons (400 million tonnes) of raw sewage enter the Mediterranean Sea. Too often, action to control sewage pollution takes place only when it is a visible public health hazard that threatens local tourism.

Managing fishing

Assuming that fisheries scientists have got their calculations right about the level of sustainable fishing, then limits of various kinds can be set on what fishers can catch. Fishers can be given quotas for the number and type of fish they are allowed to catch. They may be permitted to use only certain types of gear. Nets may have large mesh sizes to allow small fish to escape. Fishers may be allowed to keep only large fish so that immature fish are returned to the sea to grow and breed.

Unfortunately, fishing gear does not just catch the intended fish. When catching their quota of haddock, North Atlantic trawlers catch cod as well. And small fish and unwanted species are caught as bycatch. When dumped back in the sea, much of the bycatch dies. The solution is for trawlers to avoid trapping bycatch in the first place, but how to do this is an open question. At present, fishers dump bycatch at sea or grind it into fish meal.

The use of "no-take" reserves is one approach to fisheries management. The "no-take" area is a safe haven for fish in which no fishing is allowed. The argument goes that fish grow large in this safe area. They lay plenty of eggs that hatch to provide abundant supplies of fish larvae. This provides a source of fish fry (young fish) for nearby fished areas. This approach seems to work. In Kenya, when no-take areas were set up in overfished coastal waters, the fishers' catches improved even though they had less area in which to fish. Scientists from many countries where no-take zones had been introduced met at a conference of the American Association for the Advancement of Science (AAAS) in 2001. Their results confirm the usefulness of no-take areas. In most cases, no-take areas showed greater biodiversity and larger sizes of fish than in adjacent fished areas, and fish catches nearby increased.

The use of new technologies, such as satellite remote sensing and GPS navigation, is permitting fishers to find and remove fish stocks with almost surgical precision. At the same time, these technologies offer the means to police fishing. Fishing boats can be monitored by satellite or airplane to help ensure they are not breaking fishing regulations, an approach currently used in Europe.

Marine protected areas

Marine conservation is concerned with protecting marine habitats while allowing commercial activities such as tourism and fishing to continue. People will continue to exploit the resources of the oceans. The trick is to do so in a sustainable way that does not cause undue damage to the physical, chemical, and biological marine environment. It is an understatement to say this is a tough challenge.

One approach to marine conservation involves setting aside parts of the ocean for special protection, as in the case of "no-take" areas. There are now more than 1,600 marine protected areas (MPAs) worldwide. While this is a very encouraging development, many of these MPAs are small and do not include the breeding, nursery, and adult-feeding areas of the species they contain. One stage in the life cycle of a species may be protected within the MPA, but other stages that live outside the MPA are not. Marine biologists now recommend enlarging MPAs—or establishing networks of MPAs—that include critical areas for different stages of the protected species' life cycle.

Many MPAs offer only poor protection. For example, some activities may be banned within an MPA, such as mining and oil exploration, while other activities, such as commercial fishing, are allowed. Many developing countries do not have the resources to protect their MPAs even if they wished to. Even in developed countries, marine conservation may lose out in competition with other interests. For instance, some coral reefs in long-established marine sanctuaries in

Florida have been devastated by sewage pollution from coastal housing developments. There are moves in the United States to tighten control of its MPAs and to create new ones. In 2003 there were 13 marine sanctuaries in U.S. waters, covering a total area of almost 18,000 square miles (47,000 km^2)—nearly the size of Vermont and New Hampshire combined. This amounts to about 1 percent of U.S. waters.

Species protection

Despite problems getting countries to cooperate, there are some outstanding successes in protecting targeted species. The International Fur Seal Treaty of 1911 protected the northern fur seal and the sea otter, both of which were endangered by intensive hunting for their fur. Since then, their numbers have dramatically increased. In some parts of the United States and Canada the sea otter has been reintroduced where previously extinct.

The International Halibut Commission, established in 1924, protected dwindling stocks of the Pacific halibut, the world's largest flatfish. The California gray whale, reduced to a population of fewer than 500 by the 1930s, has risen to more than 8,000 since gaining complete protection in 1938.

Agencies that work to protect species often work best where they target one or a few species in a particular geographic region. Even then, they are not always successful. Despite efforts of the International Commission for the Conservation of Atlantic Tuna (ICCAT) to limit catches of tuna, by the late 1990s the bluefin tuna population in the western Atlantic had collapsed to 10 percent of its 1975 size. Undoubtedly, one reason was the incredibly high market price of this fish. A large specimen can be worth as much as $60,000—the price of a luxury car.

The North Atlantic right whale has been protected since the 1930s, but its numbers have failed to recover. These slow-swimming, coastal whales have to contend with marine pollution, entanglement in fishing nets, and collisions with ships. Fewer than 500 remain, and their future looks bleak.

International cooperation and environmental treaties

Pollutants from freshwater, land, and air can travel hundreds or thousands of miles to affect a particular region of the ocean. For example, cutting down forests inland leads to soil erosion, which adds extra sediment to rivers. Some of the sediment eventually enters the sea, where it can smother coral reefs. Nations over a wide geographical area need to cooperate to deal with environmental problems that threaten a single stretch of seawater.

International treaties such as the Mediterranean Action Plan (see "Managing pollution," pages 218–220) seek to coordinate countries in tackling marine pollution, coastal development, and other environmental problems. Progress is slow, but an encouraging sign is that political enemies do meet and work toward finding solutions for shared environmental problems.

Dozens of international environmental treaties directly concern the marine environment. However, environmental treaties work only to the extent that their regulations are agreed upon and enforced. Wealthier countries are better equipped to deal with environmental problems than are most developing countries. Moreover, when many industrialized countries amassed their wealth decades ago, environmental issues were much less of a concern; many of their actions would now be illegal. It is only fair that developed countries assist developing nations to meet the stricter environmental controls sought today.

There are success stories. One example is the stabilization of the ozone layer in the stratosphere. This layer helps block ultraviolet radiation in sunlight reaching the surface of the Earth. In the last two decades thinning of the ozone layer over the Southern Ocean has resulted in a decline in the production of phytoplankton. Chemicals called chlorofluorocarbons (CFCs) released into the atmosphere react with oxygen atoms in the stratosphere (see "Atmosphere," pages 69–70). This prevents the ozone layer forming as thickly as usual. A thinner ozone layer is a sign that more UV light is getting through, damaging phytoplankton near the sea surface. An environmental treaty called the 1987 Montreal Protocol has

Humpback whale (Megaptera novaengliae) *tail flukes at sunset in Alaska* (Courtesy of Michio Hoshino/ Minden Pictures)

encouraged countries to curb their release of CFCs from aerosol sprays, the manufacture of foamed plastics, and coolants in refrigerators and air-conditioning systems. The thinning of the ozone layer seems to have leveled off, and we can expect the ozone layer to thicken in the next decade.

Two major international treaties include regulations to protect the global oceans. One is the Law of the Sea (described earlier in this chapter), to which extra features have been added since 1982, such as rules about conserving and managing fish stocks. The other is the Convention on Biological Diversity (CBD) forged at the Rio de Janeiro Earth Summit in 1992. Both treaties highlight the importance of biological resources and focus attention on the need to conserve them in their rich variety. Both seek to ensure that developing countries have access to biological resources.

Enshrined in the Convention on Biological Diversity is the idea of "sustainable development"—the belief that development that improves the lives of people today should not use up natural resources or increase environmental problems for future generations. To turn these treaties into practical action there needs to be the political will to do so. However, at the time of this writing, the state of the marine environment continues to worsen. In addition, the specter of global warming looms large.

The future of the oceans

Many scientists suspect that global warming is the greatest short-term threat to the well-being of life on land and in the sea. It is likely that the carbon dioxide from the burning of fossil fuels is enhancing the greenhouse effect and contributing to global warming. If so, cutting back on the burning of

Sunset over Sanibel Island Beach, Florida (Courtesy of Jim Brandenberg/ Minden Pictures)

Seven actions to help the oceans

- On the beach, clear up any trash you see, and don't leave any of your own.
- Find out where the seafood you eat comes from. Is it caught or farmed in a sustainable way that minimizes damage to the environment?
- Visit aquariums and sea-life centers. What are they doing to conserve marine creatures? If they keep marine mammals captive, do they intend to return them to the wild?
- Ask your local politicians what they are doing to improve the quality of our seas. What are their opinions about global warming? Are they doing anything to reduce the burning of fossil fuels?
- Don't buy seashells or other marine souvenirs unless you know their origin and how they have been gathered. If in doubt, don't buy.
- Join a marine environmental group that campaigns for wildlife protection and organizes action to clean up the seas.
- With friends and fellow students, find out more about the marine environment by subscribing to natural history magazines, reading the environment section of national newspapers, and researching books and Web sites (see "Bibliography and further reading," page 237, and "Web sites," pages 239–242, for some examples). Deepen your understanding of environmental issues by discussing and debating what you discover.

fossil fuels is the best way to deal with the problem. This would require people to be less wasteful in their use of gasoline and other oil-based fuels. Methods could include using vehicles that consume less fuel; living and working in better-insulated, more energy-efficient homes; and using cleaner, renewable sources of energy rather than coal, oil, or natural gas. As it is, the United States still produces more than 20 percent of the world's industrial greenhouse gases.

If global warming is happening, then it could cause ocean currents to change direction, and weather and climate patterns to alter, in ways we cannot predict. If the seas warm slightly over the next century—as many scientists suspect they will—then sea levels will rise. A rise of only 20 inches (50 cm) would threaten low-lying parts of the land surface with devastating floods. Countries such as Bangladesh and low-lying island states of the Indian and Pacific Oceans would be worst affected. By comparison, North America and

Europe would get off lightly, but even there, hundreds of square miles of coastal land would be threatened in most countries.

Scientists do not yet understand enough about how ocean currents and climate interact, or how ecosystems adjust to environmental change, to be able to make reliable predictions about the effects of global warming. It is vital that researchers have the resources to monitor the ocean-atmosphere system to keep track of physical, chemical, and biological changes. We, too, can play our part, whether at home, in school or college, or when visiting the coast. We can make choices that lessen our waste, reduce the energy we consume, and cut down on the pollution we cause. We can set an example to others. We can remind ourselves of the part we play by asking, "Are our actions contributing to a better environment for the next generation?" and let our answers guide our actions.

GLOSSARY

abyssal plain the broad, flat expanse of ocean floor lying at depths between about 10,000 feet (3,000 m) and 20,000 feet (6,000 m)

algae simple nonflowering plants. They include single-celled PHYTOPLANKTON (plant plankton) and seaweeds

autonomous underwater vehicle (AUV) a robotic under-water vehicle that operates on its own, without being attached to another craft

bacteria simple, single-celled organisms that lack a nucleus

barrier reef a coral reef that grows parallel to the shore but is separated from it by a wide strip of water (LAGOON)

benthic having to do with organisms that live in or on the seabed

biodiversity the variety of life-forms in a locality

bioluminescence light produced by living organisms

biomass the combined mass of life-forms in a locality

continental drift the slow movement of continents over Earth's surface

continental margin the edge of a continental landmass comprising the continental shelf, the slope, and the rise

continental rise the gentle rise at the base of a continental slope formed by accumulating sediment

continental shelf the shallow, submerged edge of a continental landmass

continental slope the steep slope at the edge of a continental shelf

convergent plate boundary the boundary where two tectonic plates move toward each other. In the ocean, the boundary is associated with a TRENCH

coral atoll a ring of coral reef surrounding a LAGOON

coral polyp a tiny anemone-like animal, with a ring of tentacles surrounding its mouth, and a tube-like body supported by an external skeleton. The limestone skeletons of hard coral polyps build coral reefs

coral reef an underwater, rocklike mass formed mainly from the skeletons of hard coral polyps. It harbors the most biodiverse communities in the oceans

Coriolis effect the effect of Earth's rotation on moving bodies such as winds and ocean currents. The Coriolis effect causes mid-latitude ocean GYRES to turn clockwise in the Northern Hemisphere and counterclockwise in the Southern Hemisphere

crust the solid, rocky outer layer of the Earth on which the land and sea lie

cyanobacteria (blue-green algae) photosynthetic, single-celled organisms related to bacteria

delta a triangular or fan-shaped deposit of low-lying land formed at the mouth of a river

deposit feeder an animal that consumes particles that lie in or on the seabed sediment

divergent plate boundary the boundary where two plates are moving apart. Mid-ocean ridges are divergent plate boundaries

ecosystem the system comprising a community of organisms and their habitat, found in a particular locality

El Niño a southeastward-moving current of warm surface water that flows off the coast of Peru, usually around Christmastime It also refers to a widespread climatic feature that occurs in some years when the El Niño current develops much earlier in the season

erosion the breakdown and removal of rock by the action of wind, temperature change, or moving water or ice

estuary the locality where a river meets the sea and freshwater mixes with seawater

food chain the sequence of organisms in which each is food for the next organism in the chain

food web the interconnections between food chains for a community of organisms

fringing reef a CORAL REEF that develops alongside the shore

global warming a sustained rise in average surface temperatures across the world

greenhouse effect the warming effect caused by greenhouse gases in the atmosphere, such as carbon dioxide, trapping some of the infrared radiation emitted from Earth's surface

gulf an alternative name for a sea partly enclosed by land

guyot a flat-topped seamount

gyre a circular system of ocean currents in the mid-latitude region of an ocean basin. Typically, such gyres flow clockwise in the Northern Hemisphere and counterclockwise in the Southern Hemisphere, under the influence of the CORIOLIS EFFECT

habitat the place where a specific organism or community of organisms lives

hot spot a region in Earth's mantle, distant from a plate boundary, where heat burns through the crust, giving rise to volcanoes

hurricane a rotating tropical storm with wind speeds in excess of 74 mph (120 km/h). Hurricanes are called cyclones in the Indian Ocean and typhoons in the western Pacific

hydrothermal vent an opening on the seabed that discharges volcanically heated water. Unusual communities of organisms live close to such vents on mid-ocean ridges

ice age (glacial period) a cold period in Earth's history, lasting thousands of years, when glaciers and ice sheets are more extensive than usual and sea levels are lower. The most recent ice age ended about 15,000 years ago

iceberg a floating block of ice that has originated from land. Icebergs form either by being shed from glaciers (calving) or by breaking off ice shelves

ice sheet an extensive, thick layer of ice covering a major landmass. Ice sheets cover most of Antarctica and Greenland

ice shelf the outer edge of an ice sheet, extending from a landmass. An ice shelf floats on the sea surface

intertidal zone the expanse of shore that is submerged by the highest tides and uncovered by the lowest tides

invertebrate an animal without a backbone (vertebral column)

ion an atom or molecule with an overall positive or negative electrical charge

krill the common name for euphausiids. They are shrimp-like, planktonic crustaceans that form a major part of the diet of baleen whales

lagoon an area of shallow seawater separated from the open sea by reefs or low-lying land

latitude a measure of angular distance in a north-south direction. The equator is zero degrees latitude, the North Pole 90°N, and the South Pole 90°S

lava   molten rock (MAGMA) on Earth's surface

limestone   sedimentary rock containing mostly calcium carbonate

lithosphere   the outer rocky layer of the Earth comprising the crust and upper part of the MANTLE. About 20 plates make up the lithosphere

longitude   a measure of angular distance in an east-west direction. The Greenwich Meridian (an imaginary line passing north to south through Greenwich, London) is zero degrees longitude. The International Date Line is 180° longitude

longshore drift   the movement of sediment along a shore caused by waves, winds, and currents.

magma   molten rock beneath Earth's surface

mangrove   common name for any of several species of trees and shrubs that dominate the INTERTIDAL ZONE on many tropical and subtropical shores

mantle   the layer of dense, hot rock lying between Earth's crust and core. The lower mantle flows slowly, like a thick molasses, causing plates to move

mariculture   the farming of marine organisms

marine protected area (MPA)   a region of the ocean under special legal protection, typically to conserve its habitats and communities of organisms

meiofauna   minute animals that live between sediment particles

mid-ocean ridge   a mountain chain on the ocean floor formed where plates are moving apart. It is the birthplace of new ocean floor

migration   the mass movement of animals from one region to another, usually to find food or a breeding place

monsoon   a seasonal reversal in prevailing wind direction that occurs in the Tropics

navigation   the process of establishing location and direction to find the way to a particular destination

nekton   aquatic animals that can swim powerfully against currents

nutrients   substances, such as nitrates and phosphates, that plants need in small amounts to make organic (carbon-based) substances by photosynthesis

ocean   the continuous expanse of salt water that covers 71 percent of Earth's surface. The term also refers to one of the five oceans: Arctic, Atlantic, Indian, Pacific, and Southern

ocean basin a low-lying region of Earth's CRUST that contains an ocean. The continental slope marks the edge of an ocean basin

oceanography the scientific study of the ocean and its inhabitants

overfishing harvesting a fish population at a level beyond which its numbers can be replaced by natural breeding

pack ice floating platforms of ice in polar regions that form when seawater freezes

pelagic having to do with organisms that live in the ocean's surface waters or in midwater

photosynthesis the process by which plants, and some protists and bacteria, trap sunlight in order to make organic (carbon-rich) substances such as carbohydrates

phytoplankton plant plankton; plankton that photosynthesize

plankton organisms that float freely in the ocean at the mercy of currents. They swim weakly, if at all

plate (tectonic or lithospheric plate) a segment of Earth's rocky surface consisting of CRUST and attached upper MANTLE. About 20 slowly moving plates make up Earth's surface

plate tectonics the modern theory that Earth's surface is divided into moving plates. Their movements generate continental drift and are responsible for phenomena such as earthquakes and volcanoes close to plate boundaries

prokaryotes various forms of bacteria. They are single-celled organisms that lack a nucleus

protists single-celled organisms that have a nucleus. They include plantlike forms, such as diatoms and dinoflagellates, and animal-like forms, such as radiolarians

radar (radio detection and ranging) the use of radio waves to measure the size, position, and motion of objects

remotely operated vehicle (ROV) a robotic underwater vehicle attached to and operated by a surface vessel or a submersible

respiration the process inside cells by which organisms break down food molecules to release energy

salinity a measure of the saltiness of water. Most seawater has a salinity close to 35, or 35 grams of dissolved salts in 1,000 grams of seawater

satellite remote sensing the use of satellites to detect features of Earth's surface

scuba (self-contained underwater breathing apparatus) a portable device for breathing air underwater. The aqualung is the best-known type

sea a named part of an ocean, such as the Sargasso Sea. Also, an alternative name for the water in an ocean

seafloor spreading the process producing new oceanic CRUST at mid-ocean ridges

sea grasses types of flowering plants, related to lilies, that grow in the sea

sea ice ice that forms when seawater freezes

seamount a submerged volcanic cone that rises at least 3,280 feet (1,000 m) above the ocean floor

seaweeds multicelled marine algae

sonar (sound navigation and ranging) a technology that uses sound to detect the direction and distance of an object underwater

species the world population of genetically similar individuals that interbreed to produce fertile offspring

subduction the process by which one plate is forced beneath another one

submarine a cigar-shaped, piloted underwater craft

submarine canyon a steep V-shaped valley in the CONTINENTAL SHELF

submersible a small, piloted underwater vehicle with a viewing cabin

suspension feeder an animal that feeds by sifting particles out of seawater

symbiosis a close relationship between individuals of different species by which one or both benefit

thermocline a layer in the WATER COLUMN across which the temperature rapidly changes

trade winds prevailing winds in low latitudes that blow toward the equator

transform plate boundary (transform fault) the boundary where two plates slide alongside each other

trench a deep region of the ocean floor that forms where one plate is being forced (subducted) beneath another one

tsunami (seismic sea wave) a giant wave or series of waves, produced by an earthquake, volcano, landslide, or other major water displacement

turbidity current an underwater avalanche of sediment that forms or enlarges a submarine canyon

upwelling the rising of cool, nutrient-rich, deep water to the surface waters

vertebrate an animal with a backbone (vertebral column) or similar structure

water column the vertical expanse of seawater from surface to seabed

wave (sea wave) a vertical disturbance that travels along the sea surface

wetland a flat, low-lying area of land that is covered in water or has water-saturated soil

zooplankton animal plankton

BIBLIOGRAPHY AND FURTHER READING

Ballard, Robert D. *Adventures in Ocean Exploration.* Washington, D.C.: National Geographic Society, 2001.

Broad, William J. *The Universe Below.* New York: Simon & Schuster, 1997.

Byatt, Andrew, Alastair Fothergill, and Martha Holmes. *The Blue Planet.* London: BBC Worldwide, 2001.

Carson, Rachel L. *The Sea Around Us.* Rev. ed. New York: Oxford University Press, 1961.

Castro, Peter, and Michael E. Huber. *Marine Biology.* 4th ed. New York: McGraw-Hill, 2002.

Couper, Alastair, ed. *Atlas and Encyclopedia of the Sea.* 2nd ed. London: Times Books, 1989.

Doubilet, David. *Water, Light, Time.* London: Phaidon Press, 1999.

Earle, Sylvia A. *Atlas of the Ocean.* Washington, D.C.: National Geographic Society, 2001.

Ellis, Richard. *Deep Atlantic.* New York: Alfred A. Knopf, 1996.

Köhler, Annemarie, and Danja Köhler. *The Underwater Explorer.* London: New Holland, 1997.

Nybakken, James W. *Marine Biology: An Ecological Approach.* 5th ed. San Francisco, Calif.: Benjamin Cummings, 2001.

Paxton, John R., and William N. Eschmeyer, eds. *Encyclopedia of Fishes.* 2nd ed. San Diego, Calif.: Academic Press, 1998.

Pirie, Gordon, ed. *Oceanography: Contemporary Readings in Ocean Sciences.* 3rd ed. New York: Oxford University Press, 1996.

Prager, Ellen. *The Oceans.* New York: McGraw-Hill, 2000.

Sobel, Dava. *Longitude.* London: Fourth Estate, 1996.

Summerhayes, C. P., and S. A. Thorpe, eds. *Oceanography: An Illustrated Guide.* London: Manson, 1996.

Thurman, Harold V., and Alan P. Trujillo. *Essentials of Oceanography.* 7th ed. Upper Saddle River, N.J.: Prentice Hall, 2001.

Van Dover, Cindy Lee. *The Octopus's Garden.* Reading, Mass.: Addison Wesley, 1997.

Weber, Michael J., and Judith, A. Gradwohl. *The Wealth of Oceans.* New York: W. W. Norton, 1995.

Wilson, Edward O. *The Diversity of Life.* Cambridge, Mass.: Harvard University Press, 1992.

Worldwatch Institute, ed. *Vital Signs 2003: The Trends That Are Shaping Our Future.* New York: W. W. Norton, 2003.

WEB SITES

American Association for the Advancement of Science

URL: http://www.aaas.org

An international nonprofit organization dedicated to advancing science around the world.

California Coastal Conservancy

URL: http://www.coastalconservancy.ca.gov

A state agency that adopts business approaches to purchase, protect, restore, and enhance coastal resources.

CSIRO Marine Research

URL: http://www.marine.csiro.au

Australia's national marine research agency.

FAO Fisheries Department

URL: http://www.fao.org/fi

The Fisheries Department of the Food and Agricultural Organization (FAO) of the United Nations.

Great Barrier Reef Marine Park Authority (GBRMPA)

URL: http://www.gbrmpa.gov.au

The organization that advises the Australian government on the care and development of the Great Barrier Reef Marine Park.

Harbor Branch Oceanographic Institution

URL: http://www.hboi.edu

The Florida-based oceanographic institution.

International Maritime Organization

URL: http://www.imo.org

The United Nations agency responsible for improving maritime safety and preventing pollution from ships.

National Oceanic and Atmospheric Administration (NOAA)

URL: http://www.noaa.gov

The U.S. federal government agency specializing in atmospheric and oceanographic sciences.

NOAA's *Aquarius*

URL: http://www.uncw.edu/aquarius

Aquarius is an undersea laboratory owned by NOAA and operated by the University of North Carolina at Wilmington.

Scripps Institution of Oceanography

URL: http://sio.ucsd.edu

A leading oceanographic institution based at the University of California at San Diego.

Seaweb

URL: http://www.seaweb.org

A nongovernmental organization based in Washington, D.C., that campaigns to protect the ocean and the life within it.

Southampton Oceanography Center

URL: http://www.soc.soton.ac.uk

The United Kingdom's largest oceanographic center for learning and research.

The Ocean Conservancy

URL: http://www.oceanconservancy.org

A nongovernmental organization with its headquarters in Washington, D.C., that raises awareness of ocean issues through science-based advocacy, research, and public education.

The World Conservation Union (IUCN)

URL: http://www.iucn.org

The world's largest organization that brings together nongovernmental organizations, governments, and international agencies to foster wildlife conservation alongside sustainable development.

UNEP World Conservation Monitoring Center (UNEP-WCMC)

URL: http://www.unep-wcmc.org

UNEP-WCMC compiles and publishes data on the state of the world's biodiversity.

United Nations Environment Program (UNEP)

URL: http://www.unep.org

The United Nations agency with a focus on environmental conservation and sustainable development.

Woods Hole Oceanographic Institution (WHOI)

URL: http://www.whoi.edu

Based in Woods Hole, Massachusetts, WHOI is the world's largest independent oceanographic institution.

World Resources Institute

URL: http://www.wri.org

An independent, nonprofit environmental research and policy organization based in Washington, D.C.

WWF (formerly, the World Wildlife Fund)

URL: http://www.panda.org

An international nongovernmental organization that carries out promotional and practical conservation work in many countries, including field projects and scientific research.

Note: *Italic* page numbers refer to illustrations.